PERSPECTIVES IN SOCIOLOGY

HERMAN R. LANTZ, *General Editor*

Advisory Editors

Alvin W. Gouldner, *Washington University*
Robert A. Nisbet, *University of California*
Melvin M. Tumin, *Princeton University*

The Reference Other Orientation

An Extension of the Reference Group Concept

By RAYMOND L. SCHMITT

Foreword by HERMAN R. LANTZ

Southern Illinois University Press
Carbondale and Edwardsville

Feffer & Simons, Inc.
London and Amsterdam

Library of Congress Cataloging in Publication Data

Schmitt, Raymond L   1936–
    The reference other orientation.

    (Perspectives in sociology)
    Bibliography: p.
    1. Reference groups. 2. Sociology—Methodology. 3. Social groups—Bibliog-
raphy. I. Title. II. Series. HM131.S365   301.11′3   76–156789
ISBN 0–8093–0564–X

To my mother and father

Contents

List of Tables

Foreword

Comments regarding the nature of sociology in recent years indicate discontent, both from the student and the professional. Many in both quarters have been concerned with the relationship of sociological research and writing to matters of social relevance. Much of this concern has centered on the relation of sociology and sociologists to the power hierarchy, the so-called establishment, in our society. Thus, it has been argued that sociologists are too implicated in the needs of funding agencies, studying what has been suggested they study, too concerned with the establishment of their own careers, too accommodating without questioning, and that sociologists have become largely alienated from the basic ongoing social problems of the society. At different periods in the history of sociology, sociologists were especially self-conscious about the number who came from ministerial backgrounds and who were bent on reform and "doing good"; sociologists were conscious about the status of sociology as a science and reacted to this by moving toward a natural science model involving quantitative measurement. After several decades of empirical research, a second world war, and relative affluence, there are once more serious questions regarding what sociology is and what it ought to be doing. While many are sympathetic to these criticisms, a substantial number of sociologists argue that the state of our knowledge is replete with significant gaps and that the very first priority is a closing of these gaps so that valid and meaningful social criticism and social planning can take place. Thus, if one accusation is that sociologists shun relevance, the other accusation is that we often have insufficient data for responsible social planning. Indeed, some would argue that the most basic social problems of our day still elude us in spite of lofty pronouncements, conferences, meetings, and demonstration projects, not simply because of bureaucratic opposition to change but equally because much of our knowledge is still too fragmentary. To be sure we have educated communities with respect to a whole host of variables which we believe are associated with social pathology. In identifying such variables, we have described inequalities arising out of our economic order, the problems of burgeoning cities, and related components of the broader social structure. While some have proposed radical alteration of the social structure, we have witnessed a pattern which is much less radical. For example, one of the basic ways of dealing with problems when knowledge is insufficient is to create a rhetoric which has an element of authenticity but which finally may serve to obscure problems or to make people hopeless about the understanding of problems. Thus, one can talk about the complexity of social change or the multidimensional component of social problems. After listening to these statements for at least two decades of my professional life, I am led to conclude that what is often involved is that we do not really know what variables are at work. Indeed, if everything is operative, nothing may be operative. Such perspectives also suggest that the variables at work are so complex that resolutions for social pathology are still far in the future. One major result is to create both alienation and hopelessness about our capacity to deal with major social issues in any responsible way.

Another way of dealing with a fundamental lack of knowledge regarding social problems may be to redefine the nature of problems themselves. Some of this may be noted in tendencies associated with labeling and societal reaction. While not intended by the proponents of this perspective, there is the danger that extreme proponents of this point of view may come to define some social problems out of existence. However one may agree or disagree with the present state of sociology, there is no substitute for the painstaking synthesis of concepts, research, and theory. Professor Schmitt has responded to this task by providing us with an examination of the reference group, one of the most important concepts in the sociological vocabulary—a concept which is significant because it offers a possibility of bringing us closer to linking different levels of sociological analysis. What has been consistently lacking in the understanding of major social pathologies are linkage systems that integrate concepts from different levels of analysis, the cultural, the social, and the individual. Such linkage systems, if adequately established, could move us closer, rather significantly, to an understanding of the basic social problems and pathologies in our society. Such linkage systems could enable us to understand how social and cultural factors are linked to social behavior and social pathology. Moreover, the reference group concept is a concept at a high level of generality but one which has utility for understanding social behavior at almost every level from the small nuclear family to the large bureaucracy. One of the basic problems with linkage systems is the matter of relating both social and cultural phenomena to psychological phenomena. Without such a linkage, the leap from the social-cultural to the psychological can be very hazardous. An understanding of the reference group concept may minimize such a possibility since the concept incorporates psychological needs within the context of social influences and pressures.

Professor Schmitt has been investigating the subject of reference groups for at least a decade. This book represents his attempt to assess and analyze the reference group concept and its components. The author demonstrates the explanatory power of the reference group concept and its implications for macro and micro problems. His basic and careful consideration of the reference group literature suggests that at least some of the paucity of knowledge so typically attributed to the social sciences is due to a lack of systematization of what is known. By utilizing knowledge from different areas, by recognizing the value of the simple as well as the complex, by acknowledging qualitative and quantitative methodologies, by noting the phenomenological and the nonphenomenological aspects of social behavior, and by visualizing individuals and social systems from a static and dynamic perspective, Professor Schmitt has been able to construct the skeletal features of the reference other orientation. It is anticipated that his effort will become a necessary primer for those explicitly concerned with the reference group concept and a starting point for others involved in the planning of social psychological research.

Herman R. Lantz

Carbondale, Illinois
April 1972

Preface

The reference group concept is unique in the social sciences for it takes into account the individual's orientations to groups of which he is not a member. The effects of these nonmembership groups are particularly important in our mass society since the individual is exposed to numerous groups either by direct contact or through our elaborate channels of communication. The reference group concept, however, also directs attention to the differential effects of membership groups. It is apparent that the socialization process cannot be understood unless considerable emphasis is assigned to the individual's reference groups.

Although an extensive literature has developed around the reference group concept, some ambivalence has been expressed regarding its usage. One allegation, for instance, is that it has not been employed in a systematic manner. A few have even suggested the concept be discarded. Others feel the criticism is extreme, and indicate that the elaboration of the reference group concept in the literature reflects the increased insight of the social scientist into individual-other relationships.

This book involves an intensive examination of the reference group literature. Its basic theme is that an increased awareness should be given to the existence of a set of reference group cognate concepts—or a reference other orientation—that has emerged over the years. This reference other orientation is considered from its earliest beginnings to its most recent formulation.

The reference other phenomenon is regarded as consisting of three components; the reference other, the reference relationship, and the individual. These components are regarded as generic in character, but it is recognized that their parameters are dependent upon other variables. There are, for instance, normative, comparative, and identification-object reference relationships, and each of these may vary in their scope of influence. An individual-other typology is presented in order to systematize the complexity of the reference other phenomenon.

While this book has a distinct theoretical focus, it also has implica-

tions for a number of applied areas. The critical importance of the
reference other orientation for the social and personal problems of our
day is not difficult to defend.

Raymond L. Schmitt

Normal, Illinois
March 1972

Acknowledgments

I am indebted to Herman R. Lantz for providing the opportunity to write this book and his sage advice regarding its content. Primary debts are due to Stanley E. Grupp for his detailed and realistic evaluation of the entire manuscript and to Edward Jelks, an archaeologist, who brought a fresh perspective to my effort. Ed's typological insights were particularly helpful. Appreciation is expressed to Paul Baker and Melvin M. Tumin for their mature sociological observations. The constructive criticism of the latter led to a substantial revision. Aaron Donsky rendered comments on my history and theory chapters. And David Eaton read an early draft of my methodology chapter. Their comments are acknowledged.

Warm appreciation is extended to Illinois State University for providing research time and graduate assistants. In the latter respect, a most substantial debt is due Ronald Gene Humke, who spent hundreds of hours locating, abstracting, categorizing, and assisting in evaluating a variety of scholarly material. Dovie Bryant also functioned as my research assistant and provided a number of valuable insights.

My thanks are extended to Kurt W. Back, Robert E. Clark, Archibald O. Haller, R. E. Hilbert, Donald N. Levine, Delbert C. Miller, Tamotsu Shibutani, Fremont A. Shull, Jr., Richard B. Warnecke, and Joseph Woelfel for providing me with a variety of helpful material. Benjamin J. Keeley and Dorothy Lee also brought some important references to my attention.

Much is owed the numerous graduate students who not only bore up under my focused interest on the reference other orientation but offered critical response to numerous ideas. Their lack of awe for the traditional was of invaluable assistance in helping to maintain some balance in the book.

Shailer Thomas, chairman of the Department of Sociology at ISU, is owed a debt of thanks for providing the appropriate climate for the pursuit of scholarly activities.

A book must be prepared for communication. In this regard, my typist, Mrs. Alberta Carr, cannot be surpassed.

The extensive efforts of Jane Bergman in helping to prepare the final bibliography for publication are also acknowledged.

My gratitude is expressed to my wife, Margo, and my children, Laury, Bo, and Tiffani. Were it not for their encouragement and sacrifice, this book would not have been written.

CHAPTER One

An Overview of the Reference Other Orientation

The objective of this book is to examine intensively the reference group concept. This term was formally introduced by Herbert H. Hyman in his classic 1942 work, *The Psychology of Status* (182). (The parenthetical numbers found throughout this book that do not immediately follow a colon correspond to source numbers in the bibliography at the end of the book. Any parenthetical numbers directly following a colon refer to pages within the source.) Hyman studied the individual's conception of his own status positions relative to his reference groups as well as his reference individuals, reference categories, and more abstract reference others. Although it happened to be the reference *group* concept that was popularized, Hyman's research design did allow for the consideration of different types of reference others.

Hyman's concept has enjoyed extreme success since its inception. In fact, its rise in popularity has been described as "meteoric" (186:7). Authors have emphasized that the reference group concept has been utilized in literally hundreds of theoretical and empirical studies by representatives of all the social sciences in a variety of situations. It has been noted, for instance, that (186:7): "The concept appears in Australia, Israel and India; in studies of farmers, scientists, drunkards, and newspapermen; it has been applied to problems of mental illness, formal organization, marketing and public relations, mass communication, acculturation, political behavior, consumer behavior, labor relations, and juvenile delinquency, as well as to opinion formation." It should be added, however, that our review of the literature indicates that many of the "reference group writings" have only involved this concept in a tangential manner. Nevertheless, this does not negate its frequent usage by social scientists.

The increased popularity of the reference group concept has been accompanied by a growing amount of criticism. While there are various

1

facets to these negative evaluations, the main allegations are that the reference group concept is too inclusive (195), that it has been inconsistently used (240), and that it has not yet been designated as a psychological, social psychological, or sociological concept (303). Linn, one of the severest critics, has concluded that "the term itself no longer has much meaning" (240:499). The title of his critique, "Reference Group: A Case Study in Conceptual Diffusion," vividly portrays the tenor of his remarks. Similarly, Williams has recently drawn the following conclusion from her review of the reference group literature (431: 550): "In sum, the reference group concept, despite its wide use in sociology, social psychology, and other fields, is still not conceptually clarified. Questions regarding the term's actual referents include: Should it refer only to definable groups or individuals with whom one psychologically identifies? Should the term also include groups or individuals with whom one compares oneself? Should it refer to a derivative of associations and loyalties (perspectives) rather than actual groups or persons? Should it refer to categories as well as groups? Should it refer to relationships?" (It will be pointed out in chapter six that reference group studies have also been criticized on methodological grounds.)

These adverse reactions are explainable. A number of generally distinctive and quite formidable reference group cognate concepts have developed over the years. The complex character of these concepts would have, in and of itself, provided an adequate basis for criticism, but the additional fact that they were not systematized facilitated the development of some problematic aspects in their usage. The depiction of the audience reference group concept is an example of one type of confusion in this area. This term has been used to refer to reference groups that give positive rewards (217), that evaluate ego's role behavior (410), and that function as internalized audiences (306). (The word *ego* will often be used to refer to the individual.)

The question, then, is whether or not the statement that the reference group concept no longer has much meaning is justified. Our answer is clearly no! The extensive review of the reference group literature upon which this book is based indicates that the reference group concept has been undergoing a process of conceptual clarification and elaboration. Some support is given to this statement by the fact that the editors of a recent reader on reference groups (186) entitled their first section in just this manner. Hyman's concept has been supplemented by other concepts, and more are on the way. This is not surprising to one who appreciates the complexity of the phenomenon that these concepts reflect. The reference group cognate concepts have typically focused upon new dimensions and the data that is subsumed under each of them is becoming increasingly evident.

In fact, the basic theme of this book is that the composite of reference group cognate concepts constitutes what may be regarded as *a reference other orientation*. Or to put it slightly differently, there is now a *set* of *interrelated* reference group cognate concepts that is beginning to circumscribe the boundaries of *the reference other phenomenon*. (The reference other phenomenon involves that segment of the empirical world that is circumscribed by the reference group concept and its cognate concepts.) However, it remains for us to integrate these concepts. This orientation is referred to as a reference other orientation rather than a reference group orientation because it has become apparent that ego is influenced by a variety of reference others, including individuals, groups, social categories, as well as abstract and imaginary entities.

But the critics of the reference group concept should not be ignored. The important concepts, for instance, of role-taking (410), attitude (93), and subculture (439) have been subjected to constructive criticism and subsequent modification. This is a functional and necessary step in the development of an adequate conceptual scheme. A rationale for conceptual evaluation is illustrated in the following quotation involving the subculture concept (44:124): "There seems to be something in the nature of this concept which makes it easily adaptable to a wide variety of situations. In fact, as Yinger suggests, and we are inclined to agree, it is so easily used that it may be employed without a careful consideration of its implications. It seems to us that the misuse, the overuse or the indiscriminate use of any concept not only decreases its general usefulness, but it may lead to inappropriate research design, inconsistent interpretation of data, misleading conclusions, and erroneous programmatic recommendations."

A review of the reference group concept will be enhanced if the criticisms that have been leveled against it are put in a different context. It is not only the reference group concept that needs scrutinizing but also the entire set of reference group cognate concepts; if these concepts that make up the reference other orientation can be reasonably systematized, it will not be in spite of, but because of, the temporary confusion created by the elaboration of the reference group concept. Conceptual schemes are social products. They must be created, and this process is by its very nature a digressional one.

Since it is imperative that the scientist not haphazardly add elements to his conceptual arsenal, a rationale for the reference other orientation is in order. Fortunately, this is not difficult to offer. The reference other orientation is uniquely important because it directs attention to the fact that nonmembership others may be reference others for the individual. Tamotsu Shibutani has emphasized this point in his discussion of the role of reference groups in mass societies (370:255–56): "The contention that men think, feel, and see things from the standpoint peculiar to the group in which they participate is an old one which has been repeatedly emphasized by anthropologists and students of the sociology of knowledge. But what makes this hypothesis so important for the study of modern mass societies is the fact that people may assume the perspectives of groups in which they are *not* recognized members, sometimes of groups in which they have never participated directly, and sometimes of groups that do not exist at all."

Although the fundamental idea engendered in the preceding statement is not difficult to grasp, its complete comprehension presupposes an understanding of the terms *reference other* and *membership other*. These concepts, unfortunately, are not easily explained, and literally reflect the content of this entire book. In a *preliminary* manner, then, a reference other will be defined as any actual or imaginary individual, group, social category, norm, or object that influences the individual's covert or overt behavior. Admittedly, this definition is rather broad, but the typological strategy employed in this book presupposes just such an approach. This preliminary definition of the reference other is discussed more fully in chapter three. The reference self is included in the definition at that point. An other will be regarded as a membership other for the individual if persons attribute a membership affiliation to the individual and the other.

An examination of table 1 will provide further insight into the nature of reference others and membership others. This table portrays the traditional view of these two concepts. This traditional view is modified somewhat in chapter three in that the *behavioral* influence exerted by membership others upon ego is regarded as a reference influence. The first cell represents the situation where an individual has a membership affiliation with a reference other. Most families of orientation are membership and reference others for the younger members of the family. The second cell depicts an other that is a reference other but not a membership other. This cell reflects the distinguishing aspect of the reference other orientation. In societies with an open stratification system, the upper classes occupy this type of position for many members of the less fortunate classes. The third cell describes an other that is a membership other but not a reference other. Some members of organizations may simply belong to them but not take any of their values from them. The fourth cell refers to the situation where the other is neither a membership other nor a reference other. At an earlier point in the history of civilization, the mass society for the members of most primitive societies was probably of this type.

1. TRADITIONAL VIEW OF THE MEMBERSHIP AND REFERENCE STATUS OF THE OTHER FOR THE INDIVIDUAL

		Membership Status	
		Membership Other	*Nonmembership Other*
	Reference Other	1	2
Reference Status			
	Nonreference Other	3	4

Note: The digits in this table are identification numbers for the four cells (see text).

The social scientist must consider the nonmembership others that influence individuals. Behaviors and attitudes are often influenced by nonmembership others. If this source of influence is ignored, a complete explanation of social behavior cannot be obtained. One must be careful, however, not to err in the opposite direction. The traditional view posits that *membership others may also be reference others!* Students, and scientists, occasionally ignore this fact once the distinguishing aspect of the reference other orientation is made salient. After all, it is a most critical function, and a rather exciting one. Many people simply do not think about the fact that individuals may be influenced by nonmembership others. When this point is emphasized, it is possible they will overreact.

Although the importance of the distinguishing function of the reference other orientation for explanatory purposes has been emphasized, this orientation has other significant theoretical implications for the social scientist who desires to understand social behavior. We will consider four of them.

The reference other orientation directs attention to the fact that there is much variation in the type and degree of influence that different reference others have over individuals. In this regard, Ralph H. Turner has emphasized that reference groups are *segmentally* rather than totally relevant for individuals (409), and as we will see in this book, reference others may, among other things, "exert" a normative, a comparative, or an identification-object influence over individuals, and these influences vary in their scope, direction, and intensity, and occur in or outside of role relationships.

This characteristic also merits attention, as some writers have suggested that if it were not for the nonmembership focus of the reference group concept, it would simply be a new name for an old concern, namely the search for sociological determinants of behavior. The emerging character of theory and research regarding the differential relevance of reference others does not now tend to support this view. The interest of the reference group theorist in the nature of the influence that reference others have upon individuals has resulted in a rather impressive set of insights into the complexity and diversity of the individual-other relationship. In fact, it is quite conceivable that the major contribution of the reference other orientation will prove to be its insights into the differential influence of reference others rather than its unique nonmembership focus.

The reference other concept, the central concept, within the reference other orientation, is a generic concept as it is necessarily characteristic of individual-other relationships whenever and wherever they occur. In other words, individuals are not autonomous agents within the society; many of their covert and overt behaviors are necessarily oriented to reference others. It is precisely this generic characteristic of the reference other concept that has accounted for its wide usage within the social sciences.

The nature of the human reproductive process, the dependent nature of the newborn infant, the ability of the individual to engage in symbolic behavior, the necessity of "role-taking" in human communication, the reciprocal character of most roles, the interpenetration of institutional arrangements, the functional requisites of societies, and the elaborate communication channels in mass societies are some of the factors that account for the inevitability of reference others. Although he employs different terminology than we, Olsen has described the very process of social organization as one in which the social actor moves from a self orientation to a *collective* orientation (290). Indeed, we shall even observe in this book that internalization, which may be thought of as "freedom from one's reference others," frequently presupposes a prior and positive identification of ego with one or more of his reference others.

Although the need for generic concepts in the social sciences has been stressed by some (39), only a few writers have considered the relative generic character of concepts. The predictive power of theories is recognized as a variable, however, and as concepts are the "building blocks" of theories, it is reasonable to infer that they would also vary in this respect. It is not possible for us to consider the relative merits of the reference other concept, but it must be noted that generic concepts are functional because they are amenable to broad usage and generative of theories of wide predictability. Fortunately, these characteristics can be attributed to the reference other concept *and its cognates.*

Another theoretically relevant trait of the reference other concept is its social psychological character. In a very real sense, the reference other concept somewhat uniquely "brings together" the individual and the social structure. In this capacity, it provides a meeting ground between psychology and sociology. *Individuals are the object of a reference other influence only to the extent that their behavior is influenced by reference others.* It is in this respect that the reference other concept is social psychological.

The term *social structure* in the preceding paragraph should be interpreted in a *general* manner. Writers vary in their expression of the focus of social psychology. Some define it rather broadly as the study of the effects of the social structure upon the individual while others define it more narrowly as the study of the effects of the group upon the individual. Social psychology could also, in part, be regarded as the study of the effects of the reference other upon the individual. The social psychological character of the role concept has also been emphasized (235). Comparatively, the role concept, or more correctly, the *position* concept, is a *sociological* social psychological concept while the reference other concept is more of a *psychological* social psychological concept.

The reference group concept, however, is seldom explicitly described in a social psychological context. Instead, this concept is typically depicted as a psychological concept. Reference groups are frequently portrayed as those groups with which the individual "psychologically relates." Nevertheless, as one recent proponent of the social psychological position indicates (303:301): "If a noticeable gain is to be made via the reference group construct, it should be defined at the *social psychological level* of analysis. That is, it should be a construct designed to explain an individual's behaviour as that behaviour is related to the individual's significant socio-cultural worlds."

We would disagree with Pollis, the author of this quotation, however, with respect to the basic strategy for studying the reference other phenomenon. Pollis argues for attitudinal research. This is understandable as a "role-taking" view of reference others deems it necessary to determine ego's reference others from *his* perspective, but the complete study of the reference other phenomenon necessitates a sociological approach. It should also be noted that Newcomb recognized the social psychological character of the reference group concept (286). Also, see (362:223–39).

The basic reason for the psychological emphasis on the reference group concept was to stress that *a group can only be designated a reference group from the perspective of the individual!* The point was being made that there is nothing inherent about the nature of a group, per se, that makes it a reference group. A group can be a reference group for one person but not another. This was exactly why many writers stated that a reference group did not refer to a group in a sociological sense. They were attempting to explain that even though the reference group concept might involve an actual group, the central idea engendered in this concept was that the behavior of the individual was in some manner being oriented to the group. One of Olmsted's observations has implications for our understanding of the psychological emphasis of the reference group concept. He observes that "the reference group theorist does not really study groups at all but rather those aspects of the individual's mind which may be seen as involving a group referent" (289:77 n).

The observant reader will by now have realized that the traditional psychological view of the reference group concept is identical to our social psychological description of the reference other concept. Consequently, we would underscore this historical emphasis but add the important qualification that what was deemed psychological is in fact *a social psychological dimension.*

We must be quick to state that even though the reference other concept is a social psychological one, the complete study of the reference other phenomenon *presupposes a sociological framework.* Although the socialization process requires a societal element, and this is where reference individuals and groups are important, ecological, structural, and cultural factors are also necessary prerequisites. The reference group studies are not generally reflective of this assumption, but this does not negate its validity. There have, however, been some excellent investigations that have either *explicitly or implicitly* studied reference groups from a sociological perspective. These include (1; 14; 37; 58; 112; 131; 244; 245; 246; 319; 334; 353). Theoretical discussions are found in (249; 271:281–386; 272).

The final theoretical implication of the reference other orientation only involves one kind of reference other, the reference individual. Nonetheless, this is perhaps the most critical of all the theoretical consequences of the reference other orientation. For the time being, a reference individual may be thought of as an actual person who is having an influence on ego. The theoretical point that we wish to emphasize here is that all of culture is in the final analysis always transmitted through the reference individual. (We recognize that reference groups and the mass media are also agents of socialization.) In this respect, Inkeles has observed that "all institutional arrangements are ultimately mediated through individual human action" (188:251). The reference other orientation may provide the vehicle through which our knowledge concerning the role of the reference individual in this process can be enhanced. Although our statement that the reference individual is the basic agent of socialization will not come as a revelation to any social scientist, this fundamental fact has not been extensively and systematically incorporated into the study of the socialization process.

One of the reasons for this has been the reluctance of many sociologists to grant the relevance of the social psychological approach *for sociological insights*. This lack of recognition has not only hindered the development of our knowledge of the reference other phenomenon, whose total study presupposes a sociological perspective, but ironically has also retarded our understanding of social systems. Sociologists, and others, have generally failed to realize that *one may learn about the nature of the social system through an examination of its effects upon individuals!* Sociological insights are not restricted to the analysis of social system variables. In other words, to say that social psychology is the scientific study of the effects of the social system upon the individual, does not limit the obtained knowledge to the individual nor even to his relationship with the social system. We can also, and indeed must, increase our understanding of the social system, per se. The core of this argument, although rarely made, is reflected in the following quotation from Akers' work (2:457 n, my italics): "If the explanatory variables and processes in propositions about behavior are those contained in or arising out of social interaction (as contrasted, for instance, with intrapsychic, individual constitutional, personality, or unconscious variables) then one is justified in naming them sociological. *If the independent variables are social-environmental, then we have a sociological theory, whether the dependent variables be individual or collective behavior.* It is in this sense that both structural and processual theories can be sociological."

The reference other orientation is not only of theoretical interest to the social scientist but it also has definite pragmatic implications for the members of societies. Irrespective of one's viewpoint of the fundamental goal of science, the undesirable plights of the human race should not go unnoticed. While we should certainly heed the warning of those who have wisely indicated that the reference group concept is not a panacea, the social psychological and generic character of the reference other concept simply make it very amenable for applied objectives.

The reference group concept has been directly related to a number of very specific areas that have obvious implications for the improvement of human societies. For instance, this concept has been considered in regard to social work practices (222), crime rates (112), marital adjustment (429), juvenile delinquency (72; 165), ambition (366: 443–47), adolescent conformity and deviation (365), negotiations (169), social justice (337), suicide (168:54–65), alienation (33; 366:420), drinking behavior (324), illness behavior (299), conformity (282), mental health (292), racism (253), racial attitudes (124), racial preferences (13), racial integration (66), social control (371), self-development (258), role-socialization (418), societal integration (115), marihuana usage (241; 264), achievement motivation (217), occupational satisfaction (131), occupational employment (116), educational aspirations (405), educational satisfactions (88), blindness (396), and the internalization of norms (64). Other writers have more generally observed that knowledge concerning man's reference others is important as the relationships between the individual and his reference others are becoming an increasing source of concern in complex contemporary societies (268). In this context, the practical importance of the autonomous selection of reference others by the individual has been stressed (180). Importantly, Watson in his *Social Psychology: Issues and Answers* has concluded that "the most effective technique for altering attitudes is to change reference groups" (423:235). There is much in Watson's book that is relevant for those interested in social application. Many aspects of his work are compatible with the ideas presented in this book.

It must additionally be emphasized that numerous writings with pragmatic implications involve the ideas that have been associated with the reference group literature but do not *explicitly* draw upon it. For example, there have been a variety of marihuana studies that do not employ the reference group concept even though considerable importance is assigned to the user's peer groups (e.g., 38). Similarly, there have been investigations of suicide where the reference group literature would have proved useful. Some content analysis type studies have even concluded that actual suicide notes were more "other oriented" than simulated suicide notes, but these results have not been extensively interpreted within the reference group perspective. [Some of these suicide studies are cited in (175).] *One must conclude that if the reference group literature can be effectively synthesized, persons working in areas of this type will be able to more completely explore the significance of reference others for the behavior under consideration.* The potential of the reference other orientation for the alleviation of human problems has yet to be realized.

While the reason for the preceding thoughts has been primarily pragmatic, we should not forget that conceptual insights may also be attained through an examination of areas of human concern. A statement from Rokeach's provocative study of three mental patients, all of whom claimed to be Jesus Christ, exemplifies this point (325:196): "If real external, positive referents are missing in paranoid mental patients—and this seems to be the case with Clyde and Joseph and Leon—then obviously it is not possible to initiate changes in their delusions and behavior through external referents. But this does not mean that these mental patients have no positive referents whatsoever. Again and again we were struck by the fact that the three men would mention certain referents to whom they obviously looked in a positive way. But these referents were either completely delusional or only quasi-real." [Rokeach states that part two of his book is intended as a contribution to reference group theory (325:24 n). It has not, however, been so recognized. This is unfortunate as it is an excellent study of imaginary and quasi-empirical reference others.] Perhaps, however, the keenest insights into the theoretical and applied dimensions of reference others have been expressed not by a social scientist but by Thoreau in the following quotation (402:216): "If a man does not keep pace with his companions, perhaps it is because he hears a different drummer. Let him step to the music which he hears, however measured or far away."

While it is somewhat unusual to devote an entire book to a single concept, the reference group concept merits such attention. The literature in which it is either directly or implicitly involved is quite extensive and needs to be critically organized. A variety of topics is considered, beginning with the history of the reference group concept and terminating with directives for future research. Our effort is primarily based upon an analysis of the relevant articles in the volumes of *more than two hundred scientific journals* and numerous published books. The comprehensiveness and careful organization of the book make it valuable for the advanced undergraduate student, the graduate student, the professional social scientist, and anyone else who desires to learn about the complexities of the individual-other relationship.

The severe criticisms that have been leveled against the reference group concept suggest the need for an individual-other typology. Such a classification scheme is presented in this book, and it clearly demonstrates that the reference group literature has utilized a number of interrelated concepts. While the typology is an original contribution, it is based upon existing and theoretical evidence. It is hoped that this typology will alert future researchers to the necessity of designating that aspect of the reference other orientation that is of concern to them and thereby provide a framework for the systematization of works pertaining to the reference other orientation.

Further insights are also offered into the reference other phenomenon. A variety of rarely discussed subjects is considered. Methodological recommendations are made in the areas of measurement, research design, and causal inference. The explanatory role of the reference group concept in the literature is documented. Parallels between the primary group or relationship concept and the reference other concept are made. Certain voids and inaccuracies within the literature are noted, and particular attention is given to the sociological ramifications of the reference other orientation.

Considerable emphasis is assigned to the criticisms by reviewers (265; 301; 309) of a recent reader, *Readings in Reference Group Theory and Research*, edited by Herbert H. Hyman and Eleanor Singer (186). While these professional critics were in agreement regarding its scholarship, objectivity, and accomplishment, they observed that Meadian social psychology was not related to reference group theory, the role conflict literature was not utilized, no theoretical paradigms were offered, the relationship of the creation of reference groups to the socialization process was not extensively discussed, and the role of the reference group concept for theoretical developments was not emphasized. These observations are considered and assessed.

Finally, this book will help to sensitize social scientists from different disciplines to each other's work. Unfortunately, reference group writers have shown a distinct tendency to employ materials from their own scholarly domains.

CHAPTER Two

History of the Reference Group Concept

This chapter considers the historical development of the reference group concept, a challenge in view of the differential and wide usage the concept has received. Fortunately, its history is essentially limited to the twentieth century and entails three rather distinct stages. While the chapter provides a broad and intensive history of the reference group concept, those readers who wish to pursue particular points even further will find the references interposed throughout the chapter especially valuable. The stages involved in the development of the reference group concept follow.

1. The Hyman study was preceded by several *immediate fore-runners*, including the symbolic interactionist branch of social behaviorism, early psychological influences, and those writings that had begun to stress the fact that all aspects of ego's environment do not exert the same influence over him.

2. The reference group concept was originated and expanded during the 1940s and the early fifties to which the classic works of the period testify.

3. Hyman's concept enjoyed an extensive increase in popularity during the remainder of the fifties and the sixties, and experienced a conceptual expansion at this time.

Our discussion will only include those forerunners that had a direct influence upon the development of the reference group concept. The term *precursor* is employed in this book to refer to other prior sources that were characterized by ideas similar to those within the reference group literature, but which apparently did not directly influence it. Other histories of the reference group concept include (100:191–97; 184; 185; 186:3–21; 229; 272:101–5; 300; 337:9–35; 339; 364:157–81; 121). The last source contains the most *comprehensive* treatment of the subject. Its helpfulness is acknowledged.

This overview will provide the reader with factual information, familiarize him with the classic studies, and confirm the complexity of the reference other phenomenon. *We will, more than past chroniclers of the reference group concept, stress its diffuse origins as well as the analytic and comparative character of its development.* This approach allows us to relate intelligently the historical dimensions of the reference group concept to current theory and research, and to our individual-other typology in particular. [Smelser has correctly observed that an historical treatise is of no scientific value unless this is accomplished (381:20).] We will focus on the first two periods as developments since the middle fifties form the foundation for the remainder of the book.

Recalling our preliminary definition of the reference other as an other that influences ego in some manner, it is evident that the essential idea of social influence engendered in this concept had been considered by numerous philosophers, educators, and social scientists long before Hyman introduced his concept in 1942. To cite one of numerous examples in the literature, it has been suggested that Marx's notion of "false class consciousness" had a membership-nonmembership connotation. Nevertheless, it was not until the time of Hyman's monograph that writers began to focus upon the differential character, determinants, and consequences of ego's reference others. Importantly, the relevance of nonmembership others became apparent, and a body of empirical evidence about reference others began to emerge. The Hyman study and later efforts involving reference others have come to be circumscribed under the label of reference group theory. This area has been influenced by three immediate forerunners.

One of the most important forerunners of the reference group concept was the early school of symbolic interactionism. The adherents of this school are recognized as having a significant impact on American sociology, and include among its members William James, John Dewey, James M. Baldwin, William Isaac Thomas, George Herbert Mead, Charles H. Cooley, and Ellsworth Faris. Symbolic interactionist theory had its American origin around the beginning of the twentieth century. As many of its proponents were at one time associated with the University of Chicago, this approach is also known as the Chicago School of Social Psychology.

The history of early symbolic interactionism is described in (122; 172; 259). Discussions of the more recent development of symbolic interactionism may be found in the following sources: Its current status is considered in (267; 384). Its assumptions are particularly well portrayed in (42; 96; 171; 329). The relationship of symbolic interactionism to methodology, role-identities, and the self-concept is discussed in (42; 96; 97; 98), (250), and (157), respectively. Collections of readings involving theoretical and empirical works based on this approach include (167; 257; 330; 388). For two excellent social psychology texts employing this orientation, see (239; 370).

Symbolic interactionism was partly a reaction to instinctual theories of human behavior, prevalent in psychology during the later nineteenth century. According to the symbolic interactionists, instincts were not the determining factors in the formation and growth of personality (172:30). Although the biological side of man was not forgotten, social factors were emphasized. Given the diversified origin of interactionist theory, it is impossible to accurately categorize all its contributors in terms of ideas, concepts, and views, but the symbolic interactionists placed an accent on *attitude* and *meaning* (259:339). More specifically, this school was concerned with human association, the social development of the self and personality, and the meaning of symbolic behavior (267).

A relationship between the early school of symbolic interactionism and the reference group concept is frequently recognized in the literature, and symbolic interactionism is typically portrayed as a precursor rather than as a more immediate forerunner of the Hyman study (e.g., 100:191; 272:100–105). It is possible, however, to delimit some more direct influences of this early school upon the development of the reference group concept. One must proceed cautiously in tracing the history of an idea but it appears that *certain of the basic assumptions of the early school of symbolic interactionism anticipated various dimensions of the reference group approach as it has emerged over time, while certain of its other components have had, and are continuing to have, a direct impact upon its development.* The school of symbolic interactionism has "influenced" the reference group literature in a variety of ways but its emphases upon the actual others in the individual's environment, the reflective character of the self, ego's symbolic others, and the "generalized other" have had the major consequences for its development.

Two sources that give more than passing attention to the relationship between the early school of symbolic interactionism and reference group theory are (100:191–97; 229). The latter and more intensive discussion implies that symbolic interactionism was a precursor of reference group theory and queries as to what is new in reference group theory. Kuhn laments that the reference group writers did not draw more fully from the early symbolic interactionists.

Symbolic interactionism assumes that society, a network of interacting individuals with a culture, precedes any existing individual (329:13–15). This assumption implies that the individual must of necessity come into contact with external reality and be socialized. Mead, the most influential of the early symbolic interactionists, for instance, recognized that the formation of action by the individual through a process of self-indication always takes place in a social context. The individual forms and aligns his own action on the basis of an interpretation of the acts of others (41:183–84). Dewey observed the problematic aspect of this process in his 1927 discussion of multiple membership but was unable to resolve it (103:191). This emphasis of the symbolic interactional school on group association parallels an implicit but critical assumption behind the reference group concept. Ego *is* a product of his social environment. *His behavior must necessarily be oriented to selected reference others during the socialization process.*

The symbolic interactionists' interest in the development of the self foreshadowed another aspect of the reference group literature. The Hyman study was concerned with what Harold H. Kelley later called a comparative reference group. Kelley employed this term to "denote a group which the person uses as a reference point in making evaluations of himself or others" (213:79). *It was the emphasis of the early school of symbolic interactionism upon the role of the other in the individual's self-appraisals that foreshadowed the comparative reference group concept.*

The concern of the symbolic interactionists for self-appraisals is not difficult to illustrate. To cite a few examples, Cooley's now-famous concept of the "looking-glass self" most vividly documents the interest of the school in the relationship between the individual's self-appraisals and his others. "A self-idea of this sort seems to have three principal elements: the imagination of our appearance *to the other person;* the imagination of his judgment of that appearance; and some sort of self-feeling, such as pride or mortification" (81:152, my italics). It was Mead, however, more than anyone else who emphasized the social nature of this process (122:95–96). James stressed the importance of the totality of ego's others upon the self-concept, and suggested that *"a man has as many social selves as there are individuals who recognize him* and carry an image of him in their minds" (199:42). Baldwin in describing the dialectic of personal growth even stated that *"the ego and the alter are to our thought one and the same thing"* (18:162).

Symbolic interactionism both anticipated and directly influenced the development of the reference group concept through its emphasis on the *symbolic other*. The symbolic interactionists used a variety of terms to describe the symbolic other, including an audience, an other, and an internalized audience and other. The essential idea involved here is that the individual is able to take symbolically other persons into account. This view was extremely pervasive in the writings of the symbolic interactionists, and was implicit in a number of their concepts. For example, Cooley's concept of the "looking-glass self" presupposes that ego symbolically takes the other person into account in his imagination, and in other instances, Cooley describes the symbolic other as an "imaginary interlocutor."

Several writers have suggested that Cooley's discussion of the *"imaginary interlocutor"* anticipated *the reference individual* concept (e.g., 185:354). While this may be true, Cooley's writings in this regard more significantly indicate that scholars were becoming cognizant of the fact that individuals are *symbolically* influenced by reference others irrespective of whether they are physically present or not. Cooley's often cited discussion of the individual's psychological environment is perhaps the best evidence of this (see also 185:354). Mead's very important concept of "taking the role of the other" also presumes that ego symbolically considers the other person, although Mead was apparently emphasizing that ego must take the *perspective* of the other person in the socialization process (369:564). It was the symbolic interactionists' concept of internal conversation that most explicitly illustrates the symbolic other. An apt description follows (229:7, my italics): "Thinking, for all the symbolic interactionists, is *an internal conversation among the self and internalized others.* And the meaning of internalization is simply the covert segment of the general communicative process. The figures of speech differ—an internal audience, an inner forum, a covert conversation of gestures—but the meanings coincide. *They all make the other crucial to the self and to meaningful action."*

The symbolic other relates to the reference group concept in two ways. First, this concept influenced several reference group cognate concepts that emerged since the Hyman study. For instance, it had a direct impact upon Turner's concept of the audience reference group. Turner indicated that "the actor takes the role of the audience reflexively" (410:328). Turner utilized a number of ideas from the early symbolic interactionists in this work. One of his objectives was to "note the light which our analysis of role-taking may shed *upon the idea of reference group"* (410:316, my italics). Other writers (306) have explicitly utilized Cooley's thoughts on "imaginary interlocutors" and studied the individual as he was influenced by the audience about which he thinks. Pool and Shulman note that (306:145, my italics): *"What we are here describing is a reference group phenomenon.* 'Imaginary interlocutors,' who may also be described as reference persons, enter the author's flow of associations at the time of composition and influence what he writes or says." Some writers (e.g., 441) have also extended Cooley's concept in this manner, but have not utilized the reference group literature.

The emphasis of the early symbolic interactionists upon the "reality" of the symbolic other was also a prelude to the latter realization of the importance of nonmembership reference others. It is difficult to say whether this influence was direct or not, but the realization that ego could be influenced by symbolic others had to be made before the full impact of nonmembership others could be appreciated. It is important to note that Merton, who was the first person to *explicate* the importance of the nonmembership group, acknowledged that Mead recognized the role of the membership group as a significant frame of reference for the individual; Merton also stated that Mead did not extend his insights to the nonmembership group (272:57).

Additional authors have taken this same position (e.g., 258), but Gregory P. Stone criticized Merton's statement and indicated "for the fact is that Mead had nonmembership groups explicitly in mind, though not systematically" (387:559). We think Stone, an informed symbolic interactionist, is correct, but even if he were not, *the more basic fact* that Mead, and the other symbolic interactionists, saw the other as having *a symbolic influence* remains intact. Our following discussion of classic reference group works in this chapter will also indicate that other writers prior to Merton were aware of the importance of non-membership groups.

Symbolic interactionism also influenced the reference group concept in still another way. Mead's concept of the "generalized other" was a precursor of what Kelley later referred to as a normative reference group. Kelley described the normative reference group as a group that sets and enforces standards for the individual (213:80).

This contribution of the earlier symbolic interactionists, and Mead in particular, is extremely important as it has been suggested that the normative reference group be regarded as *the* reference group concept; Shibutani argued for this position in his highly influential 1955 article, "Reference Groups as Perspectives" (369). Shibutani extended Kelley's definition of the normative reference group *explicitly* in terms of Mead's "generalized other" concept. The impact of Shibutani's effort is found in the fact that sociologists have cultivated the study of the normative reference group while the comparative reference group has been relatively neglected. Hyman (184) was the first to make this observation regarding the differential study of the normative and comparative reference group in sociology. The attribution of this to Shibutani's article is an inference on our part. The fact that Kelley (213) designated the comparative reference group concept within the psychological realm may have also been a factor.

Some confusion exists concerning the meaning Mead intended to assign to the "generalized other." In fact, some argue that all of Mead's concepts are vague (266:20). The early symbolic interactionists have also been criticized for not generating any empirical evidence (e.g., 272:57). Without negating these two observations, it should be added that *the identification of variables is in one respect the most critical step in the entire scientific process.* In my judgment, this is what these men were doing!

The general consensus concerning the meaning of Mead's "generalized other" concept is captured in an important statement from Shibutani's influential article: "When Mead spoke of assuming the role of the generalized other, he was not referring to people but to perspectives shared with others in a transaction" (369:564). This led Shibutani to define a reference group as "that group whose outlook is used by the actor as the frame of reference in the organization of his perceptual field" (369:565). Shibutani's work emphasized *the perspective of the reference other* rather than *the reference other who provides the perspective,* although both elements are included in his definition.

Clearly the early symbolic interactionists had a significant impact upon the reference group literature. The influence of this school was in part due to the fact that most of its members were physically situated in a single location and able to exert a unit effect upon students by their presence and through their writings. (An excellent discussion of this aspect of early symbolic interactionism has been provided by Darnell Rucker, *The Chicago Pragmatists* [Minneapolis: University of Minnesota Press, 1969].) Their influence was both in terms of *specific ideas and basic assumptions.* The symbolic interactionists' concern for self-appraisals, symbolic others, and generalized perspectives was related to the eventual development of the comparative reference group concept, one version of the audience reference group, and the normative reference group concept, respectively. Its assumptions regarding existing sociocultural situations emphasized the inevitability of individual-other relationships; its emphasis on the reality of symbolic others seems to have logically paved the way for the view that ego could be influenced by nonmembership groups as well as by membership groups, and its very concern for the other drew attention to its significance.

It is also important to appreciate the differences between the early symbolic interactionists and the later reference group writers. (a) The symbolic interactionists did not extensively consider the nature of ego's reference others, i.e., who are they? (100:191) while those utilizing the reference group perspective have given more attention to this question. (b) The nonmembership reference group was not emphasized by the symbolic interactionist (272:57), but this is generally regarded as the distinctive focus of reference group theory. (c) The symbolic interactionists did not generate a body of empirical evidence regarding reference others (272:57). In contrast, a host of such studies characterizes the reference group literature. (d) The reference group literature has given more attention to reference categories and multiple and conflicting reference groups than did the early symbolic interactionists, while the latter focused *much more* upon the complexities of the self-other process (229). (e) The early symbolic interactionists had a set of ideas that were to some extent integrated about a model of man and his relationship to society. But the reference group writings are characterized by a *diffuseness* that at least in part stems from the fact that its authors have failed to formulate a fundamental view of the individual. (f) Finally, and in some respects most significantly, the other was not as much of a focal point for the symbolic interactionist as it has generally been for the reference group writers. In this regard, Manford H. Kuhn has observed (229:6): "I wish to observe at the outset that while *the other* plays an incontestably crucial role in the conceptions of Cooley, Dewey, Mead, Faris, and the other writers who developed the symbolic interaction orientation, nevertheless *the other* is never attended to with the discerning and analytic interest which they give to the actor."

The question could now be raised as to what consequences reference group theory has had for symbolic interactionism, but we will reserve this discussion until after the reader has been fully exposed to the reference other orientation; it will now suffice to say that, with a few *important* exceptions (e.g., 171; 370), the modern symbolic interactionist, as his earlier counterpart, does not regard the reference other as a focal point of inquiry. It must also be emphasized that although symbolic interactionism has had a meaningful impact upon the reference group concept, its potential influence has only been realized to a very minimal extent. Reasons for the lack of integration of these two areas are offered in our final chapter.

The work of psychologists prior to the Hyman study also influenced the development of the reference group concept. While it is difficult to summarize the effects of what was already a sophisticated discipline, the major lines of influence stem from the psychologists' concern for *social facilitation, levels of aspiration, and frames of reference.* These influences had a much greater effect upon Hyman's study than did the ideas of the early symbolic interactionists. Many of Hyman's references reflect this fact *for his study was basically an extension of previous psychological efforts.*

It was the work of Merton and Kitt (272), published eight years after the Hyman study, that had the single greatest effect upon the popularization of the reference group concept. However, they gave very little attention to earlier psychological efforts. The fact that sociologists would also assign considerable emphasis to the normative reference group concept but very little to the comparative reference group concept, while the minor interest that is eventually shown in psychology in the reference group concept moves towards a version of the comparative reference group concept, commonly referred to as social comparison theory, suggests the following conclusions.

1. Symbolic interactionism had no direct impact upon the Hyman study and very little influence upon the work by psychologists, since then, involving social comparison theory; its influence, which has been significant but not exhaustive, has been upon the development of the normative reference group concept and other reference group cognate concepts in sociology.

2. Early psychological influences had a direct and significant impact upon Hyman's original study and bear some relationship to later developments in psychology involving social comparison theory; this forerunner, however, has had very little influence upon the development of reference group theory in sociology.

These two conclusions would hold in the same way if the terms sociological social psychology and psychological social psychology, or their equivalents, were appropriately substituted for sociology and psychology respectively.

The earliest beginnings of experimental psychology did not exhibit a concern for social variables but eventually interest centered on *"what change in an individual's normal solitary performance occurs when other people are present?"* (6:46). In fact, Triplett's 1897 study of this question (407) employing children winding fishing reels alone and together is regarded as the first experiment in social psychology. "After Triplett's experiment, psychologists became concerned with analytically separating the various factors which could produce faster performance in groups. Among other things, the effect could be due to (1) mere observation of someone else performing the same task, (2) a feeling of competition, or (3) being observed by others" (426:2). A generation after Triplett's study, F. H. Allport introduced the concept of social facilitation to distinguish effects due to the mere presence of other persons from emulation or competitive effects (6:47). Allport attempted to eliminate the competitive effect from all his experiments. Interest in social facilitation remained quite active until the late 1930s, but it suddenly died with the outbreak of World War II.

An interest in social facilitation has been revived in the sixties. While many of these studies concern animal behavior, e.g., rats, dogs, and cockroaches, social situations are also considered, and the implications of the animal studies for human behavior have been offered. Current sources on this revival include (373; 426). These studies, and the earlier social facilitation studies, differ from the traditional reference group studies in that no strong identification bonds are presumed among the experimentally manipulated human subjects and the "orienting" influence of the other seems to be at a minimum. Nevertheless, these studies could be important for the reference other theorist *for just these reasons.* One of the important assumptions of our individual-other typology is that *the range of ego's reference others must be considered!*

The social facilitation studies are rarely related to the development of the reference group concept. This is understandable as they did not consider the nonmembership other, and they have had very little influence upon sociology, where the reference group concept has flourished to the greatest extent. We should recognize, however, that these studies (1) exhibited a concern for the other, primarily in the form of physically present individuals, (2) demonstrated the influence of these persons in that the quantity of work done by the subject generally increased or decreased (360:70), (3) showed in some instances that the other did not have to be physically present in order to influence the individual (85), and (4) originated in the discipline that was to exert the main influence upon the Hyman study and in which the social comparison branch of the comparative reference group concept was to emerge.

A more direct early psychological influence upon Hyman's study was reflected in his utilization of *the frame of reference concept.* The idea of a frame of reference had been frequently employed by psychologists before Hyman's work. Gordon Allport summarized the psychologist's work with the frame of reference concept in his 1940 presidential address to the American Psychological Society. He stated that "frame of reference has to do with any context whatever that exerts a demonstrable influence upon the individual's perceptions, judgment, feelings, or actions" (5:24). The relationship of this rather broadly defined frame of reference concept to the earlier usage of the reference group concept has been recognized in the literature. The Sherifs observed in their 1953 book, *Groups in Harmony and Tension*, that "psychological studies which demonstrated the effect of reference groups, whether or not the term was used, have stemmed from the more general concept of frame of reference" (364:164).

A number of studies in psychology prior to the Hyman study were beginning to bring into prominence the idea *that the group itself, or individuals, could function as part of the frame of reference.* For example, Asch, Block, and Hertzman (12) studied the role of the standards of congenial and hostile groups upon the principles of judgments and attitudes. Interestingly, these researchers distinguished groups to which the individual belonged from the groups to which he did not belong. Lewin observed in a typological study of the problems of a minority group that "one of the most important constituents of the ground upon which the individual stands is the social group to which he 'belongs'" (237:175). However, it was the employment of the frame of reference concept in the level of aspiration studies *that most explicitly brought attention to the relationship between the groups and individuals within a person's frame of reference and his self-evaluations,* and both of these elements are germane to Hyman's study.

The level of aspiration studies directed attention to the scales of reference which helped to determine the relative attractiveness of different points along a difficulty continuum (6:208). The researchers, who initially explored this area, were generally interested in experimentally examining the effects of ego's success or failure on a given task to his future level of aspiration in regard to that task, but it was eventually suggested that certain aspects of the social environment might also be influencing the individual's level of aspiration in given areas. Consequently, the psychological frame of reference concept, which now included individuals and groups, was incorporated into the study of levels of aspirations. It was the 1939 study by Chapman and Volkmann (70) that apparently first extended the study of levels of aspiration to specifically include the others in ego's environment. The following quotation is offered as evidence of this (70:91): "One way in which the social environment might determine the level of aspiration of a given individual would be through his knowledge of the achievement of groups whose status or ability, relative to his own, he could assess. In actual life, men do not usually approach tasks in a vacuum of ignorance about the achievement of others."

It remained, however, for Hyman in his 1942 study to relate the individuals and groups within a person's frame of reference to the evaluation of his ranking on a variety of statuses. The level of aspiration studies had related the individuals and groups within a person's frame of reference only to his self-evaluation of his future performance on a given task. In other words, Hyman introduced a new dependent variable. Even here the complex history of the reference group concept is apparent. Hyman not only cites the types of studies that we have considered in our discussion of frame of reference and level of aspiration, but he notes a number of prior sources that had distinguished between objective and subjective status, the latter being the main concern of Hyman's work. For example, Roper (327) through his public opinion studies had recognized the relevance of other persons and groups for a person's self-evaluation of his own economic status. [The reader should consult Hyman's work (182) for the additional sources that involved this notion of subjective status.] Nevertheless, the Hyman study remains unique not only because the author coined the concepts of reference group and reference individual, but also because he related these and more abstract and imaginary reference others to a variety of statuses and determined the salient reference others of his subjects rather than relying upon presented stimuli. He employed open-end questions to determine the salient reference others of his subjects, a method which was quite unique at the time.

In reviewing the effects of early twentieth century psychology upon Hyman's pioneering effort, we see that the social facilitation, frame of reference, and level of aspiration studies had an impact upon it. The social facilitation investigations only had an indirect influence but the incorporation of the frame of reference concept into the level of aspiration experiments led directly to the realization that individuals and groups impinge upon self-evaluations. It was these comparative reference groups, as Kelley later labeled them, that were of most interest to Hyman.

The frame of reference concept had the closest conceptual relationship to Hyman's work in that reference others were initially regarded as constituting part of ego's frame of reference. Consequently, it is of some interest that the frame of reference concept was never conceptualized in a manner that was generally acceptable to psychologists. Allport observed, for instance, that "the relation of frame to attitudes and to traits is a problem yet to be worked out" (5:24). Rommetveit emphasized the ambiguity in this concept (326), and Israel had the following reservation regarding one meaning that had been attributed to the reference group concept (193:126): "Furthermore, 'reference group' has sometimes been used as equivalent to the expression "a group serving as a frame of reference." In this case the ambiguity inherent in the concept 'frame of reference' so clearly demonstrated by Rommetveit, has been added to the ambiguity of the concept proper." As the psychological frame of reference concept *appears* to be very similar to Shibutani's notion of a perspective, it should be emphasized that the historical impact of the frame of reference concept was upon the *comparative reference group concept* and not the normative reference group concept.

During the fifty-year period prior to Hyman's work, sociologists and social psychologists began to emphasize that all aspects of the social environment do not exert the same influence over the individual. As we will observe, a fundamental assumption of reference group theory is that all reference others are not of equal importance for ego. This line of thought is illustrated in the works of William Graham Sumner, Harry Stack Sullivan, and Charles Horton Cooley. In contrast to the previous two forerunners of the reference group concept, these men had diverse origins and are not regarded as members of a common school.

William Graham Sumner, an important American sociologist and Yale professor, employed the concepts of the in-group and the out-group to refer respectively to ourselves, the we-group, and everybody else, the others-group, in his classic 1906 book, *Folkways* (399:27). This distinction formed the foundation for his influential discussion of ethnocentrism. Merton and Kitt later concluded that this "initial distinction put Sumner well on the way toward opening up a series of problems regarding reference group behavior" (272:102). Although Sumner did not employ the terminology of the current reference group theorist, he clearly realized that ego could be influenced by negative nonmembership reference groups and that ego's membership groups could become positive reference groups for him. Sumner apparently did not grasp the fact that nonmembership groups could become positive reference groups for the individual (272:101) and that membership groups could become negative reference groups.

Although Sumner's work is recognized as a progenitor of the reference group concept (e.g., 185:354; 272:101–5), it did not have much of a direct impact upon either the early beginnings of reference group theory or its later development. Merton and Kitt, however, noted Sumner's ideas in their discussion of concepts kindred to reference group theory (272:101–5), and they presumably gave some direction to their thinking. Sumner was also one of the most insightful of the early writers in regard to the nature of the reference other phenomenon. His view on ethnocentrism, alone, is evidence of this. Sumner's ideas were also popularized in the same cultural milieu as, and not too many years prior to, the classic reference group writings of the 1940s. It must also again be emphasized that Sumner's work was a significant part of a growing body of literature that was beginning to demonstrate that all aspects of the social environment do not have the same effect upon the individual.

It was the work of Harry Stack Sullivan, a more recent figure than Sumner, *that most explicitly pointed to the differential relevance of the others in ego's environment!* Sullivan, the psychiatrist who is given the most credit for having brought about the fusion of psychiatry and social science, coined the term "significant other" to refer to those individuals who are of unique significance for ego. Though there is some question as to whether Sullivan was referring to those individuals responsible for socializing ego or to all persons the individual held in high esteem (95:298 n), Sullivan, as much as anyone before him, understood the importance of the reference other. This is aptly portrayed in the manner in which the "significant other" is utilized by Sullivan in his explanation of the developmental stages of the child's socialization.

The following quotation from Sullivan's 1940 book, *Conceptions of Modern Psychiatry*, is one evidence of his insights in this regard (398:38): "The era of childhood ends with the maturation of a need for compeers. The child manifests a shift from contentment in an environment of authoritarian adults and the more or less personalized pets, toys and other objects, towards an environment of persons significantly *like* him. If playmates are available, his integrations with them show new meaningfulness. If there are no playmates, the child's reverie processes create imaginary playmates. In brief, the child proceeds into the *juvenile era* of personality development by virtue of a new tendency towards cooperation to doing things in accommodation to the personality of others. Along with this budding ability to play with other children, there goes a learning of those performances which we call competition and compromise." Sullivan's intellectual ideas were influenced by a number of sources, but it is of particular interest to us that one of them was the Chicago School of the Social Sciences. For an infrequently cited discussion of this point, see (298).

Although Sullivan's work is often cited in discussions of reference group theory (e.g., 95; 229), it unfortunately has not had a major impact upon this area. But his ideas are specifically related to some of the later developments within the reference group literature. For instance, they have had an influence upon the formation of two reference group cognate concepts, the orientational other (229) and the role-specific-significant other (95), and Shibutani employed several of Sullivan's ideas in his symbolic interactional treatment of reference groups, including a discussion of social status in reference groups (370:249–80). In spite of Shibutani's effort, which has utilized Sullivan's writings more than anyone else in the reference group literature, the potential of Sullivan's views on the role of the "significant other" in the socialization process for the generic study of the other has not been realized.

Charles Horton Cooley, the symbolic interactionist discussed earlier, also differentiated between various aspects of the social environment. As is well known, Cooley introduced the concept of the primary group to refer to groups that are characterized by warm, frequent, and intimate interactions. In this respect, Cooley, more so than the other early symbolic interactionists, appreciated the importance of positive identification in social relationships. Interestingly, Cooley's ideas on the primary group have not had much of an impact upon the development of the reference group concept, but they are occasionally cited in discussions of this concept (e.g., 95; 185:354; 271:358), and Shibutani has incorporated some of them into his symbolic interactional treatment of the reference group concept (370).

It should now be apparent that the men considered in this section did not have as much direct effect upon the development of the reference group concept as the previous two forerunners. However, this simply reflects the not unimportant fact that certain ideas that were later to emerge in the reference group literature had been anticipated by other sources. While some writers might include more or different men under this difficult third forerunner, there is evidence of the influence of Sumner, Sullivan, and Cooley upon the development of the reference group concept.

The only other person that we seriously considered classifying as an immediate forerunner was Georg Simmel. Merton includes him in his discussion of nonmembership groups (271:288–97); one of Simmel's articles is often recognized as having anticipated reference group theory (375), and Donald N. Levine recently brought to my attention a generally unknown work of Simmel's (374) adumbrating the basic idea of reference groups as perspectives. Nevertheless, Simmel appears to be more of a precursor of reference group theory than an immediate forerunner, as his direct impact upon the area is slight.

Sumner, Sullivan, and Cooley realized that all aspects of the social environment are not of equal importance for the individual, and they had begun to indicate the significance of this for social behavior. It is of interest that the element of positive identification is common to each of their works. Sumner spoke of the comradeship in the we-group. Cooley stressed the importance of intimacy in the primary group, and Sullivan emphasized the emotional attachments that develop between the individual and his "significant others." As we shall see, positive identification takes on an important role in the reference group literature.

It was during the forties and early fifties that the reference group concept was formally introduced and extended. We will stress the theoretical and historical aspects of the classic works of this period even though some of them involved empirical results. If there were any themes that emerged from this era, *they were those of the legitimacy and the complexity of individual-other relationships.* It became apparent that *the individual may compare himself to his reference others, identify with them, and take various norms from them.* While these classic writings insured the lasting place of the reference group concept in the social sciences, some confusion regarding the meaning of the reference group concept had developed by the mid-fifties.

Hyman's two-part study involved controlled interviews with thirty-one subjects, and three experiments that were based upon the interview results. Hyman's concern was with "subjective status." This was defined "as a person's conception of his own position relative to other individuals" (182:5). Linn (240:490) notes that the behavior studied by Hyman involved three dimensions: "(1) a comparison of oneself on some characteristic, (2) a social category which was the basis for the comparison (i.e., the 'reference group'), and (3) the evaluation of oneself as a result of this comparison (i.e., 'status')." Hyman was concerned with what Kelley (213) was later to call the comparative reference group. Sampson has emphasized that Hyman "*assumed* that reference groups are groups of which the individual is aware, with which he may or may not be ego-identified or related, and which serve the individual as anchorages for the judgment of his own status" (339:17, my italics).

The major contribution of Hyman's pioneering study was that it focused the psychologist's frame of reference concept upon ego's reference groups and related this variable to a status dimension rather than to the more popular dependent variables involving task behavior and levels of aspiration. Hyman's results lent support to the conclusion that ego's reference others influence his "subjective status." This study was also a major stimulus for the general development of the reference group concept and the examination of comparative reference groups in particular.

The setting for Theodore Newcomb's classic 1943 study of attitude change (284) was Bennington College, an isolated college located a mile and a half from a tiny Vermont village, and four miles from the village of Bennington, whose population was under 10,000. Bennington College was a new, experimental college for women that had opened during the early thirties, the era of the New Deal. The faculty of fifty was largely male, young, and generally nonconservative. Newcomb studied the entire student body at Bennington, more than 600 individuals, between the years 1935 and 1939.

Newcomb examined the influence of the rather liberal milieu of the Bennington College community upon the attitudes of the female students. The general trend of attitude change was from freshman conservatism to senior nonconservatism. "The net result of the study showed that the greater the degree of identification with the college community (i.e., the actual membership group) the greater was the change in attitude. On the other hand, the more the individual was under the influence of his previous groups serving as his reference groups, the less the attitude change" (361:138–39).

The first publication of Newcomb's Bennington study (284) did not utilize a reference group perspective. At this time, he was still employing the frame of reference concept of the psychologist. Newcomb later recast the Bennington study in a reference group framework (361:139–55). This was not the first time Newcomb had revised this data (339:37).

Newcomb's study had a number of important implications for the development of the reference group concept. 1. It helped to usher in the reference group concept. Newcomb's work proved to be very influential as is reflected by the fact that it was reprinted in several places and has received wide recognition.

2. Newcomb was the first person to empirically examine the *normative* dimension of reference groups. In fact, Kelley cites Newcomb's study in his discussion of the normative reference group (213). Newcomb was concerned with the effects of reference groups upon *attitude change* while Hyman had studied reference groups and reference individuals as standards for comparison.

3. Although the current emphasis on normative reference groups has overshadowed an explicit concern for identification reference groups, Newcomb's investigation also focused on this dimension. His discussion of reference groups as negative and positive illustrates this. For instance, some students were influenced by their families because they wished to please them while other students were influenced by their families because they were hostile to them. Newcomb's study clearly demonstrated that the individual could be influenced by reference groups he "liked" and by reference groups he "disliked." [Newcomb clarified the distinctions between positive and negative reference groups and membership and nonmembership groups in his influential 1950 social psychology text (285).]

4. Newcomb's work also emphasized that membership groups have differential influences over their members. Bennington College did not exert the same degree of influence over all its members.

5. Newcomb was the first person to incorporate an actual study of the social structure into a reference group study. He documented the liberal climate of the college, and he appreciated the probable role of the physical isolation of the college in strengthening its effects upon the students. While it remained for Merton and Kitt to extensively relate the reference group concept to sociological theory, Newcomb's effort should be regarded as an initial step in that direction. Newcomb's study is also important as it considered the relationship between personality variables and reference group influence. This relationship becomes a focal point for Newcomb's second study of these Bennington college students twenty-five years later (288).

The Information and Education Division of the United States Army sponsored a massive research project that was concerned with the American soldier during World War II. These volumes, which reported the attitudes, sentiments, and behaviors of large numbers of servicemen, represented the single greatest research effort in the social sciences up to that time (100:192). [For a history of the events leading up to this study, see (256:287–332).] The first volume of this work, written by Samuel A. Stouffer and his distinguished associates and published in

1949 (392), considered a variety of topics. However, it was the concept of *relative deprivation* that had the greatest influence upon the development of the reference group concept. Stouffer notes in chapter 1 of the first volume that a theory of relative deprivation was introduced to account for otherwise disparate empirical findings (392:52). Hyman and Singer have referred to the concept of relative deprivation as a close cousin to the comparative reference group concept (186:6). While Hyman's work is not cited in Stouffer's study, it was stated that "the idea would seem to have a kinship to and, in part, include such well-known sociological concepts as 'social frame of reference,' 'patterns of expectations,' or 'definitions of the situation' " (392:125).

Relative deprivation was not explicitly defined in Stouffer's work but it is clear what the authors intended to imply by this concept. They indicated, for example, that "becoming a soldier meant to many men a very real deprivation. But the felt sacrifice was greater for some than for others, *depending on their standards of comparison*" (392:125).

It is important to understand the role of *The American Soldier* study in the development of the reference group concept. While this research is not often stressed in discussion of the history of the reference group concept, it (1) maintained an interest in the comparative reference group concept, (2) *demonstrated and emphasized* the deprivation that ego may experience from comparing himself to others, and (3) served as a stimulus for the Merton and Kitt effort. As Stouffer himself commented in the companion volume to *The American Soldier*, "if the way in which we organized some of our concepts and analyzed and presented our data provides, as it has, the basis for brilliant further thinking of the kind which, I am told, may be represented in some of the chapters of the present book, our work has not been in vain" (390:202).

Merton and Kitt employed a reference group framework in their 1950 reinterpretation of *The American Soldier* study (272). The Merton and Kitt chapter was to have implications for numerous aspects of the development of the reference group concept but, like Hyman's original study, its focus involved the comparative reference group concept.

There are a number of reasons for the critical importance of the Merton and Kitt effort. (1) It introduced the reference group concept to sociologists (229:10). Until this time, in fact, the concept had generally enjoyed little prominence (186:6). (2) This source has been extremely influential over the years. It was reprinted by Merton (with Kitt's name changed to Rossi) in his very significant book, *Social Theory and Social Structure* (271:225–80), and Linn concluded from an empirical examination of selected sociology journals that this work was the most often cited authority in the sociological literature (240:492). (3) Most importantly, it was the Merton and Kitt effort that *most fully placed the reference group concept within a sociological perspective.*

Several factors prompted Merton's and Kitt's reexamination of *The American Soldier.* (1) They desired to expand the theoretical ideas presented in this study. Merton and Kitt observed that the analytical concepts presented in Stouffer's effort may not only apply to soldiers but have wider implications for the development of social theory (272:41). (2) They particularly wanted to extend the concept of relative deprivation. Merton and Kitt concluded that Stouffer and his associates stressed the *deprivation* rather than the *relative* in their treatment of the relative deprivation concept (272:51). The implication of this important statement, which unfortunately *has not been realized,* seems to be that the reference group theorist should place his emphasis on *the other* with whom ego compares himself rather than on *ego's reaction* to this comparison. (3) There were a number of contradictory findings in *The American Soldier* that were not resolved by its authors. Merton and Kitt commented that although the authors of *The American Soldier* employed the concept of relative deprivation to explain a number of otherwise inconsistent findings, they would "add several research cases not subjected by the authors to interpretation in terms of reference group concepts which nevertheless seem explicated by such concepts" (272:45). [For a concise statement of the additional cases considered by Merton and Kitt, see (423:101–3).]

The major contribution of the Merton and Kitt statement was that they related the reference group concept to sociological theory. While many of these insights will be incorporated into the remainder of our book, three are of immediate importance.

The reference group concept was explicitly related to the functional approach in sociology (272:41). The positive and negative consequences of reference group processes for the social system and the individual are discussed. Particular attention was given to the functions of ego's positive orientation to nonmembership groups and *the anticipatory socialization process* was emphasized.

Substantial interest was also shown in the reference group selection process. Why does ego establish reference relationships with his reference groups? The role of the social structure in this process was emphasized (272:62), and the first reference group typology was presented (272:62). It was suggested that ego's comparative reference others are "others in the same shoes" as ego, and that ego must have some knowledge about the situation of his comparative reference groups (272:66–67). Merton also emphasized the crucial point at this juncture that an understanding of reference group processes presupposes knowledge in a number of areas.

Ego's multiple reference groups were emphasized (272:59–70). The concepts of conflicting and sustaining reference groups were employed. Considerable theoretical importance was assigned to the question of how ego revolves a multiple reference group conflict situation.

In our concluding remarks about the Merton and Kitt work, it should be noted that it was subjected to a certain amount of legitimate criticism. Nathan Glazer (145), for instance, stressed the ex post facto character of their reinterpretation, and Jahoda, Deutsch, and Cook (198:332) observed that Merton and Kitt had not really presented a *theory* of reference group behavior. More recently, Glaser and Strauss have suggested that Merton and Kitt attempted to develop a formal theory without adequate comparative empirical data (141:81). These observations, however, do not negate the essential quality of the Merton and Kitt study nor its extensive influence upon the popularization of the reference group concept.

For an in-depth history of the reference group concept in sociology and psychology from 1942 to 1962, see Sampson's thesis (339). This effort is noteworthy for its comparative analysis of the reference group concept in psychology, but many sociologists would question certain of its statements in the area of sociology. Sampson also considers a number of minor reference group sources that have not been included in this book.

Several psychologists and psychologically oriented social psychologists employed the reference group concept in their writings during the forties and early fifties. These writers include Hadley Cantril, Eugene L. Hartley, Ruth E. Hartley, Muzafer Sherif and Carolyn W. Sherif. While most of their writings were theoretical and only constituted short chapters in books, including (158; 361; 363; 364), they helped to keep the reference group concept alive. In this regard, Sampson concluded that "from 1942 until the publication of Sherif and Cantril's *The Psychology of Ego-Involvements* (1947), an interim of five years elapsed in which the concept of reference group does not appear in the literature" (339:24). It will be recalled that the reference group concept never did become as popular in psychology as it did among sociologists and sociologically oriented social psychologists. The important observation should be made, however, that the influence that it does attain in psychology is largely due to the works of the Sherifs during that period.

We should quickly add that although these writings did not have a major impact on the development of reference group theory, they made some important contributions that are not always recognized. (1) The significance of reference groups for *attitude formation* was realized! This interest was reflected in the Sherif and Cantril 1947 work on ego-involvements (363) and carried through by Sherif in his later works. Although Sherif and Cantril stated that they did not significantly modify Hyman's definition of reference group, they in fact did. Their interest was in the normative rather than the comparative aspects of reference groups. (2) Several of these writings differentiated the reference group concept from the membership group concept (e.g., 361; 363). Although the distinction between these two concepts is not always clear, it was clarified by Sherif in his 1948 publication, *An Outline of Social Psychology* (361). His discussion at this point began to reflect the traditional view of these terms that was considered in chapter one. (3) The role of identification in the reference group formation process was emphasized. This observation was also initially made in the 1947 Sherif and Cantril book (363). Sampson has drawn the significant conclusion that the distinction between group identification and the reference group concept is not clear in this work (339:28–29), but nevertheless attention is drawn to the factor of identification in the reference group formation process. We will see that most writers later come to regard identification as a necessary condition for normative influence. The following definition of the reference group that Sherif has employed in his writings illustrates the emphasis that was given to identification (364:161): "With the above considerations in mind, reference groups can be characterized simply as *those groups to which the individual relates himself as a part or to which he aspires to relate himself psychologically.*" It is of interest that the Sherifs have retained this definition in the most recent edition of their social psychology text (366:418).

(4) Certain of these writers began to show the relevance of the reference group concept for the understanding and resolution of conflict caused by multiple group membership, a topic that later became of central interest to reference group theorists. The clearest evidence of this is found in Eugene L. Hartley's article, "The Psychological Problems of Multiple Group Membership," that was published in 1951 (158). The author drew upon Stonequist's work on the marginal man. Stonequist's effort has encouraged some study of conflict situations, and these studies are occa-

sionally recognized as a subdivision of reference group theory. Relevant discussions include (105; 146; 300). The 1952 social psychology text by Eugene and Ruth Hartley (159) also gave slight consideration to this topic. Sampson has observed in regard to these writings that they were the first to attempt to relate a role and position analysis to the reference group concept (339:67).

Kelley published his influential theoretical statement, "Two Functions of Reference Groups," in 1952 (213). A majority of writers since Kelley's work appeared have differentiated between the two functions he set forth and cite him for documentation. Kelley observed that the reference group writings of Hyman, Merton and Kitt, Newcomb, and others had treated the reference group concept in two ways. Drawing on the extant literature, he distinguished between the normative and the comparative functions of reference groups, a distinction that has been maintained over the years. The normative function refers to groups that *set and enforce norms for the individual.* The comparison function described reference groups that serve as *standards for comparisons.* Kelley discussed the former in terms of motivation and the latter in terms of perception.

It is important that an identification view of reference groups is subsumed under Kelley's normative function. He observed that one usage of the reference group concept was to denote a group in which the individual is motivated to gain or maintain acceptance. Kelley consequently reasoned that in order to promote this acceptance the individual will hold attitudes in conformity with what he perceives to be the consensus among the group members. His focus, however, was upon the normative rather than the identification element.

It was during the late fifties and sixties that the usage of the reference group concept was greatly expanded. Kuhn has suggested that this was due to three factors (229). (1) The prestige of its sponsors was related to its impressive development. "With such sponsors as Robert Merton, Theodore Newcomb, Muzafer Sherif, and by implication, the late Sam Stouffer and his associates, it is little wonder the concept enjoyed—as one observer put it—a meteoric rise in popularity" (229:11). (2) The concept of the reference group came into vogue at the time survey research techniques were being increasingly used by psychologists and social psychologists on the sociological side. This emphasis on the survey approach coupled with the fact that the reference group concept was operationalized by the means of some rather simple and straightforward types of questions, which could easily be employed in surveys, facilitated its usage. (3) The reference group theorists generally employed the reference group concept in such a way that the complexities of the individual-other relationship did not hinder its development.

The field of sociology is the area in which the reference group concept achieves its prominence. Certain of the thoughts and ideas of the early forerunners and the classic writers exert a major impact upon the efforts of the sociologist, but Shibutani's article, "Reference Groups as Perspectives" (369), and a second major work by Merton (271:281–386) are quite influential. The normative reference group concept, as described by Kelley *and* Shibutani, becomes the focal point of interest, while the comparative reference group concept and the identification process, which was subsumed under the normative reference group concept, receive little attention. The reference group cognate concepts that emerge during this period, since they are not yet systematized, add increased confusion to the meaning of the reference group concept. None of them, including Turner's concept of the audience reference group, are given systematic and extensive treatment.

The reference group concept has not received much emphasis in psychology since the early fifties. The only patterned interest to be shown involves social comparison theory, which exhibits a *psychological* concern for the others with which ego compares himself. This infrequently researched area can be traced to the forerunners that were previously discussed, but it is largely a result of a number of small group laboratory studies in psychology during the early fifties, and was stimulated by Leon Festinger's 1954 theory regarding social comparisons (125). Pettigrew has recently suggested that this approach be combined with the comparative reference group literature in sociology, the existing evidence on relative deprivation, and the writings on status inconsistency (300).

Discussions of the social comparison process in psychology may be found in (202:309–30; 300; 358:277–85; 426:53–74). There is not much empirical evidence on this subject but a number of studies are presented in Supplement 1 of the 1966 *Journal of Experimental Social Psychology.* This supplement also includes a bibliography of pertinent works. In one article in the supplement, Singer (379) reviews early efforts in this area. More recent studies since the supplement include (11; 396; 427).

As we will see in the remainder of this book, the expansion of the reference group concept during this recent period is characterized by both positive and negative dimensions. A host of empirical studies are conducted involving the reference group concept, and the conceptual elements of the reference other phenomenon begin to emerge. Nevertheless, and in spite of the fact that the reference group concept is employed in a number of explanatory efforts, the reference group literature remains scattered and diffuse, resulting in confusion rather than progress. The efforts of this period are also characterized by certain methodological weaknesses and suffer from the fact that they are not organized around an explicit model of man.

CHAPTER Three

An Individual-Other Typology

We have seen that the reference group concept has been subjected to a variety of criticisms, yet it is characterized by a number of positive features. There are a number of logical alternatives to this scientifically necessary but frustating dilemma. First, the reference group concept could be discarded. While this suggestion has been made by some, it represents a drastic solution as its positive functions are too numerous for elimination from the social sciences. Secondly, a single meaning could be assigned to the reference group concept. The problem of conflicting meanings would then be resolved. This is what has happened in sociology. Shibutani's definition of reference groups as perspectives has tended to predominate. While the reasoning behind this approach must be appreciated, it ignores the complexities of the individual-other relationship. "Too many doors are closed." Another possibility is to develop a classification scheme that allows for the consideration of the various dimensions of the reference group concept. *This procedure would result in the retention of the reference group concept, provide for consistency in the usage of terms, and recognize the complexity of the reference other phenomenon.* The third alternative is the preferable solution.

Some writers have resolved the reference group dilemma by defining away the problem. Parker and Kleiner (292:138), for instance, argue that the normative, comparative, and identification elements of the reference other phenomenon are empirically linked in actual ongoing behavior. Their view is rejected because this is not always true, and even if it were, it would still be analytically necessary to make distinctions of this type.

It is important to consider the rationale behind an individual-other typology not only because additional justification is in order but because the rationale provides further documentation for the complexity of the reference other phenomenon. An adequate rationalization for the individual-other typology requires a discussion of Herbert Blumer's notion of a "sensitizing concept." In stressing the importance of concepts in science, Blumer suggests that concepts in the social sciences are necessarily sensitizing in character (39). This means that the social scientist cannot simply or definitively describe that part of the "real world" he desires to examine *because variables do not exist in isolation*—a conclusion also drawn by Howard P. Becker in his discussion of generalizations in the social sciences (24:93). Their adequate description presupposes a consideration of the *setting* in which they appear. A quotation from Blumer's work (39:7–8, my italics) will help to clarify the meaning of a "sensitizing concept": "In handling an empirical instance of a concept for purposes of study or analysis we do not, and apparently cannot meaningfully, confine our consideration of it strictly to what is covered by the abstract reference of the concept. *We do not cleave aside what gives each instance its peculiar character and restrict ourselves to what it has in common with the other instances in the class covered by the concept.* To the contrary, we seem forced to reach what is common by accepting and using what is distinctive to the given empirical instance. In other words, what is common (i.e., what the concept refers to) is expressed in a distinctive manner in each empirical instance and can be got at only by accepting and working through the distinctive expression."

If the basic idea involved in Blumer's notion of a "sensitizing concept" is applied to the reference other phenomenon, it must be concluded that its analysis should include an examination of the empirical instance in which the reference other phenomenon occurs. In effect, the uniqueness of the reference other phenomenon in particular situations must be conceptually incorporated into the very study of this phenomenon. This is what the individual-other typology which follows is intended to do. Insofar as this is possible, the basic scope of the reference group concept will be extended. Blumer's view suggests that concepts in the social sciences will never be able to entirely include the peculiarities of the setting in which they appear.

It is also possible to justify and understand the need for an individual-other typology through an examination of the reference group literature. Our discussion of the history of the reference group concept indicated that a number of reference group cognate concepts had developed. A selection of these concepts is presented in table 2. The fact that many of them refer to distinctive features of the reference other phenomenon emphasizes its complexity and suggests that this complexity should be systematically incorporated into the study of this phenomenon. *Unfortunately, students of the reference group have rarely considered more than one of these concepts in the same study.* This has prevented the full realization and consideration of the multidimensional character of the reference other phenomenon! The overlapping of some of the reference

2. SELECTED REFERENCE GROUP COGNATE CONCEPTS

Source	Concept	Meaning
Herbert H. Hyman (186:149) (1942)	Reference Group	The actual or "reified" groups or categories of people ego compares himself to in regard to the statuses he perceives as important
	Reference Individual	The particular and crucial individual ego compares himself to in regard to the statuses he perceives as important
Samuel A. Stouffer and associates (392:125–26) (1949)	Relative Deprivation	The deprivation an American soldier experienced because he compared his service status to certain categories of others
Theodore M. Newcomb (285:225–27) (1950)	Positive Reference Group	A group in which the individual desires membership status and whose norms he accepts
	Negative Reference Group	A group the individual opposes and whose norms he rejects
Harold H. Kelley (213) (1952)	The Normative Function of Reference Groups	The group or category that sets and enforces norms for ego
	The Comparison Function of Reference Groups	The group or category against which ego evaluates himself and others
Hans Gerth C. Wright Mills (138:90–91) (1953)	Intimate Others	Those few significant others who are perceived by the individual as contributing the greatest confirmation to the prized or aspired-to image of his self
Muzafer Sherif Carolyn W. Sherif (364:161) (1953)	Reference Groups	Those groups to which the individual relates himself as a part or to which he aspires to relate himself psychologically

41

Table 2.   Continued

Source	Concept	Meaning
Elizabeth Bott (46)	Direct Reference Group	An actual group whose norms can be directly internalized by ego
(1954)	Constructed Reference Group	A concept or social category where the amount of projection of norms into the constructed group is high
S. N. Eisenstadt (114)	Reference Norms	General standards that influence ego's behavior and perception
(1954)	Reference Orientation	Reference norms that are employed in particular situations
Tamotsu Shibutani (369) (1955)	Reference Group	The "other" whose perspective is used by ego as a frame of reference in the organization of his perceptual field
Ralph H. Turner (410)	Identification Reference Group	This group is the source of ego's values
(1956)	Interaction Reference Group	A group ego takes into account merely to accomplish his purposes
	Valuation Reference Group	These are groups which are defined as important by identification reference groups
	Audience Reference Group	These are the groups by whom ego sees his role performance observed and evaluated
Stanley Rosenman (335) (1957)	The Dominant Internalized Other	A "trespassing" imago, an unwelcome potentate, who batters or chicanes his way to a ruling position within the organism
Robert K. Merton (271:302–3)	Reference Individual	Person who significantly influences ego in several roles
(1957)	Role-Model	Person who significantly influences ego in one or just a few roles

Table 2. Continued

Source	Concept	Meaning
W. W. Charters, Jr. Theodore M. Newcomb (71) (1958)	Salience of a Membership Group	The degree to which a membership group is present in a person's awareness
Ernest Q. Campbell Thomas F. Pettigrew (66) (1959)	The Self-Reference System	Influences stemming from ego's self-concept rather than from external sources
	The Professional Reference System	Influences originating from several designated sources mutually related to the individual's occupational role
	The Membership Reference System	Influences stemming from one of ego's designated membership groups
Jay M. Jackson (195) (1959)	Preference Group	A person is positively attracted to membership in a group but is not accepted as a member
Ithiel de Sola Pool Irwin Shulman (306) (1959)	Reference Audience	Those audiences about whom ego thinks
Francis E. Merrill (269) (1961)	The Direct Other	Those "immediate" others through which the individual perceives himself
	The Intermediate Other	Persons or groups with whom ego is not actually communicating at the moment but whose real or supposed judgments influence his self-judgments
	The Ideological Other	The general patterns of belief that characterize a particular society at a given time

Table 2.   Continued

Source	Concept	Meaning
Leonard Plotnicov (302)	Fixed-Membership Group	Permanent groups based on bonds of solidarity between members
(1962)	Flexible-Membership Group	Groups characterized by external goals
Samuel A. Stouffer (391:14) (1962)	Sanctioning Groups	Groups or categories that have the power to exert positive or negative sanctions over a member or aspiring member
Ernest Q. Campbell (64)	Internalizer	Person who follows norms because he has internalized them
(1964)	Identifier	Person who follows norms because they are associated with the wishes of significant others
Manford Kuhn (229) (1964)	Orientational Other	An other to whom ego is emotionally and psychologically committed. This other provides ego with his general vocabulary, self-concept, and social objects
Theodore D. Kemper (216) (1966)	Reference Set	The sum total of others whom ego takes into account when he "acts"
Norman K. Denzin (95) (1966)	Role-Specific Significant Other	An other who is important for ego within a role context

Note: This selected array of reference group cognate concepts is intended to illustrate and document the complexity of the reference other phenomenon and the overlapping character of some of these concepts.

group cognate concepts also suggests that a classification scheme would help to systematize work in this area.

Furthermore, a rationale for an individual-other typology has been provided by others. Kuhn has made the most explicit statement in this regard (228:78, my italics): "At present we appear to be in that rather foolish and useless situation in which we debate what a reference group really is. Most of the suggestions point to varieties of functional relations between self and groups or categories of others. *The question ought not to be which of these is really a reference group, but rather, what special term shall we agree to use for each particular relation?"*

The importance of the Kuhn statement cannot be overemphasized. It represents a distinct departure from the manner in which the reference group concept has been historically viewed and suggests that *a different conceptual and research strategy must be employed in the study of the reference other phenomenon!* Jackson also argues that the reference group concept is too inclusive (195).

The nature of typologies in the social sciences is somewhat nebulous. While typologies are often employed in the social sciences, they represent an "underdeveloped area" (255:4). For example, little attention has been given to their construction (255:4). Basically, however, a typology is *a classification scheme.* "Types" of one form or another are involved. *A unit of analysis is divided into two or more categories on each of one or more dimensions.* Redfield's (313) initial folk-urban distinction is an example of a typology in anthropology where *societies* were classified into *two categories or types,* the folk society and the urban society, on *a single folk-urban dimension.* Redfield later suggested that societies could be subdivided into still more categories or types on this folk-urban dimension (314). McKinney, a leading student of the typological method in the social sciences, presents a consensus definition of a typology as a *"purposive, planned selection, abstraction, combination and (sometimes) accentuation of a set of criteria with empirical referents that serves as a basis for comparison of empirical cases"* (254:203).

The typological tradition in sociology has had several roots (420:1). One of these has been representative of the more traditional objective of typologies and involves the delimitation of the "cluster" of variables that characterize a given type. Given this goal, "we need to know that the variables have a combination of values in some instances and that these values are all the same in all such instances and have a different set of values in other instances" (386:45). The typological method, however, has also been given a "broader" interpretation in the field of sociology. In these situations, the interest is not just with the relative frequency of occurrence of various combinations of the categories of variables but rather the focus is more on the process of *concept formation* (255:7). It has been observed that (22:50–51): "If a typology leads us toward understanding of whole networks of related variables, as for instance the 'cosmopolitan/local' typology helped to meaningfully organize a wide range of data, it should be worthwhile to break it down into its components, to study the part played by each.

In this process we may also find combinations of properties which were overlooked in constructing the initial typology, and bring to light the assumptions which led to the bypassing of certain combinations or the ignoring of certain distinctions." It is in this second, and broader sense, that the term *typology* is employed in this book. [Social scientists often attribute different meanings to the term *typology*. We would emphasize that it is a classification system. Sociologists might find of value some discussions of the typological procedure as presented by archaeologists (e.g., 225; 336).]

The typology in this general sense enables the researcher to focus more broadly upon the entire framework of the phenomenon being considered. Have the proper dimensions of the unit of analysis been included? Have the appropriate number of categories on each dimension been considered? What is the significance of the difference between combinations of categories across different dimensions? Do these differences relate to either the cause or the effect of the phenomenon being considered? The typology, much as theory, enables the researcher to identify gaps in knowledge, generate fresh hypotheses, summarize data, and clarify concepts. Typification may be thought of as "a kind of 'scientific perception' whereby the scholar abstracts from the phenomena which comprise his reality a set of theoretically relevant and *systemically* interconnected configurations and proceeds to study them as configurations" (420:1, my italics).

It must be emphasized that typologies are to be viewed as tentative classifications. Even though initial classification schemes should be based upon the existing state of knowledge regarding the phenomenon under consideration, their structure cannot be regarded as valid. This reflects not only the nature of the typological approach but the very essence of the scientific method. Quantification is involved in the original construction of the typology, the clarification and refinement of existing typologies, and the verification of hypotheses that flow from the typology (17:249–56).

While we would then stress the tentative nature of the individual-other typology to be discussed subsequently, the fact must also be emphasized that this classification scheme has been systematically based upon the extensive reference group literature. It can consequently be argued that it possesses a degree of validity that does not always accrue to an initial typological attempt. This, of course, does not guarantee its validity. The typology will certainly profit from future modification and empirical testing. [Methods for verifying typologies are discussed in

(420; 433).] In fact, the typology has been constructed with the objective of delineating the basic dimensions of the reference other phenomenon and their major categories, *anticipating that future writers will provide additional specification.* This procedure has several advantages. (1) *It highlights the primary objective of the typology, namely to stress a change in the conceptualization of the reference other phenomenon.* Drawing upon Kuhn, our goal is not to depict the nature of a reference group but to describe the types of relationships that are maintained between the individual and his reference others. (2) The complexity of the reference other phenomenon as well as the tentative nature of science are acknowledged. (3) The typology is made researchable. A too abstract or detailed typology might have precluded or inhibited future empirical efforts.

One final aspect of the typological procedure should be noted at this point. There has been considerable controversy—see (225; 254; 255; 336)—as to whether a typology is only an heuristic device or an attempt to portray actual reality. Without pursuing the various sides of this issue, and realizing that the typology is often regarded as an instrumental tool, the individual-other typology presented in this book is intended to depict reality. It should also be noted that, although we have drawn from the works of other writers for basic insights, our typology is not intended to be a categorization of their work.

While it has occasionally been noted that the reference group concept involves the individual, an other, and some type of relationship that exists between them (369), this observation has unfortunately not been systematically incorporated into its study. These factors constitute the three components of our typology. They are described as follows.

The Reference Other: The *other* that is influencing the individual.

The Reference Relationship: The *type of influence* the reference other has over the individual.

The Individual: The *object* of the influence being extended by the reference other.

Examples of these components are presented in table 3. Each of these three components will be considered in terms of its appropriate dimensions. These dimensions will then be broken down into types, and in some instances, a further subcategorization, subtypes, will be presented.

The designation of the reference other, the reference relationship, and the individual as the components in our typology is not difficult to justify. Both theoreticians and researchers interested in the reference group concept have been essentially attempting to describe and ex-

3. THE THREE COMPONENTS OF THE INDIVIDUAL-OTHER TYPOLOGY

(A) *The Three Components*

The Reference Other (1)	*The Reference Relationship* (2)	*The Individual* (3)

(B) *Examples of the Three Components*

(1) *The Reference Other*	(2) *The Reference Relationship*	(3) *The Individual*
(a) Bennington College	(a) *Normative*: The conservative college student gradually internalizes the liberal norms of Bennington College as she moves from her freshman to her senior year.	(a) The Bennington College Freshman
(b) College Friends	(b) *Comparative*: The American Soldier in combat compares himself to his college friends at home and becomes dissatisfied.	(b) The American Soldier
(c) The Girl Friend	(c) *Identification-Object*: A young man desires to marry his attractive girl friend.	(c) The Young Man

plain the influence of reference others upon the individual. Hyman was concerned with their relationship to the individual's status appraisals. Newcomb examined the effects of Bennington College upon attitude change. Stouffer studied the relevance of reference categories for the American soldier's satisfaction with his service status. Shibutani visualized reference groups as providers of perspectives for the individual. It is evident, then, that our individual-other typology must include these components, which now will be elaborated upon.

The Reference Other

The reference other will be characterized in terms of two dimensions: (1) empirical status, and (2) membership status. These two dimensions and the remainder of the typology are presented in table 4.

4. AN INDIVIDUAL-OTHER TYPOLOGY

The Reference Other: The *other* that is influencing the individual

(1) *Empirical Status*:

(1–A) *The Reference Individual*: The reference individual is an actual person who is extending an influence over ego.

(1–B) *The Quasi-Empirical Reference Other*: The quasi-empirical reference other is in a sense "real" and in a sense not "real."

(1–B–1) *The Reference Group*: The reference group is an actual group that is extending an influence over ego.

(1–B–2) *The Reference Category*: The reference category is a social or statistical category that is extending an influence over ego.

(1–B–3) *The Reference Norm:* The reference norm is an *external* norm that is extending an influence over ego.

(1–B–4) *The Reference Self*: The reference self is ego, himself, in the symbolic role of the other, extending an influence over his own person.

(1–B–5) *The Reference Object*: The reference object is *a particularly important social object* for ego that is extending an influence over him. It may be a thing, a quality, an event, or a state of affairs (excluding the other types and subtypes of reference others considered under the empirical status dimension).

(1–C) *The Imaginary Reference Other*: The imaginary reference other is an "unreal" other that is extending an influence over ego.

(2) *Membership Status:*

(2–A) *Membership Affiliation*: Ego is characterized by a membership affiliation with a reference other if he is recognized as having a membership affiliation with the reference other.

(2–B) *Nonmembership Affiliation*: Ego is characterized by a nonmembership affiliation with a reference other if he is not recognized as having a membership affiliation with the reference other.

The Reference Relationship: The *type of influence* the reference other has over the individual

(1) *The Type of Reference Relationship*:

(1–A) *The Identification-Object Reference Relationship*: An identification-object reference relationship exists between the individual and a reference other if the individual's degree of positive or negative sentiment toward the reference other is sufficient to direct his overt or covert behavior *toward the reference other* as an object.

Table 4. Continued

(1–B) *The Normative Reference Relationship*: A normative reference relationship exists between the individual and a reference other if the individual's overt or covert behavior *is being* influenced *by the norms or values* characteristic of or attributed to the reference other.

(1–C) *The Comparative Reference Relationship*: A comparative reference relationship exists between the individual and the reference other if the individual compares himself (or others) to the reference other on some dimension(s) and is influenced in either an overt or covert manner.

(2) *The Scope of the Reference Relationship*:

(2–A) *The Scope of the Identification-Object Reference Relationship*: The scope of the identification-object reference relationship reflects (1) the intensity of sentiment that ego holds toward the reference other, and (2) the range of "non-normative" influence that the reference other extends over ego.

(2–B) *The Scope of the Normative Reference Relationship*: The scope of the normative reference relationship reflects the extent to which ego has internalized the norms and values of the reference other.

(2–B–1) *The Compliant Normative Reference Relationship*: The individual in this situation follows the norms or values of the reference other because he expects to benefit from his conformity.

(2–B–2) *The Identification Normative Reference Relationship*: The individual in this situation conforms or deviates from the norms or values of the reference other because he is identified with the reference other.

(2–B–3) *The Internalized Normative Reference Relationship*: The individual in this situation has internalized the norms or values of the reference other.

(2–C) *The Scope of the Comparative Reference Relationship*: The scope of influence of the comparative reference relationship reflects (1) the number of dimensions concerning which ego compares himself to the reference other, (2) the degree of relative deprivation or gratification that results from the comparison(s), and (3) the range of other covert and overt behaviors that flow from the comparison(s).

(3) *The Role Character of the Reference Relationship*:

(3–A) *Role-Related Reference Relationship*: The individual is characterized by a role-related reference relationship if the influence of the reference other is limited to a role relationship(s) that exists between him and the reference other.

Table 4. Continued

(3–B) *Person Reference Relationship:* A person reference relationship exists between ego and the reference other if the influence of the reference other is not limited to a role relationship(s) that exists between him and the reference other.

The Individual: The *object* of the influence being extended by the reference other.

(1) *Ego's Perception of the Reference Relationship:*

(1–A) *"Objective" Perception:* Ego's perception of a designated dimension of a reference relationship is "objective" if he perceives this dimension in an essentially accurate fashion.

(1–B) *"Subjective" Perception:* Ego's perception of a designated dimension of a reference relationship is "subjective" if he does not perceive this dimension in an essentially accurate fashion.

(2) *Ego's Awareness of the Reference Other:*

(2–A) *"Role-Taking" Awareness:* "Role-taking" awareness refers to those situations in which ego psychologically takes the frame of reference of the reference other as a basis for his own behavior.

(2–B) *"Taking Into Account" Awareness:* "Taking into account" awareness involves those situations in which ego symbolically considers the reference other but its frame of reference is not used as a basis for his own behavior.

(2–C) *Non-Awareness:* Ego is being covertly or overtly influenced by a reference other even though the influence that is being extended is not directly a function of ego's "role-taking" or "taking into account" awareness of the reference other.

Note: The typology is to be examined within the context of the qualifications cited in this chapter.

(1) Empirical Status

While there are numerous ways in which reference others could be differentiated, a most significant distinction concerns the empirical status of the reference other. Does the reference other have an actual "existence?" More technically, the question is whether the reference other has an empirical referent. (We realize the philosophical issues raised by the term existence but nevertheless the empirical status of the reference other must be considered.)

Before categorizing ego's reference others on this dimension, let us first consider the relevance of this classification. Why is it important to know if ego's reference others have an actual existence? While we will offer three reasons for the importance of this question, social psychologists have often stressed the relationship between perception and behavior. For instance, there is evidence (277; 331) that the perceived reactions of others are more important than their actual responses in the formation of ego's self-conception. It might be argued that perception is the most immediate predictor of behavior and that the empirical character of the reference other is irrelevant. But, as we will observe, this position is not tenable.

1. If we are interested in modifying an individual's behavior through his reference others, knowledge in this regard is presupposed. Rokeach, for instance, has indicated that the behavior of some types of mental patients is extremely difficult to change as their reference others are non-empirical (325). If ego's reference others have an actual existence, behavior modification may be possible through them.

2. The social scientist who is concerned with the processes involved in value transmission is equally interested in this question. The empirical character of ego's reference others has an important bearing on this process. Bott, for instance, has suggested that norms are more likely to be objectively internalized if the reference other is a group rather than a social category (46). The group has explicit norms which can be accurately internalized while the "norms" of the social category are abstract and more difficult to objectively internalize.

3. The empirical status of the reference other is also related to the processes that are involved in the formation of reference relationships. Some writers, for instance, have argued that only individuals can be a normative source of influence for ego and that it is a mistake to think of social categories as influencing agents. This important question will be discussed in our next chapter. Let us now just emphasize that the empirical status of the reference other has implications for the formation of reference relationships.

The first dimension of the reference other, its empirical status, involves three types, (1–A) the reference individual, (1–B) the quasi-empirical reference other, and (1–C) the imaginary reference other. This dimension is particularly important because it begins to focus upon the *identity* of the reference other.

(1–A) *The Reference Individual.*—The reference individual is an actual person who is extending an influence over ego. Hyman spoke explicitly of the reference individual, and although Sullivan used the term significant other, he was usually speaking of actual persons. One's own experiences in society also support the observation that individuals function as reference others. The mother, the girl friend, and the teacher are reference individuals for the son, the boy friend, and the student, respectively.

The reference individual is the *most crucial* reference other for ego because he is able to exercise a "direct" influence over him. For instance, the reference individual can exert influence by word, deed, or example. Quasi-empirical and imaginary reference others are not able to influence ego in this way. It is important to note that the individual does not have to posit the existence of the reference individual. [The important question regarding the manner in which the influence of the various types of reference others is "extended" is discussed in chapters four and six.]

(1–B) *The Quasi-Empirical Reference Other.*—The quasi-empirical reference other is in a sense "real" and in a sense not "real." This not entirely satisfactory definition is best exemplified by a consideration of the sociological term group. Various writers (382; 421) have concluded that groups are both "real" and "unreal." The group is "real" in that it consists of a collection of interacting individuals but "unreal" in that it is an analytical abstraction.

The reader may have some difficulty in grasping the nature of the quasi-empirical reference other, but this is due to the complexity of the empirical status dimension. Floyd H. Allport, for instance, regards the issue of the "reality of groups" as the master problem of social psychology (4). Let us stress, however, that irrespective of the problematic aspect of this particular type, the empirical status of the other must be included in our individual-other typology if the processes whereby the reference other comes to have an influence upon ego are to be understood. There are five subtypes of quasi-empirical reference others; the reference group, the reference category, the reference norm, the reference self, and the reference object.

(1–B–1) *The Reference Group.*—The reference group is an actual group that is extending an influence over ego. The term *group* is used in a sociological sense to refer to individuals who share common norms and role relationships in regard to activities peculiar to the group. The group may be primary or secondary. For instance, families and organizations may function as reference others for ego. Bott employed the term *direct reference group* to refer to this subtype (46).

Three aspects of this particular subtype should be emphasized. (The first two aspects apply to each of the elements in our typology. They are emphasized at this point simply because students of the reference *group* have been particularly remiss in realizing them.) (1) There is the assumption that it is the group that is influencing the individual in some manner. The organization, for example, rather than some person(s) within the organization, must be influencing the individual. (2) From a methodological perspective, it must be demonstrated that it is the group that is influencing ego. It is important in this regard that the character of the influence be carefully considered. Holden concluded in an empirical study of associations as reference groups that the associations did not exert a broad normative influence over their members (174). However, it is possible that the associations influenced ego in some other way. This indicates the importance of examining the nature of the reference relationship, the second component in our typology, as well as the identity of the reference other. Unfortunately students of reference groups have not often demonstrated that it was the group that influenced ego nor have they given much attention to the processes whereby the group was able to exert its influence. (3) It is this subtype that involves real concrete groups. Although the tendency of writers to use the term *reference group* to refer to all types of reference others has accounted for much of the confusion in the reference group literature, the reference other involved in a reference relationship may be an actual group.

(1–B–2) *The Reference Category.*—The reference category is a social or statistical category that is extending an influence over ego. A social category refers to a number of individuals who have some characteristic(s) in common about which they have a "consciousness of kind" (34:294–96). Americans, Texans, and Negroes comprise social categories. A statistical category refers to a number of individuals who have a characteristic(s) in common but do not have a "consciousness of kind" about this commonality (34:293–94). All the teachers who flunked John in college may form a category *for John,* but the teachers may not be aware of the fact that they all flunked John, much less identify with one another because of it. As the literature indicates that statistical and social categories may function as reference others (346), both are included in our definition of a reference category. Bott employed the term *constructed reference group* to refer to this subtype (46).

There are several observations to be noted in regard to reference categories. (1) Statistical and social categories have often been referred to as reference groups in the past. This was due to the historical development of the reference group concept, but, nevertheless, it has been very confusing and has negated the systematic accumulation of evidence. This procedure must be avoided in the future! The empirical status of the reference other should be circumscribed. (2) As we have observed, there is some debate regarding the exact role of reference categories as influencing agents. Although there are a sufficient number of studies to justify the inclusion of reference categories in our individual-other typology, the type of influence extended by reference categories, the processes through which this influence is extended, and the importance of reference categories relative to other types of reference others are issues that need further and careful examination. Insofar as the literature allows, these questions will be considered in the next chapter. (3) The possibility exists that in some studies the reported influence of the reference category has simply been an artifact of the type of questions that were used. Kuhn has implied that forced-choice questions do not enable the investigator to determine the salience of the reference other (229:19–21). (4) A further distinction between the reference social category and the reference statistical category may be worthy of consideration.

(1–B–3) *The Reference Norm.*—The reference norm is an *external* norm that is extending an influence over ego. By definition, reference norms are external since norms internalized by ego cannot be regarded referentially. The individual lives within a cultural world and is necessarily exposed to and influenced by its multiple expectations. Eisenstadt, who introduced this mode of thinking into the reference group literature, based his original concept upon empirical evidence (114). Pollis and Pollis also direct attention to this line of reasoning with their discussion of the sociological referents of social norms. While emphasizing the sociological character of norms, they note that "just as an individual responds to other individuals in a social situation, he also responds to the normative imperatives of the situation" (304:231).

The inclusion of the reference norm into our individual-other typology would not be accepted by all reference group writers. Kemper, for instance, explicitly excludes the reference norm from the purview of the reference group concept because norms cannot sanction, interact, or manifest expectations (217). But it will become clear throughout the remainder of this book that reference others do not have to possess these characteristics. Reference norms are included in our typology because they do have an influence over ego and he may, in fact, quite consciously orient his behavior in terms of them. It should be emphasized that the individual-other typology allows for the consideration of the reference norm as a distinct type of reference other.

(1–B–4) *The Reference Self.*—The reference self is ego, himself, in the symbolic role of the other, extending an influence over his own person. Ego is a reflexive being. The individual must necessarily become a symbolic other external to himself. Although the inclusion of this reference other in our typology may seem surprising, researchers (346) have found that when individuals are asked to list those people they think of when they are about to do something, a small percentage will mention themselves. Campbell and Pettigrew report that the reference self, or as they call it, the self-reference system, was an important variable in explaining the behavior of ministers during a racial crisis (66). McCall and Simmons, building upon the work of the early symbolic interactionists, argue that the individual is the most important of all audiences because he cannot escape himself (250:74). It is apparent that ego acts as an influencing agent over his own behavior.

The reader should also note the following in regard to the reference self. (1) Its exact nature and function remains problematic. Very little evidence has been gathered about the self as a reference other. Campbell and Pettigrew made a noteworthy beginning in delimiting the nature of the reference self when they indicated that it "consists of the actor's demands, expectations, and images regarding himself. It may be thought of as what the actor would do in the absence of sanctions from external sources" (66:513). This definition, however, does not distinguish the reference self from aspects of the "real" world, such as norms and values, that may be internalized by ego. The internalized norm may also be described in terms of the absence of external stimuli (10:18). We will give some attention to internalization in chapter four, but, for the time being, let us note that the reference self is not being equated with internalized norms or values. (2) The reference self is distinguishable from the self-concept but further consideration needs to be given to the exact differences. (3) The reference self may not be involved in all types of reference relationships.

(1–B–5) *The Reference Object.*—The reference object is *a particularly important social object* for ego that is extending an influence over him. It may be a thing, a quality, an event, or a state of affairs. The symbolic interactionist has labeled that which is given a disjunctiveness from other matters in reality a social object and indicated that the sum total of an individual's social objects constitutes his social reality (227:659). But all social objects do not extend an influence over ego. We call those that do, reference objects. Gerth and Mills employed the term intimate others to refer to a special class of significant others (138: 90–91). George Herbert Mead also spoke of the "significant symbol." Reference objects are a special class of social objects.

The reference object, a term introduced here, has not been explicitly examined in the literature, but there is some evidence of it. The Sherifs have emphasized the importance of cars for the American adolescent.

In fact, they use the phrase car "culture" to refer to this pattern (365: 203–7). The automobile is a reference object for the youth of America. It isn't just a social object they perceive nor one that they "merely" hold an attitude toward. Rather the car extends a considerable influence over their covert and overt behavior. The adolescent thinks, dreams, reads, and converses about cars; examines them, admires them, saves money for them, and drives them. Other examples of reference objects for many members of the United States include money, football, sex, clothes, prestige, mobility, marihuana, and popular music. Reference objects are often cultural and value-laden.

Other writers that are apparently speaking of reference objects in their work are John Irwin and Orrin E. Klapp. Irwin has made the interesting observation that subcultures in the United States may become "an explicit category in the minds of a broader population than social scientists and the group carrying the subculture" (192:166). As he puts it, they try to "make the scene." The subculture, in this sense, is a reference object. Klapp has woven a provocative theory of the presumed identity crisis in America that involves the concept of reference symbol (221). Klapp argues that the identity problems of our day are largely due to an absence of the reference symbols that once characterized America. He does not see the past, some places, the heroes, and tradition in general, as having the positive orienting influence they once did. Is Klapp not suggesting that we no longer have a set of reference objects to direct the populace's behavior in a functional manner in regard to identity formation?

It must be emphasized that the reference group, the reference category, the reference norm, and the reference self (as well as the reference individual) are also reference objects for the individual. But they are excluded from this subtype. Ego is exposed to numerous reference objects. For a variety of reasons, the first four are given separate listings. A more general subtype is needed, however, for the classification of additional reference objects. Similarly, the remaining type under the empirical status dimension is a reference object for ego, but as it is more "imaginary" in character, this type is also excluded from the reference object classification.

The final type is limited to those reference others that would be classified as imaginary by the modern social scientist. On the other hand, heroes and fictional characters are to be placed in the reference object subtype under the quasi-empirical type. The placement of some others will be problematic; e.g., deceased relatives.

(1–C) *The Imaginary Reference Other.*—The imaginary reference other is an "unreal" other that is extending an influence over ego. This reference other does not have an actual existence in reality but is psychologically real to the individual and has an influence over him. The imaginary reference other may exist in the person's mind as an individual, a group, a personification, or in a variety of other forms. Examples of imaginary reference others in the literature include the imaginary playmates of children (8; 27), supernatural beings or places (369), deceased relatives (346), and the distorted figures of reality reported by certain mental patients (325).

The literature does not provide many insights into the imaginary reference other. Various writers allude to its significance but they rarely have gone any further. It is difficult to explain this inattention but some speculation is in order. Western thinking has been characterized by a dichotomy between thought and fiction. This emphasis on rationality may have led to a neglect of the "unreal." Strauss makes this suggestion in his discussion of fantasy and interaction (395:65). (It would be desirable to relate the fantasy literature to the study of the imaginary reference other.) The traditional concern in the social sciences on perception may have also contributed to the neglect of this other. If perception is regarded as the central determiner of behavior, the empirical status of the reference other becomes irrelevant.

Although we do not have many definitive insights into imaginary reference others, there is no question but that they may exercise significant influence over individuals. The anthropological evidence alone indicates that millions of individuals have been affected in numerous ways by beliefs in supreme beings. Sociologists and psychologists have also suggested the importance of deceased relatives for some individuals in certain societies. Further study of the imaginary reference other is to be encouraged.

(2) Membership Status

The second dimension of the reference other, its membership status, involves only two types, (2–A) membership affiliation, and (2–B) nonmembership affiliation. These types do not have any subtypes.

(2–A) *Membership Affiliation* and (2–B) *Nonmembership Affiliation.*—Ego is characterized by a membership affiliation with a reference other if he is recognized as having a membership affiliation with the reference other. Conversely ego is characterized by a nonmembership affiliation with a reference other if he is not recognized as having a membership affiliation with the reference other.

Merton (271:285–86) included the following variables in his definition of group membership: (1) ego's interaction in the group, (2) ego defines himself as a member of the group, and (3) others define ego as a member of the group. Our more limited approach allows social and statistical categories to be characterized as membership others. These two reference categories do not contain interacting members.

While our definition is not as exhaustive as Merton's, it promises to classify correctly the individual in regard to most of his membership statuses. For instance, if we consider the reference groups of American adolescents, they would include families, peer groups, clubs, schools, and athletic teams. In these instances, the adolescent is typically recognized as a member of these groups.

There are three aspects of the membership status dimension that need to be noted. (1) The individual can not have a membership affiliation with all his reference others. While ego is able to have a membership affiliation with a reference individual, a reference group, and a reference category, it does not make sense to categorize him on this dimension in regard to the reference norm, the reference self, the reference object, or the imaginary reference other. (2) If ego has a membership affiliation with a reference other, he is subject to any normative expectations that characterize the affiliation, and the consequent penalties and rewards. Kelley equated the ability of a membership group to implement and enforce sanctions with the concept of *a reference group* (213), but we shall not, as nonmembership reference individuals, groups, and social categories do not generally have the ability to implement and enforce sanctions for the nonmember though they may function as reference others for him. We would also emphasize at this point that Stouffer's distinctive term, sanctioning reference groups (391:14), seems unnecessary as membership individuals and groups are necessarily sanctioning groups. (We do not recognize reference categories as having the ability to sanction.) Nevertheless, the ability of these membership others to sanction relative to the usual inability of nonmembership others to sanction has not been emphasized often enough. (3) Membership status is a variable that is characteristic of the reference other *and* the individual since it is dependent upon a mutual relationship between ego and the reference other, but we have chosen to characterize the reference other in terms of this attribute.

The Reference Relationship

The second component in our typology, the reference relationship, will be characterized in terms of three dimensions: (1) the type of reference relationship, (2) the scope of the reference relationship, and (3) the role character of the reference relationship.

(1) *The Type of Reference Relationship*

This dimension concerns the type of influence that the reference other has over the individual. It is apparent that the nature of this influence is quite diverse, and future research will undoubtedly result in the modification and expansion of this section of the typology. It is our judgment that the present literature supports the existence of three types of reference relationships; (1–A) the identification-object reference relationship, (1–B) the normative reference relationship, and (1–C) the comparative reference relationship.

(1–A) *The Identification-Object Reference Relationship.* — An identification-object reference relationship exists between the individual and a reference other if the individual's degree of positive or negative sentiment toward the reference other is sufficient to direct his overt or covert behavior *toward the reference other* as an object. A sentiment refers to a "feeling state" that ego has towards the reference other; it reflects what the reference other means to ego. A sentiment — see Shibutani (370) — presupposes a disposition to act toward the reference other in some circumscribed manner. If ego's sentiment toward the reference other is positive or supportive, *a positive identification-object reference relationship* exists between ego and the reference other. If ego's sentiment toward the reference other is negative or nonsupportive, *a negative identification-object reference relationship* exists between the individual and his reference other. While ego may have an identification-object reference relationship with any of the three types of reference others under the empirical status dimension, the reference norm and the reference self should probably be excluded. The membership status dimension may be involved if the reference other is an individual, group or category.

Very often, as the Sherifs have emphasized over the years, the influence of the individual's positive or negative sentiment toward the reference other will manifest itself in terms of ego's covert and overt behavior regarding his membership affiliation with the reference other. If ego's sentiment toward the reference other is positive, he will desire to maintain or establish a membership affiliation with the reference other. The girl who is in love with her boy friend will certainly wish to maintain the affiliation. If ego's sentiment toward the reference other is negative, he may desire to terminate or reject a membership affiliation with the reference other. The man who has fallen out of love with his wife may well seek a divorce.

There are three reasons why ego's sentiment toward the reference other rather than ego's attitude regarding membership affiliation has been emphasized in our definition of an identification-object reference relationship. (1) The individual's sentiment toward the reference other represents the essential character of the identification-object reference relationship. It is the "state of feeling" that is most important. One suspects that it is the sentiment that usually influences ego's attitude regarding affiliation. The desire to maintain, establish, terminate, or reject a membership affiliation is a manifestation of ego's sentiment toward the reference other. (2) There are some situations in which ego's sentiment toward the reference other will not directly manifest itself in terms of his attitude regarding a membership affiliation. An American citizen may be for one side rather than another in a war but not literally want to become a member of that country. Similarly a sports fan may be very supportive of a team but not really want to become a member of the team. (3) As we have previously observed, some of ego's reference others are not amenable to membership affiliations. This would seem to be true, for instance, of those imaginary reference others with whom ego is positively or negatively identified.

As the element of identification has been de-emphasized in the reference group literature, it is necessary to consider its inclusion in our typology; it will be recalled that Kelley (213), Shibutani (369), and others, have subsumed the identification dimension under the normative function of reference groups. Identification was regarded as the mechanism for the internalization of norms. We will suggest three reasons for the inclusion of the identification variable in our typology. The first two discussions involve a rationale for the separation of the identification variable from the normative dimension, but it is the final item that provides the distinctive explanation behind the identification-object reference other.

1. While ego's positive identification with a reference other often precedes normative influence, this is not always true. Various writers have now suggested that internalization does not presuppose identification (31; 48; 64). Ego may internalize a norm because of an acceptance of it. The separation of the identification variable from the normative dimension also allows the relationship between negative identification and the rejection of norms to be emphasized.

2. Conversely, the individual may also be identified with a reference

other but not be influenced in the manner implied by Shibutani's reference group concept. While identification often leads to a normative influence, this is not necessarily true. This point may be especially important for the understanding of change in reference relationships. One suspects, for instance, that the attitudes and opinions of many adults in the United States cease to be influenced by those of their aging parents but yet their emotional ties with their parents remain strong.

3. It is particularly important to understand that *the reference other is the primary object of concern for ego in an identification-object reference relationship*. Ego has positive or negative sentiments toward this other which are manifested in his desire to please or displease the other, be supportive or nonsupportive of the other, and to desire or deplore a membership affiliation with the other. To illustrate this, let us consider the example of a suitor who is trying to win the hand of the woman he loves. The suitor may interact frequently with this girl, think about her constantly, hold down two jobs in order to buy her expensive gifts, and perhaps even commit suicide if she rejects his marriage proposal but not really have substantially modified his attitudes or perspectives in other matters due to his association with this girl. It must also be understood that if the suitor eventually adopts the perspective of the girl in some respect, it is incidental to his behavior up to that point!

It should also be emphasized that the Sherifs in their 1953 work warned against employing the reference group concept to refer to every group towards which ego has an attitude (364:168). This recommendation, which was directed at Newcomb for introducing the concepts of the negative and the positive reference group (285:225-27), is not ill-advised. The Sherifs were attempting to restrict the meaning of the reference group concept and used it to depict the attitudinal influence of the reference other upon the individual. Nevertheless, some groups, or more generally, reference others, towards which ego has attitudes, or sentiments in our terminology, account for a significant portion of ego's behavior. These groups may or may not influence attitudes but their distinguishing characteristic is that ego's covert or overt behavior is exerted *towards* the reference other. While the inclusion of this reference relationship in our typology does tend to broaden the meaning of the reference group concept, it opens avenues of thought regarding the *two-way* relationship between ego and certain of his reference others that have not yet been fully explored at a conceptual level. There is a sense in which the reference other is either a dependent variable or an independent variable, or both, relative to ego. The systematization of this complexity is not served by the designation of identification as a mere mechanism for internalization!

(1–B) *The Normative Reference Relationship.*—A normative reference relationship exists between the individual and a reference other if the individual's overt or covert behavior *is being* influenced *by the norms or values* characteristic of or attributed to the reference other. The major identifying characteristic of a normative reference relationship is that ego is covertly or overtly influenced by the perceived or actual norms or values of the reference other. The reference other may be a reference individual, a quasi-empirical reference other, or an imaginary reference other, and ego may or may not have a membership affiliation or an identification-object reference relationship with the reference other.

This definition of the normative reference relationship is quite similar to the prevailing definition of the normative reference group popularized by Kelley and Shibutani, but there are several critical differences and extensions that need to be emphasized. While our definition should be subjected to careful scrutiny, it has the advantage of focusing upon some dimensions of the reference relationship that have not been previously considered. (1) Kelley's definition was limited to reference *groups*. Our definition encompasses three types of reference others. (2) Kelley's definition emphasized the ability of the reference group to *set* and *enforce* norms. Our definition stresses that ego is being influenced irrespective of the intentions of the reference other. (3) Kelley's definition implies that only membership groups can provide norms for ego as nonmembership groups do not usually enforce norms. Our definition recognizes membership and nonmembership reference others as potential sources of normative influence. (4) Kelley and Shibutani assume that normative influence presupposes identification. Our definition does not make this assumption. (5) Kelley and Shibutani tend to imply that if identification does not lead to normative influence it is of no importance. Our definition does not make this assumption. (6) Neither Kelley nor Shibutani incorporated ego's perception into their definition of normative reference groups. Our definition does this. (7) Shibutani indicates that ego must adapt or internalize the perspective of the reference other. Our definition does not involve this assumption. We regard the reference other as extending a normative influence over ego if ego acts in some manner with regard to the norms of the reference other. As we will see in our later discussion of the scope of influence of the normative reference relationship, it is now recognized that individuals follow norms for different reasons. As a matter of fact, *in some respects,* once ego does adapt or internalize the norms or values or perspectives of the reference other, *it ceases to be a reference other.* The individual is no longer influenced by the norms and values of the reference other in that they are now *his* values. This in no way implies, however, that it is unimportant to know what reference others *were* the sources of certain of ego's values, but it is equally important to determine what reference others are *now* providing ego with his perspectives. This is why we have included the words *is having* in our definition of a normative reference relationship. We would take the same position in regard to the identification-object and the comparative reference relationships. The time perspective is emphasized at this point simply because students of the normative reference group have been the most guilty of overlooking this important element!

(1–C) *The Comparative Reference Relationship.—*A comparative reference relationship exists between the individual and the reference other if the individual compares himself (or others) to the reference other on some dimension(s) and is influenced in either an overt or covert manner. There is some doubt as to whether ego would compare himself to all types of reference others if the empirical dimension of the reference other is taken into account, but clearly the reference individual can be a comparative reference other, and ego may or may not have a membership affiliation, an identification-object or a normative reference relationship with this reference other.

Since Kelley's coining of the comparative reference group term, various writers have argued that it should not be regarded as a reference group (369). The basic premise of these authors has been that the comparative reference group is not a source of norms, values, or perspectives. While we would concur with this rationale, the comparative reference other does have an influence over individuals. It should be kept in mind that our objective is not to define what a reference group is but to begin to depict the types of influences that prevail between the individual and his reference others. Various illustrations of the effects of comparative reference others will be noted throughout the remainder of this book. For the present we will cite a quotation from Klapp's recent book, *Search For Identity,* to suggest the influence of the comparative reference other (221:64, my italics): "I think the rebels of our modern affluent society are reacting to a frustration compounded *of a sense of relative deprivation, from comparing themselves with others and their own exploding expectations,* and from symbolic disturbances to identity. Only a fraction of this frustration is attributable to sheer economic hardship or political injustice." Klapp does not use the term *comparative reference group*, but he speaks of the frustration ratio (221:63–70). He cites an abundance of evidence for the frustration ratio on pages 344–45. Any attempt to document the relevance of the comparative reference other requires a mention of the self. The role of this other for the study of self-appraisals is an area that has not yet been exploited.

There has not been much variation in the definition of the comparative reference group concept in the literature. Following Kelley, most writers regard it as a reference group with whom ego compares and evaluates himself or others. We stress the individual's reaction to his comparisons with the reference other more so than past writers. In order for a reference other to be a comparative reference other, ego must be influenced in either a covert or overt manner. He may, for instance, experience relative deprivation or modify his behavior in an attempt to "catch up" with the comparative reference other. It is in this sense that the comparative reference other is something more than just a reference point!

A few distinctive types of comparative reference relationships are beginning to appear in the literature. Since we are attempting to keep our typology within manageable limits, this work will not be considered in detail. But a brief examination of Kemper's effort (217) will illustrate some of the further categorizations that can be made in regard to the comparative reference relationship. Kemper has made a useful distinction between an equity comparison reference group and a legitimator comparison reference group. Kemper also regards the role model and the accommodator group as types of comparative reference groups. We have not done this as these terms seem to portray a normative influence more than a comparative influence. It is important to note, however, that the role model literature can be related to the reference group literature. In our terminology, an equity comparative reference relationship exists when ego employs the reference other for judging whether or not his situation or fate is fair or unequal. This is the meaning of the comparative reference group that has received the most attention. Considerable interest has been shown in ego's reaction to his equity comparison. Does ego experience relative gratification or relative deprivation? We consider this point further in our discussion of the effects of reference others in chapter six. A legitimator comparative reference relationship exists when ego employs a reference other to answer a question about the legitimacy of his own behavior or opinions. Kemper notes, for instance, that the statement "Everyone cheats on his income tax; why shouldn't I?" is an illustration of a legitimator comparison (217:33). Kemper's observations which regard comparative reference groups as involving problematic situations are further evidence of the complexity of the individual-other relationship.

(2) The Scope of the Reference Relationship

The scope of the reference relationship concerns *the extent of the influence* that the reference other has upon ego. This is an important dimension as reference others are not of equal significance for individuals. Although the reference group literature has focused upon ego's most influential reference others, the scope of influence of the reference other is a *variable*. Turner's concept of the interaction reference group does acknowledge a normative reference group that is not too important for ego (410). Sharples has also presented evidence regarding the importance of insignificant others among a population of amputees (357). The solution to many questions will be more easily obtained if this perspective of variability is systematically incorporated into the reference other orientation. For instance, an understanding of the formation and modification of reference relationships presupposes an examination of ego's less influential reference others.

(2–A) *The Scope of the Identification-Object Reference Relationship.*—The scope of the identification-object reference relationship reflects (1) the intensity of the sentiment that ego holds toward the reference other, and (2) the range of "non-normative" influence that the reference other extends over ego. It is difficult to say much more about the scope of this particular relationship as the identification process has been given so little emphasis in the reference group literature. But we should note that Sullivan's concept of the significant other (398) and Kuhn's concept of the orientational other (229) involve a reference individual that is very influential, and these two concepts reflect to some extent the attributes we have ascribed to the identification-object reference relationship.

(2–B) *The Scope of the Normative Reference Relationship.*—The scope of the normative reference relationship reflects the extent to which ego has internalized the norms and values of the reference other. While Turner's concepts of the identification reference group and the interaction reference group were concerned with the extent of normative influence exerted by ego's normative reference groups (410), we will base our consideration of normative influence upon Herbert Kelman's discussions of attitude change (214; 215). Kelman speaks of compliance, identification, and internalization. Other sociologists have recognized the relevance of his work for the understanding of the reference group concept (290:124–27; 297). The following three subtypes are based upon his efforts.

(2–B–1) *The Compliant Normative Reference Relationship.*—The individual in this situation follows the norms or values of the reference other because he expects to benefit from his conformity. He hopes to gain rewards or escape punishments. It is the individual's *overt behavior* that is influenced rather than his attitudes and perspectives. There is not any internalization of norms but there is *behavioral* influence. Ego's participation in certain of his membership groups may entail compliance of this type. This is what earlier students of the reference group meant when they said that all membership groups are not sources of values for ego. We are not modifying this position but emphasizing it and adding the important insights that ego is influenced in a behavioral manner in situations of this type and that the compliant reference relationship may be changed to an internalized normative reference relationship, which is reflective of an attitudinal influence. It appears that ego may have this type of normative reference relationship with most types of reference others, but it may be most common among membership reference individuals and groups as they are in a position to apply sanctions.

(2–B–2) *The Identification Normative Reference Relationship.*— The individual in this situation conforms or deviates from the norms or values of the reference other because he is identified with the reference other. If ego holds positive sentiments toward the reference other, he conforms to its norms, while, if he is negatively disposed toward the reference other, he will deviate from its norms. It should be emphasized that the norms are again not internalized by ego in this situation. The actual or perceived norms or attitudes of the reference other do not become the attitudes of the individual. The teenage girl, for instance, may refrain from behavior that her parents deem improper out of a love for them, rather than because she actually believes the norms are improper or because of a fear of punishment. It would seem that this type of reference relationship could occur among membership reference others or nonmembership reference others as it is not dependent upon sanctioning behavior.

It should be noted that the identification normative reference relationship differs from the identification-object reference relationship in that its stress is upon the normative influence of the reference other rather than the fact that the reference other serves as a focal point for ego. The girl may follow certain norms set by her mother and father out of a love for them, but yet they may not serve as focal objects for her behavior as does her peer group. Similarly, the latter may affect much of her behavior but its normative impact would only constitute part of its influence. Also, the norms of the peer group could be followed out of compliance or because the girl had internalized the norms. These are "pure types," however, and the individual may have an identification normative reference relationship and an identification-object reference relationship with the same reference other. The fact that both of these relationships involve identification is not unimportant and further empirical evidence is needed to determine the extent to which they in fact do overlap in reality.

(2–B–3) *The Internalized Normative Reference Relationship.*—The individual in this situation has internalized the norms or values of the reference other. (The internalized normative reference relationship may or may not stem from an identification-object reference relationship. It should be *emphasized* that while our discussion of the scope of the normative reference relationship has largely involved a consideration of ego's *acceptance* of norms, this reference relationship also includes those instances where ego reacts *against* the norms or values of the reference other.) The norms of the reference other have become ego's own standards for behavior. Ego has incorporated them into his personality. This aspect of normative influence has been given the most attention by reference group theorists probably because it represents the instance where the impact of the reference other is the greatest. It is precisely the purpose of this subtype to emphasize this extreme normative influence of the reference other. From somewhat of an ironic stance, and as suggested previously, it is necessary to add the thought that it is exactly when the individual internalizes the norms of the reference other that its influence declines. The individual almost seems by definition to be acting according to "his own norms" rather than the norms of the reference other. Clearly the individual is not now involved in a role-taking process with the reference other in regard to the norms that have been internalized. Even so, the reference other in this situation remains the source of the internalized norm, value, or in Shibutani's terminology, perspective.

(2–C) *The Scope of the Comparative Reference Relationship.*— The scope of influence of the comparative reference relationship reflects (1) the number of dimensions concerning which ego compares himself to the reference other, (2) the degree or relative deprivation or gratification that results from the comparison(s), and (3) the range of other covert and overt behaviors that flow from the comparison(s). It is difficult to say more about the scope of comparative reference relationships as they have not been systematically studied from this perspective. We would emphasize, however, that the *recognition* of the preceding three variables should provide a significant foundation for an intensive examination of the scope of the comparative reference relationship!

(3) *The Role Character of the Reference Relationship*

The third dimension of the reference relationship, its role character, involves two types, (3–A) the role-related reference relationship, and (3–B) the person reference relationship. This dimension is limited to those reference relationships that ego has with reference individuals.

(3–A) *The Role-Related Reference Relationship* and (3–B) *The Person Reference Relationship.*—The individual is characterized by a role-related reference relationship if the influence of the reference other is limited to a role relationship(s) that exists between him and the reference other. A person reference relationship exists between ego and the reference other if the influence of the reference other is not limited to a role relationship(s) that exists between him and the reference other.

This third dimension, as is the second, is somewhat concerned with the scope of influence extended by the reference other, but more of a *generic* distinction is involved in this instance. To cite Merton's work in this regard (271:302–3), the question is whether ego is influenced by the reference other within one or a few role relationships that he has with him, or whether the influence of the reference other extends beyond these role relationships. Some evidence is provided on this question by Denzin (95) and Moore (278). They found that if subjects are asked to name who is important to them as students and as persons, differential responses are obtained. The responses given to the person question in the Denzin and Moore studies were apparently identification-object reference individuals. But this does not have to be the case. The influence of a physician may extend beyond his role even though he is not an identification-object reference individual for the persons he is so influencing.

We must emphasize the importance of the role-related reference relationship and the person reference relationship. These begin to get at a situational component! In this regard, our role-based distinction may not be adequate. Vander Zanden cites a study involving southern white migrants to Chicago (413:88). He suggests that the South was a reference group for their attitudes toward Negroes while Chicago was a reference group for their behavior towards Negroes. This appears to be more of a situational than a role phenomenon.

The Individual

There are two dimensions of the individual that must be taken into account in our typology: (1) ego's perception of the reference relationship, and (2) ego's awareness of the reference other. We would stress the importance of this final component because in some respects the role of the individual in reference relationships has been ignored, and certain of the dimensions subsumed under this component reflect the most confusing and problematic aspects of the reference group literature. This is particularly true of our final dimension involving ego's awareness of the reference other.

(1) Ego's Perception of the Reference Relationship

The first dimension of the individual consists of two types, (1–A) "objective" perception, and (1–B) "subjective" perception.

(1–A) *"Objective" Perception* and (1–B) *"Subjective" Perception.* —Ego's perception of a designated dimension of a reference relationship is objective if ego perceives it in an essentially accurate fashion while his perception is subjective if he perceives it in an inaccurate fashion.

Perception is important with regard to normative and comparative reference relationships. In the former situation, the question is whether ego has attributed the correct norms and values to the reference other. In the latter instance, one queries if the individual has correctly perceived the reference other's standing on the dimension(s) employed for comparative purposes. The role of perception in the identification-object reference relationship is less clear at this time but it could prove to be important.

An understanding of the accuracy of ego's perception of a reference relationship is important for a number of reasons. The individual's behavior may be incomprehensible unless this variable is considered. Merton, for instance, found that the behavior of the raw recruit in battle was only understandable once the inaccuracy of his perception of certain norms became apparent. More generally, the problem of value transmission presupposes knowledge in this area.

(2) *Ego's Awareness of the Reference Other*

The second dimension of the individual involves three types, (2–A) "role-taking" awareness, (2–B) "taking into account" awareness, and (2–C) non-awareness. These types do not have any subtypes.

(2–A) *"Role-Taking" Awareness.* – "Role-taking" awareness refers to those situations in which ego psychologically takes the frame of reference of the reference other as a basis for his own behavior. This is the Meadian version of role-taking and assumes that ego symbolically considers the "viewpoint" of the reference other and employs it as a basis for his own behavior. Turner, for instance, observes that the "confidence man" often succeeds because of his ability to identify the feelings and attitudes of the person he is attempting to swindle (410).

While *emphasizing* that the awareness dimension is a complex one and subject to significant qualifications (see 410), a "role-taking" awareness is most characteristic of the normative reference relationship. Ego almost by definition must anticipate the norms, values, attitudes, or perspectives of the reference other as a guide for his own behavior. It is of some interest that Turner has observed that "taking the role of another may or may not include adopting the standpoint of the other as one's own" (410:319). In two of the subtypes of the normative reference relationship, the compliant normative and the identification normative reference relationships, ego does not adopt the standpoint of the reference other as his own, but this does occur in the internalized normative reference relationship.

(2–B) *"Taking Into Account" Awareness.* – "Taking into account" awareness involves those situations in which ego symbolically considers the reference other but its frame of reference is not used as a basis for his own behavior. Ego is symbolically aware of the reference other in this situation, but he does not guide his behavior by the norms, values, attitudes, or perspectives that he attributes to the reference other. *The reference other is taken into account more so than the normative features of the reference other.* Turner has made this point in his discussion of the comparative reference group (410:327, my italics): "However, the actor may or may not take the role of a member of the reference group. So long as the actor is using the reference group only as a point of comparison in estimating his own social standing or in deciding whether to be satisfied or dissatisfied with his lot, *external* attributes of the other alone are involved." However, we would emphasize more than Turner that ego's behavior may be significantly influenced by his "taking into account" awareness of the reference other.

The normative reference relationship is not amenable to a "taking into account" awareness on the part of ego. This relationship assumes that ego is in some manner being guided by the normative aspects of the reference other. The identification-object reference relationship, on the other hand, can not only be, but probably is, typified by this kind of awareness. This makes a good deal of sense as the behavior of the individual is directed toward the reference other in an identification-object reference relationship, but ego's *anticipation of a reaction of the other* involves "role-taking" awareness. Comparative reference relationships are characterized by "taking into account" awareness.

Before considering the final item in our typology, some discussion must be given to the salience concept. This term is often mentioned in the reference group literature, and its importance will become apparent in our statement regarding reference group conflict in chapter five. In contrast to previous writers, we do not regard salience as a distinct variable. *Rather, salience is an index of the individual's awareness of the reference other.* The reference other ("taking into account" awareness) or its normative elements ("role-taking" awareness) may be more or less prominent (salient) in ego's thoughts. Similarly, some writers have employed the term audience reference group to refer to those audiences that ego symbolically takes into account (306). This is quite legitimate, but again these audiences should be regarded as a component of the awareness dimension. *The nature of the influence extended by the reference other must still be determined.*

(2–C) *Non-Awareness.*–Ego is being covertly or overtly influenced by a reference other even though the influence that is being extended is not directly a function of ego's "role-taking" or "taking into account" awareness of the reference other. It is doubtful, for instance, that the attitude change that occurred among many of the students at Bennington College was dependent upon their "role-taking" or "taking into account" awareness of this college.

Some writers have argued that reference group behavior is limited to role-taking situations (329:11 n) while others regard this as unimportant (434:79). We allow for both extremes in the typology. It is no longer fruitful to debate the point. Empirical evidence is needed to determine the type of influence extended in these different instances. *But we would suggest that the term "reference other" be reserved for those situations in which the influence that is being extended by the reference other is dependent upon a "role-taking" or a "taking into account" awareness on the part of ego.*

Our third type includes these instances where ego is influenced by an other of which he is not at all aware—a situation that would be quickly dismissed by some critics. But it also circumscribes those relationships where the influence of an other upon ego is *in some respects* dependent upon ego's awareness of the reference other but not *in other respects*. This alternative clearly merits further study.

Now that the three components of the individual-other typology have been detailed, the typology will be briefly overviewed. It is recommended that the student of the individual-other relationship initially consider the reference other, one of three components in our typology. Attention should first be given to the empirical status of the reference other. Is the reference other a reference individual, a quasi-empirical reference other, or an imaginary reference other? If the reference other is quasi-empirical, the appropriate subtype must be determined. Is the reference other a group, a category, a norm, the self, or an object? The membership status of the reference other should next be considered. It must be remembered that this dimension only pertains to the reference individual, the reference group, and the reference category.

The reference relationship, the second component in the typology, now becomes the focal point. It has three dimensions. The initial question concerns the type of reference relationship. Is it an identification-object, a comparative, or a normative reference relationship? It should be stressed that while *any particular reference relationship* is either an identification-object, normative, or comparative one, ego may have more than one type of reference relationship with the same reference other. The second dimension to be considered involves the scope of the reference relationship. If the reference relationship happens to be normative, one of three subtypes must be determined. The reference relationship may be compliant, identification, or internalized. Finally, if the reference other is an individual, the question must be asked if the reference relationship is a role-related or person reference relationship.

The third component in our typology is the individual. It has two dimensions. The first is ego's perception of the reference relationship. Is his perception objective or subjective? The nature of the perception that is involved varies with the type of reference relationship being considered. Ego's awareness of the reference other represents our final dimension. Three types are involved: "role-taking" awareness, "taking into account" awareness, and non-awareness. It might be said that the question is whether the reference other is truly a *reference* other or an influencing agent.

The basic purpose of the individual-other typology is to illustrate the complexity of the individual-other relationship. The reasonable position is taken that all individual-other relationships are necessarily characterized by three essential components; the reference other, the reference relationship, and the individual. Although these components constitute a framework for the examination of individual-other relationships, it is always necessary to introduce additional variables; that is, relevant dimensions of each component must be considered. In this way, some of the peculiarities of the particular setting in which the reference relationship occurs are to some extent built into the reference other orientation. This typology should prove useful for the development of scientific hypotheses and facilitate the systematic accumulation of data.

The distinguishing characteristic of the typology is that it synthesizes and extends present work within the reference group literature. While the reference group dilemma proved to be a reality, the basic difficulty with the reference group literature was the absence of a guiding framework. Indeed, the fact that various ideas had been adequately developed provided the basis for the typology!

Our final remark concerns the tentative nature of the typology. The objective has been to sketch the basic components of the reference other phenomenon and their central dimensions. Although this approach will facilitate the future study of the reference other phenomenon, the typology will need to be modified. In some respects, it may be too broad. Perhaps the reference self and the reference norm should not have been included. On the other hand, the typology is too narrow in some respects. This is particularly true in regard to the type of influence that the reference other extends over the individual. In fact, we ourselves have omitted some promising leads in this regard. But this is a most complex dimension, and our typology does bring attention to this important fact. Some will regard our failure to characterize certain reference others in terms of *their perceptions and intentions toward ego* as an omission. While we noted that membership groups almost by definition set and enforce norms while nonmembership groups do not, this is an avenue worthy of further investigation. In spite of these observations, it is necessary to start somewhere. And writers should now no longer *just* ask the question "What is a reference group?"

CHAPTER Four

The Formation of Reference Relationships (1) The Sociocultural System

The objective of chapters four and five is to explain the development of reference relationships between ego and his reference others. Conflicting reference relationships are not discussed in this chapter. A consideration of this more complex question occurs in chapter five. The processes involved in ego's acquisition of his reference others are not easily understood due to the complexity of the "real world" into which the individual is born and socialized. The individual in a typical modern society, for instance, is exposed to a host of potential reference others. Why do some become actual reference others while others do not? Why does ego establish positive identification-object reference relationships with some but negative identification-object reference relationships with others? And what about changes in reference relationships? How constant is ego's reference set? [The reference set refers to the totality of ego's reference others (216).] These are but a few of the questions that face the social scientist.

Although many aspects of the processes involved in the formation of reference relationships remain problematic, substantial insights have been made in this area. This chapter considers the role of the sociocultural system in the formation of reference relationships. *Its theme is that the sociocultural system is the central explanatory variable in this process.* Reference relationships are sociocultural products. Chapter five focuses upon the dynamics of the process. A failure to include this discussion would result in legitimate criticisms of sociological determinism and oversimplification (437).

The individual is provided with many of his reference others directly or automatically through his very participation in society. That is, many of his reference others are socially structured (272:62) or ready-made (180:123). This is true at all stages of the socialization process.

Socially structured reference others are patterned by the sociocultural system. Merton has observed (271:302, my italics): "Almost irrespective of provenience, sociological theory holds that identification with groups and with individuals occupying designated statuses does not occur at random but tends to be patterned by the environing structure of *established social relationships and by prevailing cultural definitions.*" Berger and Luckmann have also stressed the importance of relating studies of internalization to the social structure (31:207), and Nelson has argued that the development of reference group theory presupposes the recognition of the role of structural variables (283).

A sociocultural system involves two components; social structure and culture. While elaborate and necessary discussions exist regarding social structure (281) and culture (16), it is adequate for us to consider these terms in the following manner.

Social Structure.—Social structure is the system of positions and roles that characterize a total society or some segment of the society. A position represents the place that an individual occupies in the social structure while a role is the set of expectations that accompanies the position.

Culture.—Culture is the totality of norms, values, and beliefs that characterize a society or some segment of the society.

In other words, reference others and relationships are provided and influenced by the sociocultural system if they are patterned by the positions and roles that the individual occupies and enacts, and the norms, values, and beliefs of the society. While our discussion necessarily reflects a general discussion of the nature of the sociocultural system, the more intimately familiar one is with this phenomenon the more he will be able to understand the formation of reference relationships.

It must be emphasized that the critical role we have attributed to the sociocultural system presupposes the existence of an ongoing sociocultural system. This assumption is quite reasonable. It not only reflects everyday observations but certain quite opposing theories of human behavior involve this premise. Orthodox Freudian theory posits that adult personality is largely a consequence of the individual's adjustment to the demands of "external reality" and symbolic interactionism assumes that *"society—a network of interacting individuals—with its culture—the related meanings and values by means of which individuals interact—precedes any existing individual"* (329:13). The reader should realize that an ongoing sociocultural system may be assumed without denying the importance of determining its initial origins, or adopting a static view of human behavior.

Although we have already implied that the individual's reference others and reference relationships are not "simply" explained by his exposure to the sociocultural system, let us now consider three reasons for this. (1) All of the individual's reference others are not socially structured. The individual may acquire some idiosyncratic reference others—reference others that are not patterned by the sociocultural system. Idiosyncratic reference others have not been given much study, but they may be important precisely because they are not socially structured. For one discussion of this subject, see (272:61–62). (2) The differential influence of the individual's socially structured reference others has to be explained. Why does one socially structured reference other take priority over another in a given situation? (3) The processes through which reference relationships are developed must be carefully considered. The dynamics of these processes are not just due to the sociocultural system. We must determine how the sociocultural system comes to "impinge" upon the individual. All human experience is *interpreted* by the individual (42:1–60).

The relevance of the sociocultural system for the formation of reference relationships has been suggested, but some supportive evidence for this position is in order. The impact of the sociocultural system in this regard will also be illustrated in our later discussion of the steps in the reference relationship formation process.

One of the simplest and most convincing observations to make about the role of the sociocultural system in the development of reference relationships is that reference relationships vary across sociocultural systems. *Individuals in different sociocultural systems simply have access to different reference sets, and the differences between these reference sets are largely a function of differences between the sociocultural systems.* To cite just one example, the American college student may aspire to go to law school but a male of the same age in a more primitive society has no such aspirations. The sociocultural system in the latter instance simply does not have law schools. The sociocultural system in no way provides for the creation of this reference relationship. There are no socially structured mechanisms to direct ego's attention to this positively defined reference other.

Anthropological studies lend substantial support to the role of the sociocultural system in the formation of reference relationships. While evidence could be provided for each of the institutions of society, it is necessary for us to limit our discussion to the institution of the family. This institution is not only a major determinant of personality but a very important mechanism in the transmission of culture from one generation to another.

There are many ways in which the impact of the family on the development of reference relationships could be demonstrated but a place to begin is with the newborn infant. The typical child is born into a family of orientation. The child later marries and establishes a family of procreation. The individual may be a son or daughter and a brother or sister in the family of orientation, a husband or wife and a father or mother in the family of procreation. This membership of the individual into two families is of considerable moment. Murdock has observed (279:94): "It is this universal fact of individual membership in two nuclear families that gives rise to kinship systems. If marriages normally took place within the nuclear family, there would be only family organization; kinship would be confined to the limits of the family. But by virtue of the fact that individuals regularly belong to two families, every person forms a link between the members of his family of orientation and those of his family of procreation, and ramifying series of such links bind numbers of individuals to one another through kinship ties." In a nontechnical sense, this means that the individual's "world of others" is divided into "family others" and "non-family others" at the very moment of his birth. There is no society that does not recognize a system of culturally patterned relationships between kinship systems (279:96).

Kinship patterns exhibit considerable diversity across sociocultural systems. While it is not appropriate to consider the numerous variations between kinship systems, the differences between kinship patterns in industrialized and nonindustrialized societies will be observed. Even a consideration of these two types of societies lends substantial support to the role of the sociocultural system in the formation of reference relationships. The differences in the kinship systems of these two societies—and their importance for the formation of reference relationships—are aptly portrayed by the social anthropologist, John Beattie (23: 93): "Very few of the interpersonal relationships which make up a Western European's social world are kinship ones. Kinship plays little or no part in his relations with his friends, his employers, his teachers, his colleagues, or in the complex network of political, economic and religious associations in which he is involved. But in many smaller-scale societies kinship's social importance is paramount. Where a person lives, his group and community membership, whom he should obey and by whom be obeyed, who are his friends and who his enemies, whom he may and may not marry, from whom he may hope to inherit and to whom pass on his own status and property—all these matters and many more may be determined by his status in a kinship system. Where everybody is or thinks of himself as being related to nearly everybody else, almost all social relationships must be kinship or affinal ones too. But even where kinship is less pervasive, it usually plays a much more important part than it does in modern urban and industrialized Western societies."

Anthropologists have given extensive attention to structural differences between kinship systems. Murdock has demonstrated that three distinct family structures characterize human societies; the nuclear family, the extended family, and the polygamous family (279). These three structures are characteristic of the American family structure, the traditional Chinese family structure, and many African family structures respectively. The nuclear family consists of a married man and woman with their offspring. The extended family consists of two or more nuclear families affiliated through an extension of the parent-child relationship. The polygamous family structure consists of two or more nuclear families affiliated by plural marriages. It is apparent that the individual's reference others will vary with each of these family structures. The reader is referred to Murdock's work (279) for evidence in support of this statement. Caplow's discussion of the formation of triads in various types of societies is also of interest (68:62–94).

The attempts of anthropologists to relate kinship differences to variations in the ways of life of individuals have not always been successful but Francis Hsu (178) has offered an explanation for this which is of substantial importance for our discussion of reference relationships. Hsu argues that anthropologists have focused upon kinship *structure* but have ignored kinship *content*. In our terminology, we would suggest that positions have been the major object of attention while roles have been de-emphasized. This is of obvious importance as the nature of role expectations may vary within the same type of family structure.

It is Hsu's thesis that societies differ according to the interpersonal relationship that is of prime importance to them. Hsu believes that this fact accounts for many outstanding differences in thought and behavior among the people living in societies. For example, among a majority of the Oriental peoples, including Chinese, Japanese, Koreans, Siamese, and others, emphasis is given to the relationship between the son and father. In other words, the relationship between the son and father is institutionalized. Its identificational and normative qualities are largely dictated by the sociocultural system. Hsu observes (178:408): "The great importance given to the father-son axis reduces, modifies, or dominates all other relationships, including that between husband and wife. Indeed the married woman's primary duties are not those to her husband but to her husband's parents or her sons. Similarly the married man's duties to his parent and to his sons take precedence over those to others."

Hsu also discusses how other societies give priority variously to different relationships—mother-son, husband-wife, or brother-brother—and the consequences of these relationships for individuals and society. While Hsu's thesis as to the causal significance of the emphasis placed on a particular relationship by a given sociocultural system should be regarded as tentative, his empirically based discussion of differences between various types of societies indicates that for "one reason or another" sociocultural systems show what is presumably a systematic variation in its members' reference others and relationships.

It is also possible to illustrate the effects of the sociocultural system upon the formation of reference relationships by examining evidence from within sociocultural systems. Most attention will be given to the American society.

Our initial example involves patterns of membership in voluntary associations in the American society. These patterns are of particular interest as they indicate the importance of the sociocultural system upon the individual's decision to join a "voluntary" organization. Organizations become membership groups for individuals and consequently exert some type of normative influence over its members. As membership in these organizations is voluntary, it is probable that large numbers of individuals may also *identify* with the organization.

A classic work in this area is the Hyman and Wright study (187) of membership in voluntary associations. Their effort involved large samples of the American adult population. Some of their conclusions were that voluntary memberships are more characteristic of whites than Negroes, Jews than Protestants, Protestants than Catholics, and urban than rural farm residents. Voluntary organizational membership was also found to vary directly with socioeconomic status.

Hyman's and Wright's finding in regard to the relationship between socioeconomic status and membership in voluntary associations in the American society is well documented. Regardless of the measures of status and organizational participation, studies show that the higher the socioeconomic status, the higher the rate of participation in organizations tends to be. While different explanations may be offered for this relationship (118), the pattern is not random. The socioeconomic position occupied by the individual "in one way or another" influences his participation in voluntary organizations.

The importance of positions and roles for the development of reference relationships is explicitly demonstrated in a study by Hadden and Rymph (154). These authors gave a group of forty-eight Protestant clergymen from seven denominations the opportunity to participate in civil rights demonstrations. They concluded (154:59, my italics): "The hypothesis, thus, becomes obvious; the more dependent the minister is upon the denominational leaders, the more obligated he is to reflect their beliefs in action. Or viewed from a slightly different perspective, *different structural positions must respond to different reference groups.*"

The effect of the sociocultural system on the development of reference relationships can also be demonstrated through an examination of social mobility in the American society. Social mobility refers to the extent to which the individual moves up or down various hierarchies in a society. There is some support for the proposition that the individual's reference others and reference relationships systematically vary with his actual or anticipated movement in the social structure.

Form and Geschwender studied the comparative reference others that 545 manual workers employed with respect to job satisfaction (131). They found that most of the manual workers were satisfied with their occupational positions, did not expect great social mobility, and employed their peer groups and the male members of their family of orientation as social referents in evaluating their occupational position. However, when the manual worker became desirous of social mobility, he tended to shift his social references to the incumbents above him, the white-collar workers. It is of interest that these authors stressed that reference group theory "must take into account structural features of the society such as the type of stratification system, patterns of adult socialization, and mobility rates" (131:228).

Some studies have applied the reference group concept to the social mobility patterns of the American Negro. Parker and Kleiner examined the relationship between status position, mobility, and ethnic identification through the use of this approach (291). Their sample consisted of 1,489 twenty- to sixty-year-old Negroes living in the Philadelphia area.

One conclusion was that "Negroes in the higher status positions tend to have values more similar to those of the white middle class, stronger desires to associate with whites, more internalization of negative attitudes toward other Negroes, and relative weaker ethnic identification than individuals in lower status positions" (291:102). This result supports a relationship between social mobility and the formation of reference relationships.

Parker and Kleiner also concluded that the identification patterns of their subjects were a function of two sets of reference others; those associated with the status position they left behind, and those related to their newly acquired status position. This is not only an important substantive result but it has *broader theoretical implications* and again indicates the complexity of reference relationships.

Peter Blau (36) has contributed some important theoretical observations regarding social mobility that are pertinent for our discussion. Blau argues that the socially mobile person does not experience the complete enculturation of the values and styles of life of one group nor the full constraint of the reference other. These observations suggest that the effects of reference others are to some extent mediated by the individual's social mobility in the sociocultural system. Turner (412) has also emphasized the importance of the accuracy of the socially mobile person's perception of the goals and means of the nonmembership other. He suggests that the goals or ceremonial values will be more objectively perceived than the means or working values, and indicates the significance of this for the mobile individual.

The sociocultural system also influences the formation of reference relationships through its basic value system, the cultural dimension of the sociocultural system. A work illustrating this important point is Eisenstadt's study of new immigrants to Israel (115). In an effort to determine the factors influencing the immigrants' choice of new reference groups, Eisenstadt concluded that the immigrants selected groups that could confer prestige upon them. Eisenstadt's related analysis of certain youth groups in Israel indicated that the institutional values of the society significantly influenced the prestige motivations of the immigrants. The prestige preferences reflected the value structure of the society. Eisenstadt observed (115:182): "Consequently many members of these movements tend to evaluate the several roles which they perform in their various membership groups, school, family, and others, not only in terms of the satisfaction of immediate personal needs, but also in terms of their relation to the ultimate values of the society. In other words, these values and the status aspirations connected with them serve as one of the main reference standards of the adolescents."

Thus far, the role of the sociocultural system in the formation of reference relationships has been stressed and partially documented. Our attention now turns to an examination of the specifics of this influence. What are the processes through which the individual comes to acquire his reference relationships? It is suggested that five major steps are involved.

This approach necessarily represents an oversimplified statement of the reference relationship formation process. Its complexity cannot actually be described in five steps. On the other hand, these steps do entail the essential elements involved in the formation of reference relationships. The complexities are more fully considered in chapter five.

(1) *The individual is assigned certain ascribed positions at the moment of birth.* Individuals who are born on this earth are thrust into an existing sociocultural system. They are immediately assigned certain ascribed positions. An ascribed position is one that is assigned to the individual without any reference to his unique abilities or qualities. The number and character of these ascribed positions varies depending upon the nature of the particular sociocultural system the individual is born into, but he is always assigned some positions. All societies have employed the biological variable of sex as a basis for the assignment of ascribed positions (414:95), and we have previously observed that the individual is ascribed various positions within a kinship structure at the moment of birth.

(2) *Ego's occupancy of the ascribed positions exposes him to designated role-related reference others.* Once ego is assigned various positions within the existing sociocultural system, he is necessarily exposed to certain reference individuals who occupy reciprocal positions; that is, he is exposed to a set of role-related reference others. The newborn infant, for instance, is typically exposed to a mother and a father. There are three aspects of this common but critical situation that merit emphasis; (1) the *exposure* of ego to reference individuals, (2) the *reference individuals* to whom ego is exposed, and (3) the *role relationships* between ego and his role-related reference individuals.

The Exposure of Ego to Reference Individuals.—One of the important but sometimes overlooked assumptions for the development of reference relationships is that *the individual be exposed to his reference others*. The assignment of ascribed positions to ego at birth necessarily exposes him to designated role-related reference others. The possibility of the development of normative, comparative, and identification-object reference relationships thus exists.

Unfortunately, infrequent attention has been given to the factors influencing ego's exposure to the reference other. This is true even though some popular sociological theories presuppose that ego has some type of awareness of the reference other. For instance, various theories of delinquency assume that ego is aware of the norms of the upper and middle class. The single most important contribution in this area has been made by Merton (271) who relates the probability of ego becoming aware of the reference other to the actual *visibility* of the reference other in the sociocultural system. This relationship is of particular importance to us since the concept of visibility vividly portrays the role of the sociocultural system in the formation of reference relationships.

Merton describes visibility as the extent to which the reference other is available for observation (271:350). Although Merton stresses that visibility is a characteristic of the social structure, he also indicates that visibility is dependent upon ego's position within the social structure (271:350). Visibility is a function of both the "objective" character of the sociocultural system and ego's position within it. As always, the complexity of reference relationships must be taken into account. One may consider the visibility of the reference other, per se, the norms associated with the reference other, or the standing of the reference other on selected dimensions. The basic point is that the more visible the reference other is in the sociocultural system, the more likely it is that the other will be employed as a reference other. [In a study of visibility and types of social conformity, Coser concludes that the "insulation from observability and access to it are just as important structural elements in a bureaucracy as the distribution and delimitation of authority" (82:29).]

The Reference Individual.—A critical condition for the emergence of reference relationships is the reference individual. Ego would not develop any reference relationships if it were not for his exposure to actual individuals. While this might seem like an obvious point, the sociologist occasionally overlooks the individual in his enthusiastic concern for the sociocultural system. Inkeles, however, has emphasized that all institutionalized arrangements are ultimately mediated through individual human action (188). Campbell and Alexander have re-emphasized and extended this view in their discussion of structural effects and interpersonal relationships (65:284). "The value systems and normative milieus of the larger social structure typically influence the behaviors of individuals through transmission and enforcement by certain *specific* others for any given individual." Caplow (67) also stresses the importance of the individual within the organization.

The formation of reference relationships presupposes that ego be exposed to actual individuals. Ego not only forms reference relationships with these individuals but, as we will note subsequently, they direct his attention to additional reference individuals, achieved positions, and other quasi-empirical and imaginary reference others.

The Role Relationship.—Once the individual is assigned a social position, he enters into role relationships with designated reference individuals. The newborn infant, for instance, assumes role relationships with his mother and father. The social positions that ego occupies determine to a large extent the reference others in his reference set as well as the nature of his reference relationships with them. Indeed, it would not be incorrect to describe the influence of roles as "awesome." McCall and Simmons depict roles as follows (250:69–70, last italics mine): "In fact, they give the very *meaning* to our daily routine, for they largely determine our interpretations of the situations, events, and other people we encounter. By providing us with plans of action and systems of classification, our role-identities go far to determine the objects of our environment, their identity and meaning. *This is particularly true of persons as objects, both ourselves and others.*" These authors are here defining what they call role identity. As we will see subsequently, they stress the fact that roles do not "simply" impinge upon ego.

A most important component of roles with respect to the development of reference relationships is their *reciprocal* character. *Roles direct ego's attention to other individuals.* The reciprocal character of roles can be defended both conceptually and empirically. From a conceptual perspective, practically every student of roles has emphasized their reciprocal character. Ralph Linton stressed this characteristic in his influential discussion of statuses and roles (242). Merton introduced the concept of role set to refer to the complex of others associated with a given position or status (270). Although some roles do not possess this characteristic of relatedness (281), the critical importance of this typical role trait has gone unquestioned by scholars.

There is also empirical evidence to support the relevance of the reciprocity dimension of roles for the reference relationship formation process. In studies where subjects have been asked to list those others that are important for them, the others listed often reflect role-related reference others. Kemper (216) found that wife, boss(es), mother, father, and colleague(s) were the five most frequent mentions made by the 256 business executives and managers in his sample. Couch and Murray (83) found in their study of teachers, agricultural specialists, and agents that principals, parents of students, self, students, fellow teachers, and superintendents were most frequently listed by the teachers. Administrators, clients, and coworkers were most frequently cited by both specialists and agents. The results of other studies (95; 278; 328; 346; 405; 406) also reveal that many of the reference others reported appear to be role-related.

While the objective of most of the preceding studies—Denzin's (95) and Moore's (278) specifically to the contrary—was not in general to determine the role character of the responses, their results do lend support to the proposition that many of the reference others regarded as important by ego are involved in role relationships with him. Additional evidence is required to determine the extent to which this is true, the nature of the reference relationships involved in these instances, and if the role-related reference other becomes important for ego in a trans-role sense as a person reference other.

The reader will recall that the sociocultural system does not "simply" influence the formation of reference relationships. This point is very well illustrated by a further consideration of the role concept. Two additional aspects of roles must be appreciated before the relationship between assigned positions and the reference relationship formation process can be understood, namely the nature and perception of role expectations.

One of the reasons that assigned positions do not "simply" influence the formation of reference relationships is due to the nature of the role expectations associated with the assigned position. Although the very essence of roles is to provide standards for human conduct, they also allow for a latitude in behavior. Scott Greer (149:22) has made this point very explicitly in his description of roles as *minimum sets of expectations*. This characteristic of role expectations exerts a considerable impact upon human behavior. Some writers have used it as a basis for a nondeterministic view of human behavior (30; 329:14) while others have indicated that this characteristic of role expectations enables the individual to influence or "make" his role (411). While the relationship of this factor to the formation of reference relationships needs to be systematically explored, certainly such a relationship exists.

The effect of ascribed positions upon the development of reference relationships is also dependent upon ego's perception of the role expectations. McCall and Simmons (250) have stressed the importance of this variable by coining the concept of role-identity. Their position is that the effect of the sociocultural system is significantly mediated by ego's perceptions and feelings about role expectations. There is a need for explicit evidence relating this dimension of roles to the formation of reference relationships, but, as it is well established that the individual's actions are influenced by his perceptions, it is reasonable to conclude that such a relationship exists.

(3) *The scope of the individual's reference set increases as he experiences position changes in the sociocultural system.* Given the fact that positions exert an influence over the development of reference relationships, it is not surprising to find that modifications in the individual's social positions will be reflected in his reference set. During the early years of life, changes in positions bring about an increase in the scope of the individual's reference set but in many societies changes in positions during the latter part of life result in a narrowing of the individual's reference set. The following statement indicates the change in an American child's reference set as he experiences certain rather patterned position changes (73:147–48): "As the child moves outside the family there are a number of other agents and agencies of socialization to which he will be exposed. In unsupervised play with his peers he comes to participate in autonomous groupings which have their own shared activities, codes of behavior, and controls. Through family, school, or neighborhood he may be involved in church activities, in clubs, and supervised youth groups."

Various writers have suggested a relationship between the stability of the individual's social environment and various personality characteristics. Although these writers have not been explicitly concerned with reference relationships, their views are of interest. Dai (84) hypothesized a relationship between personality organization and the stability of the sociocultural environment. Kuhn (171:38) has similarly suggested that stability in personality is related to the stability of ego's roles.

Other writers have more explicitly described the relationship between position changes and reference relationships. Caplow's remarks regarding the individual's entrance into an organization are particularly relevant (67:170–71): "Joining an organization involves an encounter with 'new people,' as does promotion or demotion or transfer. Even former acquaintances seem to change. The incumbent of a new position sees them from a new angle, since they play different roles in relation to his present position than they did to his former position." Strauss (395) has emphasized that the individual *loses and acquires* significant others and reference groups via position changes. Shibutani (370) has also described the importance of position changes for interpersonal relationships.

A most relevant discussion of the effects of positions upon human association is provided by McCall and Simmons (250) in their discussion of the *career* of a relationship. These authors not only indicate the importance of positions and roles for the development of reference relationships but they also capture and emphasize the dynamic aspect of this process. They remind us that the individual must learn his role behavior, develop role agendas involving others, "take the role of the other," react to social relationships, and actively engage in the development, continuation, and termination of social relationships. It is possible to lose the very essence of individual-other relationships through a systematic analysis of them. The McCall and Simmons effort takes on special significance from this perspective. Strictly speaking, these authors are describing interpersonal relationships (250:160) rather than reference relationships. While all interpersonal relationships are reference relationships, the converse is not true.

We have previously considered some empirical evidence regarding the relationship between positions and reference relationships, but one additional study merits our attention at this time. It not only considers the relationship between position changes and changes in the individual's reference set but it also emphasizes an important dimension of this relationship that is not fully understood.

Davis and Olesen (86) examined the identity problems experienced by a group of female students who had entered a school of nursing after having spent two or more years in a university setting. The stresses produced by this change resulted in what Sullivan has described as "chumming tendencies." Intimate relationships developed between pairs of females. Part of the frustration experienced by the girls was due to the fact that the nursing role involved a separation from males. More generally, the nursing students experienced considerable identity stress because of the difficulty they had in psychologically integrating the student nurse role with a concurrently emerging identity of adult womanhood.

The distinguishing feature of the Davis and Olesen study is that the importance of examining the effects of position changes within *a broader extra-positional context is emphasized*. These authors found it necessary to consider various facets of adult socialization in their analysis of the nursing transition. They observed that many studies of occupational socialization do not take into account extra-occupational influences. The implications of this emphasis for the reference other orientation are clear. The individual typically comes to occupy a number of positions. The effect of changes in any one of these positions can not be viewed in isolation. It must be regarded within the context of the totality of the positions held by the individual within the socio-cultural system.

We can not further pursue the relationship between position changes and modifications in reference relationships. This is unfortunate as so much must be left unsaid. Our primary purpose, however, has been to indicate the importance of this dimension for the foundation of reference relationships. A detailed discussion of status passage that has implications for the development of reference relationships may be found in (142).

(4) *The scope of ego's reference set continues to increase due to his acquisition of social object reference others.* We have, thus far, stressed that once ego is assigned his initial positions in the socio-cultural system, his åssociations with his role-related reference individuals begin and any position changes will result in the acquisition of still more role-related reference individuals. These role-related reference individuals are also important in that they direct his attention to additional reference others or social object reference others. *This term is introduced to refer to those reference others that are linked to ego by his role-related or person reference individuals.* They may include other reference individuals, quasi-empirical reference others, or imaginary reference others. For instance, the parents of an American child may prepare the child for school by stressing the positive qualities of teachers, or they may teach him to love God and hate the devil. To the extent that ego acquires these social object reference others, the reference relationship formation process is successional in character.

The social object reference other has gone relatively unnoticed in considerations of the development of reference relationships. This is true in spite of Turner's emphasis on the fact that reference individuals direct ego's attention to additional reference others through his concept of the valuation reference group (410). We changed Turner's term to the social object reference other because the concept of social object is existent in the literature (227) and it reflects the meaning intended by Turner. The inattention to Turner's concept is most unfortunate as an extremely important aspect of the reference other formation process is precisely the fact that reference individuals provide ego with other reference individuals, reference groups, reference categories, reference norms, reference objects, and imaginary reference others. It is particularly critical to understand that they also direct ego's attention to *achieved positions* which in turn may expose ego to still other role-related reference individuals. Achieved positions are alloted to ego on the basis of his capabilities.

There is some supportive evidence for social object reference others. Turner (410) introduced the concept of the valuation reference group to refer to exactly this phenomenon, and Kuhn has emphasized that ego's reference individuals provide him with his reference categories (226:580, my italics): "A person derives from his reference groups his norms, attitudes and values and *the social objects these create.* He also derives *significant social categories,* both the ones to which he is assigned and the ones with which he is, in one way or another, contrasted." Shibutani has also described the "overlapping quality of primary groups" (370:404–6). (The primary relationship and the positive identification-object reference relationship reflect a "similar" phenomenon.) Litwak has additionally attributed a "stepping-stone" function to certain reference groups (245).

Empirical evidence in support of social object reference others is provided by a few studies. Berreman in an anthropological study of a North American group explicitly indicated that the "white society" became a valuation group for the members of the Aleut society (33). The Aleuts wanted to be accepted by the "white man" and had defined him as important. In this instance, the social object reference other happened to involve a positive identification-object reference relationship. Schmitt and Audas found support for "connecting audiences" in their study of adult Catholic females (346). Their husbands' coworkers, their husbands' coworkers' wives, their children's friends' parents, and the parents of their close friends became important to them. Goode is also referring to this phenomenon in his sociogenic consideration of multiple drug use among marihuana smokers. His apt term "intimate of intimates" is evidence of this. (See his discussion in *Social Problems,* vol. 17, pp. 48–64.)

The consideration of social object reference others is of particular importance since it focuses attention upon the processes whereby the individual's reference relationships are created. Let us take the example of reference categories. Kuhn has indicated that reference individuals direct ego's attention to certain reference categories. How is this accomplished? It seems that ego is necessarily an active agent in this process. His reference individuals direct him to certain reference categories rather than other reference categories but at some point ego must "*symbolically form*" these categories. Bott has provided some initial insight into this complex symbolic process in her study of social classes as reference categories. She suggests that the creation of reference class categories consists of three steps (46:265, my italics): "first, he internalizes the norms of his primary membership groups—place of work, colleagues, friends, neighborhood, family—together with some more hazy notions about the wider society; secondly he performs an *act of conceptualization* in reducing these segregated norms to a common denominator; thirdly, he projects his conceptualizations back on to society at large. This is not a conscious, deliberate process; it happens for the most part unwittingly. Moreover, modifications and revisions are constantly being made, and there are often inconsistencies and contradictions between the constructions made at different times and for different purposes. *The main point is that the individual himself is an active agent.* He does not simply internalize the norms of classes which have an independent external existence. He takes in the norms of certain actual groups, works them over, and constructs class reference groups out of them." We have assumed that, in this quotation, ego has a "role-taking" or "taking into account" awareness of the reference other.

It should be quickly emphasized that ego symbolically considers all the reference others with whom he has a "role-taking" or a "taking into account" awareness. The fact that all of ego's reference others, including the reference individual, quasi-empirical reference others, and imaginary reference others are symbolically considered in the same way by ego is of extreme importance! *The implication is that the totality of these reference others shares a "symbolic commonality" in the phenomenal world of the individual.* [For an important discussion of ego's awareness of inanimate objects, see (19).]

We have observed on a number of occasions that questions have been raised regarding the role of reference categories as reference others. Our conclusion is that the individual can symbolically create or form reference categories and that these reference categories can and do function as reference others. But very significantly, it is *only* because of the symbolic capability of ego that reference categories can serve as reference others. This is certainly true of imaginary reference others. The extent to which reference categories are reference others for ego, nevertheless, remains a moot point. There is evidence indicating that reference individuals are more influential than reference categories (100:197). It cannot be emphasized too often that only the reference individual can be the *source* of normative influence.

There are three more points that need to be emphasized in regard to social object reference others. (1) The term social object reference other is an analytical term. The individual in the "real world" experiences all his reference others in the same manner. The source of the reference other may not be known to the individual. (2) It is, of course, possible for a social object reference individual to direct ego to additional social object reference others. (3) Idiosyncratic reference others are *not* social object reference others!

(5) *The influence of ego's reference others increases as his identification with his reference others increases.* An underlying theme of the reference group literature is that there is a relationship between the degree to which an individual identifies *positively or negatively* with a reference group and the extent of influence of the reference group. It will be recalled from the discussion of our typology that identification is involved in identification-object and normative identification reference relationships.

It is extremely difficult to explain the processes through which the individual comes to identify with his reference others. There are at least four reasons for this. (1) The formation of identification is a very complex process. It is not easily understood. (2) The very meaning of identification poses a problem of no small moment for the social scientist. Some writers have suggested that the term be discarded (340) while others have made the observation that there are different types of identification (51). (3) A variety of factors may influence the process by which ego comes to identify with the reference other. For instance, the individual may identify with an organization because of a desire for prestige but identify with an athletic team because one's son is a member of it. (4) A number of factors at different levels influence the identification formation process. There are sociological, sociopsychological, and psychological determinants of identification.

It is impossible for us to consider the complex process of identification in detail but we shall indicate several very important factors that influence this process: the sociocultural system, additional sociological factors, actual or perceived characteristics of the reference other, and various attributes of ego.

We have already illustrated how the sociocultural system influences reference relationships. Many of the individual's sentiments toward reference others are circumscribed by the sociocultural system. Shibutani has aptly depicted the influence of the sociocultural system in this regard with his phrase, the social control of sentiments (370:383). The nature of the sociocultural system is the single most important variable influencing the identification formation process.

But the structural and cultural elements of the sociocultural system are not the only sociological factors to influence the process by which identification is formed. For instance, it is generally accepted that the size of a group, the frequency of interaction of its members, their degree of homogeneity, and the period of time over which they interact influence the formation of *primary* relationships. And we have generally recognized a similarity between Cooley's notion of a primary group or relationship and the element of positive identification involved in some reference relationships.

Identification formation is also influenced by the actual or perceived characteristics of the reference other. While one would anticipate that this variable would be related to identification formation, the problem is to determine the relevant characteristics of the reference other, and the conditions under which they are operative. To cite just a few of many possibilities, there is some evidence to indicate a relationship between identification formation and the degree of power attributed to the reference other (280), the affection-giving tendencies of the reference other (349), and the extent of control the reference other exerts over ego (3).

As one component of the individual-other typology is ego, it is understandable that some consideration would be given to this variable. The basic idea is that individuals vary in regard to characteristics that are related to their patterns of identification. For instance, the psychoanalytical literature suggests that the early socialization of the individual may "condition" the identification patterns of individuals, and Schachter (342) has presented evidence supporting a relationship between the anxiety status of the individual and his affiliation tendencies.

Irrespective of the difficulties involved in the explanation of identification, this remains a critical area for the reference other theorist. It will not suffice to just regard identification as a mechanism for normative influence. The manner in which positive and negative sentiments develop between ego and his reference others must receive additional attention if the reference other phenomenon is to be more fully understood. We shall now consider the relevance of identification for internalization.

The internalization process has been of major concern to past and present scholars. Such men as Freud and Mead attached considerable significance to this process. This interest has been maintained by modern social scientists. It is now apparent that the individual's relationships with his reference others constitute an important part of the internalization process. In this regard, we have noted that attitude formation may involve the stages of compliance, identification, and internalization (214; 215). The observation was also made that the normative influence of the reference other may diminish when ego does internalize the perspective of the reference other, and a host of authors have in one way or another incorporated reference others into their analysis of socialization in general and internalization in particular (73).

The relevance of reference others for the internalization process is even seen in the arguments of those scientists who question the reality of internalization. Bandura and Walters, for instance, state that (21: 259): "The size of the group by reference to which a particular person evaluates his behavior may vary considerably; when a person's immediate reference group is small and select, and does not share the values of the majority of persons of his social class, it may sometimes appear that he is making an independent self-evaluation, and displaying 'inner-directed' behavior, whereas he may be, in fact, highly dependent on the actual or fantasied approval or disapproval of a few individuals whose judgments he values highly." While only a few writers question the reality of internalization, this view focuses upon the relationship between the process of internalization and the reference other orientation.

While the internalization process has been given extensive consideration by some authors (10; 57), these efforts have usually involved a psychological or a limited social psychological perspective. There is a need for a broader and a more sociologically oriented approach to internalization. In this regard, Parsons has noted that "any theory that is to do justice to the range and complexity of socialization as a phenomenon must cover the whole range of social system levels" (294:64).

More sociologically oriented discussions of internalization include (48; 49; 64; 73; 293; 294). Vincent's study of unwed mothers (417) is also of interest in that he concluded that the internalization of traditional sexual norms presupposed that the norms be taught by positive significant others in a nonauthoritarian fashion. In my judgment, the Gerth and Mills effort (138) has important implications for a sociological approach to internalization. A recent book by John Finley Scott is also pertinent in that internalization is approached through a synthesis of Skinner's "operant behaviorism" with some contemporary forms of sociological theory (see *Internalization of Norms: A Sociological Theory of Moral Commitment* [Englewood Cliffs, N. J.: Prentice-Hall, 1971]).

The reference other orientation represents one perspective that offers numerous implications for the study of internalization. The fact that internalization must be mediated by reference others within a sociocultural context provides full justification for this view. The reference other would be central to such an approach, but the *entire* reference other orientation should be included in such an analysis. For example, we have discussed internalization at this point in the book because it is an intimate dimension of the reference relationship formation process. To the extent that this is true, it is imperative that ascribed and achieved positions, reference individuals, role expectations and relationships, position changes, social object reference others, identification—as well as the entire scope of the reference other phenomenon—be specifically incorporated into the study of internalization.

The basic theme of this chapter has been that the sociocultural system is extremely instrumental in the formation of reference relationships. The individual is born into an existing society with a given social structure and culture. Ego is assigned a set of positions at birth which exposes him to designated role-related reference others. The very nature of the reference relationships that ego enters into with these reference others is further structured by the sociocultural system. These role-related reference others direct ego's attention to various social object reference others, and as ego undergoes position changes, the entire process begins again. The individual will enter into reference relationships of one type or another with his newly acquired role-related reference others and will be exposed to still more social object reference others. The reference relationship formation process is somewhat of a successional process in that the positions and roles of the society are patterned, and ego's social object reference others are brought to his attention by his role-related reference others.

The reader should be careful, however, not to regard this sociocultural view of the formation of reference relationships as either deterministic or simplistic. We have also tried to depict *the variability and the complexity* of this process. Ego must always interpret his experiences; role expectations are minimum standards for behavior; psychological and social psychological factors influence the development of reference relationships; individuals do not negate their entire reference set with a position change. It should also be emphasized that other factors that we have not been able to discuss are involved in this process, and in part add to its variability and complexity, such as chance, idiosyncratic reference others, the mass medium, the "self-directing" character of the individual, and the actual dynamics of the reference relationship formation process.

Shibutani more than anyone else has emphasized that the mass medium is a source of perspectives (371). There is the question, however, in any particular instance of whether the mass medium is the *source* of the perspective. It should also be added, and emphasized, that the mass medium directs attention to *reference objects*. Some excellent insights regarding the reference relationship formation process are to be found in the writings on the modeling process. In particular, see Bronfenbrenner's (53:120–51) and Bandura's (20) discussions.

CHAPTER Five

The Formation of Reference Relationships (2) Multiple Reference Others

The individual's reference set expands due to his maturation in the sociocultural system. While the extent to which this occurs is dependent upon the nature of the sociocultural system and the individual's position within it, this is an inevitable experience for individuals in all societies. One consequence of this enlarging reference set is that ego will be exposed to multiple reference others. These multiple reference others may exert either compatible or conflicting expectations upon the individual. In the words of Merton, the individual's multiple reference groups may be sustaining or conflicting (272:59–69). Merton is speaking of normative reference relationships at this point. It is also possible for ego to experience conflict in his identification-object reference relationships. Comparative reference relationships are not usually considered from a conflict perspective. Their development will be considered in chapter seven.

Various writers have suggested that the most important question confronting the reference group theorist is the explanation of ego's behavior when he is the subject of conflicting reference others. While this view may be exaggerated, there is no doubt that this is a critical question for the social scientist. Its solution promises both theoretical and pragmatic rewards.

To the extent that the social scientist comes to understand the differential influence of ego's multiple reference others, he will necessarily have gained insights into the formation and the effects of reference others, and, as some of ego's more critical behaviors involve situations in which his reference others exert conflicting demands upon him, the practical relevance of knowledge in this area is crucial.

The differential influence of multiple reference others is not often considered from a reference relationship formation perspective. The reason for this seems to be that discussions of multiple reference others presuppose that the individual has established reference relationships with two or more reference others while considerations of the formation of reference relationships assume a reference relationship is to be established. While these assumptions are not untrue, there are reasons for viewing multiple reference others from a reference relationship formation perspective.

The essential point is that the factors accounting for the initial formation of reference relationships are often the same ones that tend to maintain the reference relationship. For instance, the basic values of the society are not only important in regard to the initial formation of many of the individual's reference relationships but they also continue to be important for their maintenance. This argument is particularly appealing as it explicates the fact that the social scientist has to explain both the initial formation and the continuation of reference relationships. The social scientist may increase his understanding of the formation of reference relationships through an examination of multiple reference relationships and gain increased insight into the individual's behavior in multiple reference other situations through the study of the initial origins of reference relationships.

Judson Brown, in a review of research on intrapersonal conflict, suggests that it may be necessary to reorient its study emphasizing "the principle *that the important determinants of behavior in conflict-producing situations are indistinguishable from those in ordinary unambivalent situations and that no sharp dividing line can be drawn between the two kinds of behavior*" (55:136). Preiss and Ehrlich take a similar position in regard to role conflict (307:94).

Our focus in this chapter concerns ego's *conflicting* reference others. The reasons for this emphasis are that unfortunately very little attention has been given to Merton's concept of sustaining reference groups, and conflicting reference others represent somewhat of a "test case" for the social scientist. The differential importance of crucial variables can be determined in this situation. (Chapter eight contains an analysis of the negative methodological consequences resulting from the inattention given to Merton's concept of sustaining reference groups.)

It is possible for the individual to experience conflict in either his normative or his identification-object reference relationships, but, as the latter have not been given much consideration, this chapter will focus upon conflicting normative reference relationships. Let us briefly, however, discuss conflicting identification-object reference relationships. The lack of concern with this phenomenon should not be taken as an indication of its importance.

The individual experiences conflict in his identification-object reference relationships if he experiences some type of conflict involving his identification reference others as focal points. In this situation, the *identification-object reference others are most salient.* For example, the young man may have to decide upon a steady from between two girl friends, or the newlyweds may each experience some conflict in deciding whether to live near the wife's or the husband's parents.

There is one study that contains a particularly good illustration of conflicting identification-object reference relationships. This is Killian's study of the significance of multiple-group membership in disaster (219). Killian found that the disaster produced conflicts that did not exist under normal conditions. When faced with the aftermath of a tornado, the conflict faced by the largest number of workers in two oil refineries was whether to stay on the job or go home to their family. Although Killian did not employ our terminology, ego's reference others were at the focal point of this conflict. Killian concluded that the largest number of individuals decided to go home in spite of the fact that in some instances this decision could have contributed to a second disaster if explosions had occurred in the oil refineries.

There are three situations that involve conflicting expectations; normative conflict, role conflict, and normative reference relationship conflict. *An expectation is a standard for behavior.* Although these three types of conflict have not been often compared, it is necessary for us to do so if normative reference relationship conflict is to be understood.

The Similarities.—These three types of conflict involve two similarities. (1) All three conflict situations presuppose that ego *consciously* perceives two or more expectations as *contradictory.* [The last term is used in the manner suggested by Preiss and Ehrlich (307:95). Its meaning is discussed subsequently.] It should be emphasized that the actual expectations may not be contradictory. As we suggested earlier, the distinction between objective and subjective perception is crucial for the reference other theorist, but this distinction is not of focal interest here. (2) The individual is faced with contradictory expectations that cannot be ignored in each of the three conflict situations. In other words, ego must behave in some way regarding the perceived conflicting demands; inaction is not permitted under this concept. According to Preiss and Ehrlich, "a set of *contradictory* expectations is one in which all cannot be fulfilled *and* one in which all cannot be ignored" (307:95). But it should be emphasized that there are many instances when ego will experience conflict and learn to "live with it"

The Differences.—These three types of conflict also differ in certain aspects. If each type of conflict is considered separately, we can better illustrate the differences.

Normative Conflict.—Normative conflict is the least complicated of the three types of conflict to grasp. An understanding of this type of conflict presupposes that the concept of a norm be understood. *A norm is a single expectation for behavior that is not distinctively related to a particular position that the individual occupies.* Ego would experience normative conflict if it was necessary for him to act in a situation that he perceived to be characterized by two or more conflicting norms.

An example of normative conflict experienced by many American middle-class males involves the values of honesty and achievement. The American male is expected to be honest but he is also expected to be financially successful. Occasionally these norms may conflict, and ego will have to decide to abide by one or the other. Does the second-hand car salesman, who is having great difficulty with his car sales, tell the truth about the mileage on a particular car (honesty) and lose the sale (no achievement), or does he lie about the mileage on the car (dishonesty) and eventually obtain the sale (achievement)? Strictly speaking, this example may reflect a conflict in values.

Role Conflict.—An understanding of role conflict presupposes that the concept of a role be understood. *A role refers to the set of expectations that accompanies a given position.* The foreman is a classic example of role conflict. More generally, ego experiences role conflict if he is required to act as an occupant of a position or positions which he perceives to be characterized by two or more conflicting role expectations.

This definition of role conflict involves one dimension which has not been discussed; namely, the distinction between *intrarole* and *inter-role* conflict. In intrarole conflict, ego perceives certain role expectations associated with a *single* position he occupies to be in conflict. The school superintendent, for example, may be required by the teaching staff to be their spokesman, but the school board may expect him to represent them to the teaching staff (151:248–49). Inter-role conflict involves perceived conflicting expectations associated with *two or more positions* occupied by ego. The same superintendent might be expected by the school board to spend many of his after hours at P.T.A. meetings and other educational functions while his wife may expect him to be with her most evenings. In this instance, the expectations associated with the positions of superintendent and husband would conflict (151:248–49). While some authors limit their definition of role conflict to intrarole conflict (293; 351) *or* inter-role conflict (59; 389), our definition of role conflict includes both intrarole and inter-role conflict.

Normative Reference Relationship Conflict.—The essential characteristic of normative reference relationship conflict is that the individual must act in a situation where *he perceives a conflict in the expectations associated with two or more of his reference others.* As always, a reference other cognate concept must involve an other. One example of this type of conflict is illustrated in Rosen's (332) study of the attitudes of Jewish adolescents toward the use of kosher meat. Certain of these adolescents' membership groups, and presumably reference groups, had conflicting attitudes toward the use of kosher meat. This is an excellent example of normative reference relationship conflict in that some adolescents were faced with conflicting expectations from their family and peer group concerning the use of kosher meat. This situation involved conflicting expectations that were explicitly associated with specific others.

Our discussion is limited to a general consideration of conflicting normative reference relationships. It will be recalled that the normative reference relationship has three subtypes; the compliant, the identification, and the internalized. Also, it should be noted that the factors considered in regard to normative reference relationship conflict resolution would appear to apply to any conflict situation.

While there is no problem in distinguishing normative reference relationship conflict from normative conflict, the relationship between normative reference relationship conflict and role conflict must be more carefully considered as they may overlap. In fact, if the normative relationship conflict involves two or more of ego's membership others and if the role conflict is "other oriented" rather than "normatively oriented," they will be identical. While this latter distinction concerning roles has apparently not been explicitly made, it is of importance.

Role conflict is "other oriented" if the conflicting role expectations saliently involve ego's role partners. The foreman, for instance, is supposed to be loyal to labor and management. This is an example of role conflict and normative reference relationship conflict. *Role conflict is "normatively oriented" if ego's role partners are not saliently involved in the conflicting role expectations.* The university professor, for instance, is expected to teach and do research. When these two role expectations come into conflict, we have a situation of role conflict that is not also normative reference relationship conflict.

Now if role conflict that is "other oriented" is identical to normative reference relationship conflict when membership others are involved, the question arises as to whether or not there are ever any instances of "pure" normative reference relationship conflict involving membership others. While this still remains a problematic issue, the answer appears to be in the negative. If one assumes that ego cannot have a membership affiliation without having a corresponding role relationship with a membership other, it seems that role conflict that is "other oriented" and normative reference relationship conflict involving membership others refer to exactly the same phenomenon.

Let us now consider normative reference relationship conflict when at least one nonmembership other is involved. It should be initially emphasized that ego can experience conflict in this situation. Suppose ego has a good friend, Joe, a membership other, and that he also admires Frank, a nonmembership other. Now Joe does not intend to go to college and tries to involve ego in numerous nonacademic activities, but ego realizes that Frank, who intends to go to college, spends a great amount of time studying. Ego may find this to be a conflicting situation. Does he develop regular study habits or not?

Although ego is experiencing normative reference relationship conflict in a situation of this type, he is not experiencing role conflict, as the conflict does not involve two or more role partners. There is an important difference between normative reference relationship conflict involving two or more membership others and normative reference relationship conflict that only involves one or fewer membership others. Ego is not typically subjected to external sanctions from his nonmembership others. Any sanctions stemming from ego's nonmembership others are usually internal or self-imposed. This fact is of importance for our understanding of the resolution of normative reference relationship conflict.

As the individual's reference set increases, he will experience some degree of normative reference relationship conflict. The alternatives available for the resolution of individual conflict are of particular interest. A consideration of these alternatives will provide further insight into the nature of normative reference relationship conflict and lead into a discussion of the variables that influence ego's behavior when he acts according to one of the conflicting expectations rather than another.

There are apparently only a limited number of alternatives available for the individual to select when he is faced with normative reference relationship conflict. An extremely important question concerns the relative frequency with which these alternatives are selected. Only a few researchers such as Gross, Mason, and McEachern (151) have given it any attention. Toby, in his discussion of role conflict, suggests the fact that alternatives are limited in number (403). There is some consensus regarding five alternatives that the individual has in a conflict situation.

(1) *Rejection of all Conflicting Expectations.*—The individual may reject all of the conflicting normative reference relationships involved in a given situation. This will at least eliminate the overt conflict for him. The young assistant professor who cannot decide to employ the grading standards set by his peers or the more liberal expectations of the students with whom he has considerable rapport may simply throw up his hands and go into the insurance business.

Merton has observed in regard to this alternative in role conflicts that it "can be effectively utilized only in those circumstances where it is still possible for the status-occupant to perform his other roles, without the support of those with whom he has discontinued relations" (271:379). Goode has also observed in regard to this alternative in role conflict that ego becomes psychologically dependent upon the positions he occupies, and he cannot leave them without some psychic cost (147). The professor's self-image, for instance, may be very reflective of his position as teacher. Ego faces this same psychological dilemma if he employs this alternative to resolve his normative reference relationship conflicts.

(2) *Compromise.*—Students of role conflict have indicated that individuals may compromise their role conflicts in some manner. For instance, one superintendent who was caught in a conflict between the hiring of personnel on the basis of professional competence or the preference of certain school boards said (151:262): "I compromise. It's a matter of the degree of differential between the two candidates. If the difference in competence is too wide, I operate on the professional criteria. If there is little difference, there's no harm in recommending on the basis of the school committee's preferences. If I do this the committee will help me on the big picture—it's for the greater good of the school system. If you can justify it as being for the greater good of the system, then it's all right." This alternative is also available to individuals who are experiencing normative reference relationship conflict. For an excellent example of the compromise and the rejection alternatives to conflict, see (324:252–53).

(3) *Avoidance.*—The individual may resolve normative reference relationship conflicts by psychologically or overtly avoiding one or more

of the conflicting expectations. In this situation, ego does not relinquish his position in his membership groups nor does he sever his psychological relationship with his nonmembership others. The avoidance solution is distinct from the rejection solution.

Students of role conflict have detailed a number of avoidance mechanisms. Ego may psychologically compartmentalize the conflicting expectations in order to "ignore" the problem of inconsistency (147), delegate work to others in order to help alleviate the conflict (147), employ tact to legitimately avoid those situations in which the conflicts might become very salient (403), use stalling techniques to temporize conflicting situations (403), actually extend role obligations in order to provide a rationale for his inability to live up to conflicting expectations (147), and employ excuses of one type or another in order to explain any inconsistent behavior (403). These avoidance mechanisms can also be employed by ego for the resolution of normative reference relationship conflict.

(4) *Innovation.*—The individual may respond to conflicting normative reference relationships with a certain degree of creativity. While this alternative has not been given much attention, probably because of the fact that social structures show a considerable degree of stability (270), it remains a logical alternative, and under some conditions it is an actual alternative. The assistant professor caught in the grading dilemma may succeed in passing some type of new grading policy in the department, or he may obtain a new title for his course which would give it somewhat of a "special status" and provide a rationale for the assignment of higher grades to the students in this class. For another example of innovation, see (206).

(5) *Conformity to One of the Conflicting Expectations.*—The individual may overtly resolve normative reference relationship conflict by conforming to one of the conflicting expectations. As this alternative is the most revealing of the variables that influence the formation and the resolution of normative reference relationship conflict, it is the focus of the remainder of the chapter.

There is merit in reviewing the general logic of the following section. The assumption is that the individual is caught between two or more conflicting reference relationships that are relatively similar in their influence over him. If the individual conforms to one of these conflicting expectations, the social scientist posits that some factor(s) "swayed the balance" in that direction. In other words, differential influence is explainable. The factors presently suggested by the literature are considered below. There are certainly, however, other variables that operate in situations of this type. Future research should reveal their importance.

While there is evidence regarding the variables that account for the differential influence of ego's normative reference relationships, there is very little evidence concerning the *joint* influence of these factors. We do not know what happens when several of these variables are present in the same situation. While one might infer the combined effect of a set of factors from the separate effects of each of the included variables, this inferential process will not always result in correct predictions. The categories of variables may combine in either a "logical" or an "illogical" manner. This significant observation should not be forgotten by the reader. Technically, of course, the point is that the categories of variables may combine in an additive or an interactive manner.

An excellent example of the complexity of the variables influencing reference relationships is provided by Rosenberg's study, *The Worker Grows Old* (334). Rosenberg investigated the friendship and kinship patterns among a sample of white working class Philadelphians. Rosenberg, whose major objective was to determine if these patterns were primarily related to the aging process or the social stratification system, concluded (334:186): "Were we now to evaluate these traditional orientations to the problem of social isolation on the basis of the preceding chapters, perhaps we would be forced to conclude that elements of the stratification approach are more fruitful than those of the gerontological approach. However, as the epigraphical fragment above implies, this would serve little better purpose than trying to describe the gods by skin or eye color while neglecting to define them by their divinity. We have found that at all levels, within the portion of the socioeconomic hierarchy we examined, neighborhood contextual dissonance isolates people from friends. Although socioeconomic rank dictates the differential response made to a given neighborhood context and age signifies a role transition from breadwinner to neighborhood which sensitizes a person to the influence of the neighborhood context, nevertheless, in themselves, age and rank have no direct relation to isolation from friends. And neither age nor socioeconomic rank in themselves restrict a person's contact with kin. It is a history of economic deprivation which does that along with disrupted family arrangements."

We will now consider some of the factors that account for the differential influence of ego's normative reference others. A factor that is quite important in accounting for the differential influence of the individual's conflicting normative reference others is the salience of the reference other. It will be recalled that we are using the term *salience* to refer to the extent to which ego is aware of the reference other in either a "role-taking" or a "taking into account" manner. Although there is very little research on the role of salience in conflict situations per se, the available theoretical and empirical works on salience in general indicate that, if ego is involved in a normative reference relationship conflict, he may resolve it in the direction of the reference other that is the most salient for him. The reference group studies that have employed the salience variable in one way or another include (61; 71; 143; 144; 210; 212; 376). Charters and Newcomb have described the theoretical rationale for the role of the salience variable in conflict situations in their study of the attitudinal effects of the experimentally increased salience of a membership group (71:276): "We have attempted a simple test of the proposition that attitudinal response is a function of the relative strengths of momentary forces toward or away from membership in groups with conflicting norms. By increasing the potency of one of an individual's membership groups, we would expect to find that his expressed attitudes would resemble more closely the attitudes prescribed by the norms of that group."

If ego's reference others are truly in conflict, their differential effects might be due to the *momentary* salience of one of ego's reference others. This suggests that *situational factors*, such as the physical proximity of the reference other, may be of substantial importance in explaining the differential effects of ego's reference others. Lewin has frequently reminded us that the characteristics of a situation have a considerable influence upon human behavior, and studies (127) have demonstrated the importance of ecological factors on group formation. On the other hand, one may speculate that if ego is not truly in a conflict situation, the effects of situational factors would be considerably less.

The classic study involving the salience of the reference other has been the Newcomb and Charters effort (71). They found that an experimental group of Catholic subjects, who were reminded of the fact that they were Catholics, responded to a set of attitudinal items more as Catholics would be expected to respond than a control group of Catholic subjects who were not reminded of the fact that they were Catholics. Differential results were not obtained for Jewish and Protestant subjects who had been placed in similar situations.

Kelley (212) in a rigorous extension of the Newcomb and Charters study concluded that Catholic high school students whose religious affiliation was made salient were more resistant to change in matters contrary to Catholic norms than Catholic high school students whose religious affiliation was not made salient. Significant differences were not observed among Catholic college students who were placed in a similar situation. Kelley makes the important observation in this regard that if the Catholic Church was not a reference group for the college students, the increased salience of the Church would not have any effect upon their behavior.

Other types of studies have also shown a relationship between the salience of reference others and their effects upon individuals. For instance, some researchers have demonstrated the increased ability of individuals to withstand pain when their religious affiliation is made salient for them. Buss and Portnoy (61) have presented evidence that pain tolerance varied directly with the individual's degree of identification with the religious group that was made salient.

The salience variable is a particularly important factor to consider in regard to ego's resolution of normative reference relationship conflict because it encompasses other situational variables. We have already mentioned the physical proximity of the reference other in this context. One might also question whether ego's present or past reference others exert the greater influence in a conflict situation, or if ego's membership or nonmembership reference others would be the most influential in a normative reference relationship conflict situation.

We would anticipate from a salience perspective that if ego was involved in a normative reference relationship conflict situation, present reference others would be more influential than past reference others, and membership others would take priority over nonmembership others. If ego is not in a conflict situation, this would not necessarily be the case. Some past reference others are very important, and the very foundation of the reference other orientation is that nonmembership others may be more important than membership others.

Although there is not a large amount of evidence in these two areas, Kaplan concluded the following in his study of reference groups and political behavior (210:169): "In this examination of possible past and present reference group influences, the general conclusion can be reached that in those instances where there seems to be a conflict between the two, the present point of reference seems to be the more relevant and significant."

In regard to the membership-nonmembership other question, Glaser has made the following observation (143:441): "During any period, *prior identifications* and *present circumstances* dictate the selection of the persons with whom we identify ourselves. Prior identifications which have been pleasing tend to persist, but at any time the immediate circumstances affect the relative ease (or salience) of alternative identifications. That is why membership groups so frequently are the reference groups, although they need not be." This and other evidence indicates that researchers would theoretically benefit from viewing situational factors within a broader salience perspective.

Another variable that is involved in the resolution of normative reference relationship conflict is the personality of the individual. The concept of personality is employed here in a general sense to refer to selected characteristics of the individual, such as personality traits, need-dispositions, the self-concept, and the like. Our objective is to illustrate how the individual's personality may be critically involved in the resolution of normative reference relationship conflict and in the more general process of reference other acquisition.

There is evidence from small-group laboratory studies supporting a relationship between personality traits and conformity behavior. If one is willing to make the assumption that this evidence bears some relationship to the "real" world, support is lent to the basic connection between the individual's personality characteristics and the influence of his reference others upon him. [Jahoda has emphasized the absence of ego-involvement in small group experimental type studies (197).] Berkowitz and Lundy (32) for instance, in a laboratory study of the relationship between personality characteristics and susceptibility to peers or authority figures, found that college students low on interpersonal confidence were more influenced by peers than by authority figures. It was suggested that individuals with low confidence scores had a greater need for interpersonal relations.

Hochbaum in another experimental study involving college males and females was explicitly concerned with the relationship between the individual's self-confidence and his reactions to group pressures toward uniformity. One of Hochbaum's principal findings vividly indicates the relationship between personality characteristics and the ability of the reference other to influence the individual (173:687): "The effect of agreement or disagreement with an appropriate reference group on a person's perception of his ability to deal successfully with the issue concerning which the group serves as a referent is inversely related to the person's initial perception of his level of ability concerning the issue."

In a nonexperimental study that was concerned with the relationship between personal needs and the acceptance of a new group as a reference group, Hartley (163:355) found evidence suggesting "that individuals who consider their needs important are also likely to feel that their needs are satisfied in a variety of groups, and are therefore more likely to accept almost any new group more easily than those who assign a low degree of importance to their needs." While Hartley's study of 146 first-semester male freshmen at a municipal college was not concerned with a conflict situation, it supports the role of personality characteristics in the reference relationship formation process. [Clark has recognized the role of ego's needs in the formation of reference relationships and cites a variety of evidence to support this position (72).]

One study which explicitly illustrates the role of personality characteristics in conflict situations is the Stouffer and Toby study of role conflict among a group of college students (393). The students were presented with a series of hypothetical conflict situations in which they had to select between obligations to a friend and society. The most important result of this study was that individuals exhibited a pattern in their resolution of these conflicts. Students tended to resolve the conflicts in either a particularistic (selection of the friend) or a universalistic (selection of the society) direction. These results suggest that individuals may have a predisposition to react in certain ways when faced with role conflict. This same point can be made in regard to the resolution of normative reference relationship conflict.

The role conflict study by Getzels and Guba (140) suggests another way in which personality characteristics may be involved in the resolution of normative reference relationship conflict. These authors conducted a study of officers at nine teaching schools of the Air Command and Staff School of the Air University and found role conflict to exist among some of the officers in regard to military and teaching duties. One finding was that individuals showed a tendency to resolve their conflicts in terms of the *major role* to which they were committed. The authors further suggested that "an actor, therefore, placed in a role conflict situation, will probably choose as his major role the one that is most compatible with his needs" (140:174). Generalizing to normative reference relationship conflict, the implication is that its resolution may be a complex function of ego's personality needs and his basic role commitments.

In reviewing our discussion of the relationship between personality characteristics and the resolution of normative reference relationship conflict, it should be emphasized that the data is far from definitive.

While one may conclude that personality characteristics are complexly involved in both the resolution of normative reference relationship conflicts and the formation of normative reference relationships, it must not be forgotten that personality factors *always* operate within a social framework, and at least one study has demonstrated that individuals with different types of personality structures tend to resolve conflicts in similar ways (275). An understanding of social behavior presupposes an inclusion of both individual and group variables (173).

The precise role of personality variables in the prediction of conflict resolution relative to sociological factors remains an empirical question. For one study that did consider this issue, see (113). The personal preference variable in this study proved to be as predictive as the structural variables. It must be remembered in studies of this type that the human organism is a collection of acts (7). We do not know how well the personality characteristics that have been examined are representative of the total personality.

It should not be surprising that the individual's degree of identification with his reference others would be involved in an explanation of their differential influence. We have already stressed the fact that identification often precedes normative influence. This leads to the hypothesis that "all other things being equal" the individual will resolve normative reference relationship conflict in the direction of the reference other with whom he has the greatest positive identification. The reverse statement could be made in regard to reference others with whom ego negatively identifies. For an excellent study illustrating this point, see (260). Berelson and Steiner offer as a generalization in their inventory of scientific findings (29:329): "When caught in cross-pressures between the norms of different groups of which he is simultaneously a member, the individual will suffer some emotional strain and will move to reduce or eliminate it by resolving the conflict in the direction of the strongest felt of his group ties." The foregoing statement pertains only to membership groups, but it can be extended to nonmembership others.

There are a number of studies that indicate the role of identification in conflict situations. Kaplan (210) found that the intimate primary group was more important than population categories, such as Catholics or Protestants, in situations where conflicts existed regarding voting behavior. Bowerman and Kinch concluded in a study of peer-family orientations that while the majority of students were oriented toward their peers, "those students who had a high level of adjustment to the family were most likely to be oriented toward the family, particularly *in identification* and in acceptance of family norms and values" (47:211, my italics).

While there is theoretical and empirical support for the importance of ego's identification with his reference others in the resolution of normative reference relationship conflict, more evidence is needed before we can be definitive about its role *under varying conditions*. Existing studies indicate that other factors besides identification must be taken into account in any total consideration of normative reference relationship conflict. Kandel and Lesser (207) found in their study of parental and peer influence on educational plans that the influence of friends upon ego increased with intimacy but this was not true of the mother. Her influence remained the same irrespective of the adolescent's closeness to his mother.

Komarovsky (224) in a study of blue-collar marriage found that background factors, such as age, sex, and kinship fashioned intimate friendships in patterned ways. Wives, for instance, would disclose certain kinds of things to their sisters but not to their mothers. Similarly, husbands would disclose certain things to their girl friends that they would not disclose to their wives. We should also remember Turner's emphasis that reference others are segmentally important (409). Brittain's (50) study of adolescent choices and parent-peer cross-pressures demonstrated that different reference others were utilized for different types of problems. Studies of this type unmistakably indicate that identification is not the only factor that influences ego's behavior in a normative reference relationship conflict situation.

Another variable that may influence an individual's resolution of a normative reference relationship conflict situation is the degree of consensus he perceives among his significant others. While a large amount of empirical evidence has not been generated on this point, the hypothesis is that "if all things are equal" ego will resolve the conflict in the direction where he perceives the greatest amount of consensus among his significant others.

Although it was not a study of normative reference other conflict, the study by Backman, Secord, and Peirce (15) of changes in the self-concept is an excellent illustration of the effects of the consensus of the individual's significant others in some situations. The basic hypothesis of the study was that the greater the number of significant others who are perceived by ego to define an aspect of his self-concept congruently, the more resistant to change is that aspect of the self. The authors found support for their hypothesis. A deliberate attempt to modify the subjects' judgments about certain of their personality needs resulted in a significantly greater change for needs where there was low consensus among significant others than for needs where there was high consensus.

Gullahorn (153) in a questionnaire study of hypothetical role conflict situations involving a sample of union members examined the relationship between the consensus of ego's reference others and various modes of role conflict resolution. He concluded that the effects of ego's reference others were generally additive. This meant that the greater the consensus among the reference others as to the particular mode of conflict resolution ego should follow, the more often the respondent selected this alternative. Gullahorn also found that when two of the three most strong reference groups of the union members, "people you represent" and the "executive committee," were in agreement in their demands upon ego, their joint effect was greater than that of either separately. This suggested to the author that when the two stronger of three competing reference others are in agreement, their effectiveness becomes greater. The political scientist has also concluded that ego's peer associates are more likely to influence his voting behavior when group members are in agreement than when they are in disagreement (91:137).

It must be stressed that the role of the consensus variable in normative reference relationship conflict remains problematic. Explicit research in this area has not been extensive and there is some evidence suggesting that other variables, such as the size of ego's reference set, have some effect on its impact. Reeder, Donohue, and Biblarz (315), in a study of nine work groups of enlisted men at an isolated military base, found that persons whose self-ratings disagreed with the ratings assigned to them by the members of their work group had a greater number of reference groups than those individuals who agreed with the ratings of their work groups. Brim has made a relevant observation in regard to the size of ego's reference set in his discussion of adult socialization (49:193–94): "Most important is that adults have a wider set of reference figures to draw upon for counteracting sets of values and opinions. Resistance to the immediate local demands for conformity springs from reliance on non-immediate significant others in one's life, so that the person is not necessarily concerned with approval and acceptance at this time and place. The increased number of interpersonal relationships, that is, the richness of the gallery of significant others, gives the adult greater autonomy and independence from many groups. The extreme instance is the adult martyr who can pursue his distinctive purpose even though strong coercive measures may be used against him by many groups in society, because he is supported by others whose approval is of higher significance to him and so sustain him in his independent course, whether they be future generations of men, the host of dead poets, his father or his mother, or perhaps his God."

Two other variables that may be operative in the normative reference relationship conflict situation are the legitimacy of the expectations placed upon ego by his reference others and the ability of the reference other to impose sanctions upon him. These two factors are considered together because they both represent sociological factors. This is not to suggest that they could not be considered from a perceptual perspective.

While a number of writers have acknowledged the probable role of sanctions in conflict situations, let us consider the Campbell and Pettigrew study, "Racial and Moral Crisis: The Role of Little Rock Ministers" (66). This research illustrates the role of sanctions in at least one role conflict situation. The basic theme was that the churches employed rewards and penalties to "keep the ministers in line." The clergymen were caught in a dilemma between conformity to moral integrationalist guidelines as presented by official church policy and the segregationist preferences of the community. In this particular situation, positive and negative sanctions were implemented by the local hierarchy in support of the segregationist position rather than the integrationist position. The authors observed (66:514): "However exalted the moral virtue the minister expounds, the hierarchy does not wish him to damn his listeners to hell—unless somehow he gets them back in time to attend service next Sunday. Promotions for him are determined far less by the number of times he defends unpopular causes, however virtuous their merit, than by the state of the physical plant and the state of the coffer."

A legitimate expectation is one that the reference other has a right to expect of ego. Although more evidence is needed regarding the role of this variable in conflict situations, there are some conditions under which ego will view one expectation as more legitimate than another and resolve the conflict in that direction. Getzels and Guba (140) considered this factor in their study of role conflict among military personnel at Air University. It will be recalled that some of these men experienced a conflict between teaching and military obligations. The authors found that the role conflicts experienced by these men were affected by the legitimacy that they ascribed to these roles as well as by the major role that they ascribed to themselves. They concluded that "the officer-instructor at Air University who chooses as his major role the instructor rather than the officer role is more likely to be involved in conflict because his major role is not also the legitimate role" (140:175). In other words, there was *a structural expectation* that the officer role take priority on an agenda of roles.

Interestingly, the two variables being considered in this section, legitimacy of expectations and ability of the reference other to implement sanctions upon ego, have been simultaneously considered in a number of studies. The most important has been the Gross, Mason, and McEachern classic study of role conflicts faced by school superintendents in Massachusetts (151). This research also included a third major independent variable—ego's primary individual orientation towards the legitimacy and sanctioning dimensions of norms.

In regard to the latter factor, individuals were classified as having a moral orientation, an expedient orientation, or a moral-expedient orientation. The authors were attempting to determine if individuals had a predisposition to react toward conflict situations in terms of these three dimensions. Individuals with a moral orientation gave priority to the legitimacy of norms over the sanctions connected with them. Individuals with an expedient orientation gave first priority to the sanctions connected with the norms. The individuals with a moral-expedient orientation took both factors into account.

Gross, Mason, and McEachern were able to predict the reactions of these superintendents to role conflict situations in an impressive number of instances. These three variables taken together enabled the authors to make correct predictions in 91 percent of the role conflicts considered (151:299).

Other investigators have achieved a lower but an impressive accuracy in the prediction of role conflict resolution from a consideration of the legitimacy of expectations and the sanctioning ability of the reference other. This evidence further supports the importance of these two variables. The study by Miller and Shull (273) of four different groups, including two groups of business executives, a group of company training directors, and a group of labor leaders, and the study by Ehrlich, Rinehart, and Howell (113) of police officers and police trainees, resulted in a significant but somewhat reduced level of successful predictions. The overall accuracy of prediction of the Miller and Shull study was 71 percent. Ehrlich, Rinehart, and Howell obtained a similar, but slightly lower, result in their consideration of these variables (113).

While additional evidence is needed in regard to the role of the sanctioning ability and the legitimacy of the expectations provided by the reference other in normative reference relationship conflicts, the variation in the results of the previously mentioned studies suggests that the role of these two structural variables may vary with other conditions. Ehrlich, Rinehart, and Howell concluded "that, where our operations and procedures of analysis are comparable, the difference obtained between our findings and the findings of Gross and his associates are due in large measure to differences in the population studied" (113:96). The work of Cain also suggests another possibility. Her theory of conflict resolution gives considerable attention to ego's perception of the group's dependence on him. For instance, after discussing the two structural factors presently being considered by us, Cain states "but in either case, the factor affecting behavior will be *ego's perception of the dependence of the group on him*, which will no doubt be related to the actual situation but not necessarily exactly so" (62:200). [It must be remembered always that causal relationships vary under different conditions. An example of this from the reference group literature is the finding that the relationship between received evaluation and choice of significant others varied for three classes of role performance (83).]

Another factor that may enter into the formation of normative reference relationships and the resolution of normative reference relationship conflict is the attractiveness of the reference other. Festinger, Torrey, and Willerman observe in their study of the self-evaluation process as a function of the individual's attractiveness to the group that "anything which increases the importance of the group as a general reference or comparison group will increase the pressure towards uniformity" (128:162).

The attractiveness variable has been employed in a variety of ways by the social scientist, and consequently it is somewhat difficult to assign a precise definition to it. The underlying meaning of the concept is that the individual, for one reason or another, finds the reference other to be an *appealing* one. Ego may, for instance, be attracted to a reference group because of the status it offers him or the appeal of the norms of the group. Another factor that may attract ego is the congeniality of the members of the group. For one reference group type study that operationalized attractiveness in this manner, see (137).

An excellent example of the role of prestige of the reference other in the reference other formation process is Eisenstadt's study of the absorption of new immigrants into Israel. It will be recalled that we previously alluded to this study as an illustration of the role of cultural values in the reference relationship formation process. Eisenstadt concluded that "most of the choices of reference groups seem to be made in terms of status aspirations of the individual and his evaluation of the status-conferral possibilities of different groups within the institutional structure of the society" (115:183).

The attractiveness of the reference other has also been considered in terms of the similarity between the norms of the reference other and the values of the individual. Hartley found in her study of 146 male freshmen that the students who perceived the greatest differences between the college norms and the norms of their current reference groups were less likely to accept the college as a reference group than those who perceived fewer differences between the college norms and those of their current groups (162).

Although additional research is required regarding the components of what we have somewhat broadly described as an attractiveness dimension and the exact role of this variable in normative reference relationship conflict, this is a factor worthy of further study.

The objective of this chapter was to explain further the formation and the complexity of the individual's reference set. Although our focus was upon conflicting reference relationships, the perspective was adopted that many of the same variables that account for the resolution of conflicting normative reference relationships are also involved in the initial formation and the continuation of the reference relationship.

While much was said about conflicting normative reference relationships, much had to be left unsaid. Perhaps the most serious void is a characterization of the experiences of the individual actually caught up in a conflict situation. This is a difficult image to capture on paper. But it is clear that *ego is not a passive creature in this process.* Some excellent descriptions exist regarding the adjustment of individuals to role conflict within organizations (206), and we know, of course, that ego may experience dissonance in conflict situations. For two empirical studies that explicitly relate the reference group concept and role conflict to dissonance, see (248; 442) respectively. The latter article shows the influence of the social structure upon the formation of defense mechanisms. The best study, however, that relates dissonance to a reference group perspective is (296). The evidence from various voting studies and laboratory studies also indicates that individuals in conflict situations may postpone its resolution and switch back and forth between alternatives before it is resolved (78:106). It is equally clear that although conflict is dysfunctional for the individual in some ways, it is functional in others. Ego would not mature without conflict, at least in the sense of "problem solving" behavior.

Our final remark concerns the state of knowledge regarding the resolution of reference relationship conflict. Some of the central variables that are operative in this process have been identified. What is now needed is additional knowledge concerning the *conditions* under which these variables are differentially operative. One may argue that empirical evidence as much as theory is needed in this area. More attention should be given to the role of the reference other in conflict situations. Most of the evidence we have considered in this chapter has involved role conflict situations, and while the insights gained from studies in this area are invaluable, only a few researchers, such as Preiss and Ehrlich (307) have focused upon the role of the reference other in the formation and resolution of role conflict. [The reader who is interested in a more role-oriented discussion of role conflict than has been provided here is referred to (350:449–520).]

CHAPTER *Six*

The Effects of Reference Others

The purpose of this chapter is to illustrate and document the effects of reference others for individuals and society. These effects have a variety of consequences for the overt and covert behaviors of individuals and the very maintenance of the society. While the effects of reference others are discussed throughout this book, they are now our special concern. (Although they are not identical, the term *effects* and *consequences* are used in an interchangeable manner in this chapter.)

It is imperative that the effects of reference others be documented. The social scientist is occasionally criticized for developing constructs that do not have empirical referents. It is argued that the developed constructs may be useful for the intellectual consideration and expression of ideas but that they do not refer to actual "forces." The critic concludes it is an error to assert that these constructs exert an influence because they are abstractions. The social scientist is said to have committed the "fallacy of reification"—to make real what is not real.

Although the possibility of reification is not at issue, a basic assumption of this book is that *reference relationships are real.* They are not constructs. The main justification for this position is that their effects can be recognized and documented. This argument is not entirely convincing since it does not delineate the empirical referents of the reference other nor the processes whereby the reference other manifests its effects upon the individual. While there are not definitive insights in these areas, some further observations are in order.

Our previous consideration of the empirical character of the reference other resulted in a threefold classification; the reference individual, quasi-empirical reference others, and imaginary reference others. Let us first consider the type of influence the reference individual and the imaginary reference other are capable of extending over ego. *The concept of "direct influence" will be used to refer to the effects of a reference other upon ego that are the result of actual contact between ego and the reference other while the concept of "indirect influence" will be* used to refer to the effects of a reference other upon ego that are not the result of actual contact between ego and the reference other. Direct influences may be intended or unintended by the reference other and recognized or unrecognized by ego.

Reference individuals are able to extend a direct influence upon ego but imaginary reference others cannot. A reference individual may actually tell ego to study more, or ego may come to study more due to his imitation of the behavior of the reference individual. In either case, the reference individual has extended a direct influence over ego through his actual contact with him. The imaginary reference other does not have an actual existence. Its influence must therefore be indirect. The imaginary playmate of the young boy, for instance, only influences him in that *the boy attributes an existence to the imaginary playmate*. Apparently, ego must have either a "role-taking" or a "taking into account" awareness of the imaginary reference other!

It must be emphasized that the direct influence extended by a reference individual is not necessarily sustained through continued contact. College students who go away to school may feel just as guilty for not studying hard as those college students who stayed at home and attended a local college. The point is that in both instances the students are being influenced by the wishes of their parents. The reader must also understand that reference individuals may extend an indirect influence over ego. The young school boy may be influenced by his favorite sports hero even though he was never introduced to him. In this instance, the mass media was the vehicle of influence.

Let us now consider the quasi-empirical reference other. This is the problematic category as its five types are "real" and "unreal." Our position is that reference categories, reference objects, reference norms, and the reference self can only have an indirect influence over the individual. While it is true that ego is able to come into actual contact with some of these reference others, that is, certain reference objects, *the notion of direct influence presupposes that the reference other has the capability to influence by word or deed*. With this in mind, there is only one type of quasi-empirical reference other, the group, that *conceivably* could influence in this manner, but it must be remembered that the group is, in part, an abstraction. Consequently, *we regard groups as being able to have an indirect influence over ego through his symbolic consideration of them and perhaps a direct influence due to ego's actual interaction in the group context*. This area needs further study.

The remainder of this chapter will consider the types of effects that reference others have for individuals and society. A discussion of the effects of reference others for individuals will be emphasized as there are not as many empirical studies of the consequences of reference others for society. Consideration of the effects of reference others for individuals will center about the three major types of reference relationships; the normative, identification-object, and comparative. Although it would also be logical to categorize the studies in this chapter by aspects of the reference other or the individual, the existing evidence has focused upon reference relationships.

One additional point regarding our selection of illustrations needs to be explained. Reference group studies have often been criticized for being post hoc in character (e.g., 45). Stratton has observed that (394:258): "Traditionally, the reference group concept has been used as an explanation *post factum*. If an individual acts in a certain way or reports certain beliefs, it has been the practice of many social scientists to attribute this behavior, or these beliefs, to an orientation to a particular reference group which sanctions them." This is a serious and partially valid observation. It is serious as the establishment of scientific truth presupposes that successful predictions are made prior to the examination of evidence. It is partially valid since some important reference group studies have employed a post hoc approach (e.g., 272; 287).

In view of this criticism, the studies discussed in the remainder of the chapter were selected because of their methodological sophistication, the a priori character of their predictions, or the impressiveness of their results. It remains a moot question as to whether the reference group literature is more or less characterized by post hoc interpretations than other areas of the social sciences. The important point, as Merton (272:68 n) and Stratton (394:258) have indicated, is that studies of the reference other do not have to be post hoc in character.

In the following pages we illustrate the normative consequences of reference others for individuals. A normative reference relationship exists between the individual and a reference other if the individual is being influenced by the norms or values characteristic of or attributed to the reference other. Reference others have a variety of normative influences over ego.

Overt Behavior.—A number of studies have demonstrated a relationship between the individual's reference others and his overt behavior in normative areas. Relationships have been found regarding voting behavior (210), sex conduct norm violations (208), adolescent premarital sexual behavior (274; 317), and smoking behavior (377). The

Kanin article (208) is particularly important because it demonstrates that, even though the individual may be attracted to a group that has certain values similar to his own, the group may provide a very important function in that it supports and sustains these values. Reiss's study (317) is noteworthy because it is one of the few empirical attempts to develop a general theory of sexual attitude change and reference group behavior. As Reiss observes, there is little in the extensive literature of the adolescent period that relates reference group theory to sexuality through empirical research (317:139n). We shall confine ourselves here to a consideration of two studies examining, respectively, (1) adolescent premarital sexual behavior and (2) smoking behavior.

There have been several investigations of the relationship between the American adolescent's premarital sexual behavior and the sexual values of his reference others. We shall, however, limit our attention to Mirande's study of this relationship (274). Mirande focused upon the problem of delineating the time order among his variables. If it is argued that the adolescent's reference others are causally related to his premarital sexual behavior, it must be demonstrated that the reference relationships were formed prior to the overt behavior. The reference other could, among other things, be providing a reinforcing function even though the reference other was not the source of certain values.

Mirande obtained questionnaire data from 93 single undergraduate students enrolled in sociology classes at a midwestern university. He was primarily interested in whether there was a relationship between the attitudes and behaviors of the adolescents' reference groups and their own sexual activity. "With respect to sexual activity, students were asked if they had ever experienced sexual intercourse" (274:573). Mirande's basic conclusion was that a relationship did exist between the attitudes and behaviors of the adolescents' reference groups and their own sexual behavior. This relationship was more pronounced for females than males.

Mirande's most impressive result was that *all* of the male and female respondents who had engaged in premarital sexual intercourse reported that at least one of their two best friends had engaged in sexual intercourse whereas, among students without sexual experiences, 67 percent of the females and 29 percent of the males reported that their two closest friends had not experienced coitus.

Mirande gave specific consideration to the possible spurious character of the obtained relationship between the adolescent's premarital sexual behavior patterns and the sexual values of his reference others, and while he was careful to indicate the probable effect of the fact that individuals may tend to seek out groups with values similar to their own, he concludes (274:577): "The possibility that our findings reflect nothing more than a psychological mechanism through which the respondent justifies his actions seems unlikely for several reasons. First, the influence of reference groups increases as students move from the freshman to senior year. This is to be expected if peer groups actually operate as agents of socialization over a period of time and eventually as points of reference in guiding behavior. Second, peer group effect seems to be greater among categories of persons—Greek members and women—believed to be unusually sensitive to peer expectations. Finally, the overall consistency of the findings leads one to believe that the orientation of associates toward sex is an important determinant of student sexual behavior."

While there have been a number of studies examining the relationship between normative reference others and overt behavior, one of the more definitive nonexperimental studies is Simon's investigation of doctors, smoking, and reference groups (377). Simon reports that 90.3 percent of the doctors in North Carolina, the lowest percentage of any state, gave an affirmative answer to the question, "Do you believe cigarette smoking is a health hazard?" It was also found that 29.9 percent of North Carolina physicians reported to be smoking at the time of the study. This was the highest figure indicated by doctors in any of the states. Simon concluded that "to maul an old poker metaphor, the doctors of North Carolina are willing to put their lives where their mouths are" (377:647). It was also found that the other Southern tobacco-producing states exhibited the same pattern.

Simon concluded that the beliefs and behaviors of doctors in North Carolina were influenced by the people among whom they lived. North Carolina's economy is heavily dependent upon tobacco, and it is understandable that many people there would desire to see the tobacco industry prosper. The most important aspect of this study for us is the definitiveness that Simon assigned to his basic conclusion (377:646): "This finding is unusually neat, for two reasons. First, it is statistically unequivocal; the chance that North Carolina alone would head the list is 1 in 50, and the chance of the other tobacco producers following close on North Carolina is far less, taken together. Second, unlike almost any other data collected by survey rather than by laboratory experiment with randomized subjects, the cause-and-effect mechanism is very clear, and there is little danger of confounding. It stretches the imagination to propose any possible cause of this result except that North Carolina is a state of tobacco farmers. Other Southern but non-tobacco-producing states such as Arkansas, Georgia, and Mississippi show results very close to the national mean." Simon also argued that the doctors were influenced by the goals and wishes of those around them for tobacco prosperity rather than by a belief that tobacco itself was not harmful to the individual's health.

Attitudes.—The historical interest in the normative reference group concept was precisely because reference groups were regarded as a major source of attitude formation and change. Since Newcomb's pioneering investigation of the influence of Bennington College upon the attitudes of its students, a number of researchers have been specifically concerned with the consequences of normative reference others. Two exceptional methodologically sophisticated studies in this area will be discussed. In the terminology of our individual-other typology, these are illustrations of identification normative reference relationships.

The first work to be discussed is Fendrich's investigation of perceived reference group support, racial attitudes, and overt behavior (124). Fendrich was interested in determining the possible causal relationships that existed among these three variables. Previous empirical evidence indicated that each of them was correlated with one another but a question remained regarding the character of the causal relationships among them.

Fendrich obtained data from 189 students enrolled in three undergraduate social psychology courses at a Big Ten university. Reference group support referred to the degree to which the students perceived certain of their reference others as being willing to participate in various activities with Negroes. Racial attitudes were reflective of the students' attitudes toward the involvement of Negroes in various campus activities. Overt behavior was operationalized in terms of the extent to which the students participated in certain designated activities of the NAACP. All of the students were provided with a range of opportunities to participate in various activities of this organization.

Fendrich's study was characterized by a variety of methodologically desirable traits. It was a theoretically based study; the three central variables were clearly conceptualized and operationalized; considerable attention was given to the validity and reliability of the measuring instruments. Most importantly, Fendrich employed an appropriate multivariate statistical technique to filter out the causal relationships among the three variables. The mechanical analysis of the data was supplemented with an intelligent appraisal of the results.

The conclusions of Fendrich's research are most interesting. His multivariate analysis of the data indicated that reference group support was influencing racial attitudes and racial overt behavior, and racial attitudes were independently influencing racial overt behavior. This result not only supports the relationship between reference others and attitude formation but it also depicts the complexity of the "real" world. This study is also evidence of the effects of normative reference others upon overt behavior. Racial overt behavior was both directly and indirectly a function of perceived reference group support as well as a direct consequence of racial attitudes.

Perhaps the most definitive study that exists regarding the relationship between reference others and attitude change is the Siegels' study of reference groups, membership groups, and attitude change (372). These authors examined the effects of membership groups and reference groups upon the authoritarian attitudes of 28 female college students during their freshman and sophomore years. The authoritarianism scale that was developed in *The Authoritarian Personality* was used to measure these attitudes.

The Siegels' study was based largely on the fact that during the spring of each year a drawing is held for housing the following year. All freshman students were required to participate, and any other student who wished to change her residence could also participate. Some girls, for example, desired to move into the Row Houses. The Row Houses were regarded as the most prestigious residences. The girls who selected these houses were categorized as having a high status orientation.

Each student drew a number from a hopper, and the rank of that number determined the likelihood that her preference would be satisfied. The authors, by obtaining information on each subject's residence choice at the end of her freshman year, her assigned residence for her sophomore year, and her residence choice at the end of her sophomore year, were able to classify each student into one of the following three categories (372:362):

"A. Women (n = 9) who had gained assignment to live on the Row during their sophomore year and who did not attempt to draw out of the Row at the end of that year;

"B. Women (n = 11) who had not gained assignment to a Row house for the sophomore year and who drew for a Row house again after living in a non-Row house during the sophomore year; and

"C. Women (n = 8) who had not gained assignment to a Row house for the sophomore year, and who chose to remain in a non-Row house after living in one during the sophomore year."

With respect to attitude change among the three groups, it was predicted that Group A should show the least change in their authoritarian attitudes as they had spent their sophomore year in a social context that reinforced their initial attitudes. The greatest change was predicted for Group C because these girls had spent their sophomore year in the non-Row house, which is low in authoritarianism, and they had also changed their reference group from the Row to the non-Row house. Each of these girls had desired to move into the Row house at the end of their freshman year but chose to remain in the non-Row house after living in one during the sophomore year. It was predicted that the girls in Group B would be between Group A and Group C with respect to the degree of change in their authoritarian attitudes since they still desired to move to the Row house at the end of their sophomore year but had lived for a year in the non-Row house.

All three predictions were upheld by the data. This was interpreted by the Siegels as evidence of the effects of *membership groups and reference groups upon attitude formation.* This evidence has to be recognized as being supportive of the normative effects of reference others due to the outstanding methodological characteristics of the study. We would say that this effort indicates that the attitudes of the individual may be influenced by a membership group that was apparently only a compliant normative reference group and by an identification normative nonmembership reference group. Although this research had a number of desirable methodological characteristics, and it was an a priori prediction type study, three of the most important ones were emphasized by the authors (372:364): "First, the study demonstrates that it is possible operationally to define the concept of reference group. The act of voting by secret ballot for the group in which one would like to live constitutes clear behavioral specification of one's reference group, and it is an act whose conceptual meaning can be so directly inferred that there is no problem of reliability of judgment in its categorization by the investigator. Second, the study demonstrates that a field study can be conducted which contains the critical feature of an experiment that is usually lacking in naturalistic situations: randomization. The determination of whether or not a woman student would be assigned to the living group of her choice was based on a random event: the size of the number she drew from the hopper. This fact satisfied the requirement that the treatment condition be randomized and permitted sharper inferences than can usually be drawn from field studies. Third, the test behavior on which the conclusions of this study were based occurred in a context in which the salience of membership and reference groups was *not* aroused and in which no external sanctions from the relevant groups were operative. This feature of the design permitted the interpretation that the E–F scores represented the S's internalized attitudes."

Educational Plans.—Educational plans are often described as educational aspirations. It could also be argued that plans represent motives. Another illustration of the normative consequences of reference others for individuals concerns the effects of parental influence upon the college plans of their children. If the reference other has an influence over the college plans of the individual, this is taken as an indication of the normative influence of the reference other. While parental influence upon the college plans of their children has been given empirical examination by a number of researchers, these studies have suffered from various methodological limitations. The more serious of these limitations are incorporated into the following discussion, but, for a more complete listing, see (356). One of the more definitive works in this area of college plans is the Sewell and Shah study of social class, parental encouragement, and educational aspirations (356).

The data for the Sewell and Shah study are based on a survey of 1957 graduating seniors in all public, private, and parochial schools in Wisconsin. The analysis in the reported study was based on 10,318 seniors who constituted about a one-third random sample of all 1957 seniors in Wisconsin. Two of the purposes of the study were to determine (356:561): "(1) whether or not observed social class differences in the college plans of youth can be explained in terms of the differences in the level of perceived parental encouragement when intelligence is taken into account; (2) and if not, what additional influence parental encouragement has on college plans over and above the influence of social class and intelligence."

The Sewell and Shah study was characterized by a number of methodologically desirable characteristics. The large random sample enabled the authors to speak with some authority about relationships between social class, parental authority, and educational aspirations in the population of 1957 Wisconsin high school seniors and to *simultaneously* control certain selected variables statistically. Information was also gathered on the subjects' intelligence and included in the analysis. Although previous data indicated that IQ is related to both economic status and college plans, this variable has not always been considered in studies of educational aspirations and parental influence. And a sophisticated statistical analysis was made of the data. Correlational, path, and cross-tabular techniques were employed. This approach enabled the investigators to consider a variety of questions about their data.

Sewell and Shah found that socioeconomic status, the students' intelligence, and parental influence were all positively influencing the educational aspirations of the child. For instance, only 1.1 percent of the males who were low on intelligence, low on status, and low on perceived parental encouragement desired to go to college, while 85.6 percent of the males who were high on intelligence, high on status, and high on perceived parental encouragement intended to go to college. The crucial role of parental influence upon the students' educational aspirations is illustrated by the authors' following conclusions (356:571): "(3) where parental encouragement is low, relatively few students, regardless of their intelligence or socioeconomic status levels, plan on college (even highly intelligent students with high social class origin who are not encouraged by their parents are not likely to plan on college); (4) where parental encouragement is high, the proportion of students planning on college is also high, even when socioeconomic status and intelligence levels are relatively low. Thus, it may be concluded that while social class differences cannot be entirely explained by differences in parental encouragement (or intelligence) among the various socioeconomic classes, parental encouragement makes an independent contribution to social class differences in college plans of both males and females."

A variety of investigators have also examined the relative effects of parents and peers upon the educational plans of adolescents. Although some have concluded that parental influence is greater (378; 432) and others that the influence of peers is greater (79; 252), these studies definitely indicate that the adolescents' educational aspirations are influenced under varying conditions by their parents, peers, or parents and peers. This evidence further supports the normative influence of reference others. Some studies indicate that parental influence in the area of educational aspirations varies by the sex of the child (26; 355). We have previously indicated that the influence of parents and peers may vary with the issue being considered (50).

A comparative reference relationship exists between ego and the reference other if ego compares himself (or others) on some dimension(s) to the reference other and is influenced in an overt or covert manner. Although the comparative reference other has not been studied as often as the normative reference other, a body of evidence does exist regarding its effects. Most of the existing evidence concerns the relative deprivation that the individual experiences from comparing himself to the comparative reference other. In this regard, researchers have explicitly related the comparative reference other to suicide rates

(168), career decisions of college men (90), racial preferences (13), graduate student satisfaction with their academic position (88), social justice (337), job satisfaction (131; 295), metropolitan crime rates (112), mental illness (292), and Negro discontent with the American social system (150). We shall discuss three studies representative of the latter three areas.

Crime Rates.—The occurrence of crime has not often been studied in relationship to the comparative reference other, but one exception is the Eberts and Schwirian study of metropolitan crime rates and relative deprivation. Their general hypothesis was *"that variations in community crime rates are associated with variations in local structural sources of relative deprivations"* (112:44). This study is of interest not only because it illustrates the effects of the comparative reference other but also because it examined the *structural* sources of relative deprivation.

One of the independent variables in this study was the relative economic prosperity of whites and nonwhites in the local community. This variable was regarded as a structural variable, and it was operationalized in terms of the occupational distribution of whites and nonwhites in white-collar occupations in the 166 metropolitan areas that were considered in this part of the study. Sixty-two of the standard metropolitan areas were classified as having a high percentage of occupationally high whites and nonwhites. Thirty-seven had relatively low whites but high nonwhites. Twenty-two had occupationally high whites and low nonwhites and 45 had occupationally low whites and nonwhites.

The authors predicted that crime rates would be highest in those standard metropolitan areas where whites are occupationally high and nonwhites are occupationally low. This is precisely where the gap between whites and nonwhites is greatest and where the relatively poorer status of the nonwhites is probably the most salient. The next highest crime rate was predicted for those standard metropolitan areas where both whites and nonwhites have a high rate of white-collar employment. The rationale here is that "those left behind in the blue collar jobs or who are unemployed may experience greater relative deprivation, which may then be translated into aggressive criminal behavior" (112:47).

The lowest crime rates were predicted in those metropolitan areas where the nonwhites were high and the whites low on the occupational measure and in those communities where both groups are low. In the latter case, there presumably should be less relative deprivation and consequently not as much criminal behavior. In the former case, while the whites may experience deprivation relative to the nonwhites, they are able to postpone their gratifications. One of the assumptions of this study was that the "lower working class people are both more 'immediate-gratification-oriented' and 'present-time-oriented' than people in other classes" (112:44).

The results obtained in this study were very supportive of the authors' predictions. The highest median crime rate did occur in those SMSAs (Standard Metropolitan Statistical Areas) with a high percentage of white-collar whites and a low percentage of white-collar nonwhites. The next highest median crime rate occurred as predicted in those SMSAs with a high percentage of white and nonwhites in white-collar occupations. The lowest crime rates occurred as predicted in the remaining two SMSAs. It is of interest that the author's predictions were maintained when the three variables—population size, percent nonwhite, and region—were alternately controlled. It should be noted that Eberts and Schwirian did *not* consider the perceived deprivation of the subjects in the census tracts.

The American Negro.—It is somewhat of an anomaly that the American Negro should have exhibited his greatest discontent with the American social system at exactly that point in history when his economic, educational, and social position was the best it has ever been. One of the reasons that may be offered for this anomaly is that the growth of the Negro middle class, and the increased exposure of blacks to the "American dream," may have expanded the black man's reference groups and hence raised his level of relative deprivation. In this regard, Matza has observed "profound degradation in an absolute sense may be tolerable or even pass unnoticed if others close at hand fare no better or if one never had reason to expect any better" (262:622).

Some writers have subjected the discontent of the American Negro during the twentieth century to empirical investigation. Grindstaff, in attempting to explain the higher rates of unrest among urban Negroes than rural Negroes, hypothesizes that the urbanization of the Negro improves his absolute position in many respects but his position relative to urban whites degenerates (150). Grindstaff further suggests that, if this thesis is correct, the urban Negro will experience greater relative deprivation that will manifest itself in higher rates of racial unrest.

Grindstaff subjected this explanation to partial test in four Southern states: Alabama, Georgia, Mississippi, and South Carolina. The Deep South was taken as the focus of the study because of the recent growth of urbanization and the existence of a large white and Negro rural population. The specific hypothesis of the study was that there would be greater differences between urban Negroes and whites in terms of education, occupation, and income than among rural Negroes and whites. United States census data for the year 1960 was used to test the hypothesis. For analytical purposes, rural, urban, and large urbanized areas were utilized.

The results of the study gave exceptional support to Grindstaff's hypothesis. While the data clearly demonstrated that both Negroes and whites were "better off" in the areas of education, occupation, and income the more urbanized they became, there were almost without exception greater differences in each of these areas between urban Negroes and whites than between rural Negroes and whites.

Although Grindstaff did not test whether or not there was a greater amount of *perceived* relative deprivation among urban Negroes than rural Negroes in his study, his very consistent results indicate that this *could have been the case* in the four states that he studied. The findings of other researchers (139) when coupled with results such as Grindstaff's add support to the relative deprivation theory of twentieth-century racial unrest.

Mental Illness.—Parker and Kleiner conducted a large scale investigation of mental illness in an urban Negro community (292). Their research design involved the comparison of two samples, both drawn from the Philadelphia Negro community. Each of these two samples contained over a thousand individuals which enabled the investigators to engage in appropriate statistical comparisons. Although the authors' basic interest was in the stress produced by the goal-striving tendencies of the individuals in their two samples, an additional concern was with the relationship between reference group behavior and mental disorder (292:137–67).

Parker and Kleiner were interested in the relationship of the comparative reference group to mental illness. Their basic hypothesis was that *"the degree of negative discrepancy from a reference group will vary directly with the severity of mental illness"* (292:139). If an individual was below his reference group on a scale of status, he was characterized by a "negative discrepancy." The authors further hypothesized that *"within the mentally ill population, negative discrepancy from a reference group will be higher for the psychotics than for the neurotics"* (292:139) and *"within the community population, negative discrepancy from a reference group will be larger for a high symptom group than for a low symptom group"* (292:139). The authors concluded from their data that the preceding three hypotheses received striking support. They observed (292:165): "There is a direct relationship be-

tween severity of illness and degree of negative discrepancy from the
reference group, thus confirming our predictions. We find significantly
higher negative discrepancies among the psychotics than the neurotics,
and among the high symptom group than the low symptom group." It
is also of interest that these predictions were generally upheld when
statistical controls for sex and age were applied.

The Parker and Kleiner investigation is particularly supportive of the
effects of the comparative reference other because of its a priori predictions, the accuracy of the predictions, and its general methodological
sophistication. Particularly noteworthy is the fact that the authors
operationalized the reference group concept in several ways, and
utilized each operation in the analysis.

An identification-object reference relationship exists between the
individual and the reference other if the individual's degree of positive
or negative sentiment toward the reference other is sufficient to influence his overt or covert behavior. It will be recalled that the reference
group theorist has shown little interest in identification. We will consider several studies that indicate the effects of identification-object
reference relationships for pain tolerance (61), the development of the
individual's self concept (258), and ego's physical survival (132; 194).

Pain Tolerance.—Several investigators have considered the effects of
the reference other upon pain tolerance. While these researchers have
been concerned with the salience of the reference other and the comparative effect of the reference other, there has usually been either an
implicit or an explicit interest in identification. The underlying hypothesis is that there is a direct relationship between the extent of
ego's identification with the reference other and his pain tolerance.
Some of the studies in this area may be better examples of identification
normative reference relationships. The Frankl study (132), however,
definitely involves identification-object reference relationships.

A rather convincing demonstration of the effects of identification
reference others upon the pain tolerance of males at the University of
Pittsburgh was conducted by Buss and Portnoy (61). They tested the
hypothesis that there was a linear relationship between group identification and pain tolerance. Their study is of particular interest because
it was experimental in character, the groups employed in the experiment
were actually ranked for their strength of identification, and a variety of
reference others were employed: nationality, gender, and college.

Buss and Portnoy had college students at the University of Pittsburgh
rank eight groups in terms of their identification with them. On the basis
of these criteria, three identification reference groups were selected.

America was the high identification group, gender was the middle identification group, and college was the low identification group. Certain appropriate and contrasting comparative groups were also employed: Russia and Canada for the American identification group, Penn State and Carnegie Institute of Technology for the college identification group, and females for the gender identification group. Consequently there were five experimental groups employed in the experiment as well as one control group. Fifteen men were in each group.

The members in each group were subjected to pain by electric shock through a finger electrode. The pain tolerance levels of the individuals were recorded in milliamperes of current. After a three-minute rest period, subjects in each group were given a false norm regarding the ability of a comparative group to withstand pain. For instance, in one experimental group the subjects were told that "on the average Russians have a greater tolerance for pain than Americans" (61:107). This procedure was followed for all five experimental groups. The control group was not given such information. The subjects were again subjected to pain through the finger electrode. Change in pain tolerance was represented by a change score: milliamperes on Trial 2 minus milliamperes on Trial 1.

The results were very supportive of the hypothesis. The control group decreased in pain tolerance but increases were noted in all of the experimental groups, and each of these groups was statistically different from the control group at either the .01 or the .001 level. The rank order of the change was also critical. The authors concluded that "the general trend of the findings is clear: group identification does increase pain tolerance, and the stronger the identification, the greater the increase" (61:108).

Studies of this type are important for demonstrating the effects of identification-object reference relationships not only because they are conducted under experimental conditions but also because *pain is a very real result!* If we can demonstrate that identification-object reference others influence pain tolerance, we would seem to have convincing evidence of their reality.

The Self.—Social scientists agree that the individual's conception of himself is in some way related to the reactions of others to him. This belief is maintained in spite of the fact that serious questions have been raised regarding the validity of self measures employed in studies of the self (438), the correlational character of many of these studies (416), and the ability of the individual under some conditions to be insensitive to the reactions of others (331). The social character of the individual seems to be incontrovertible. The self is being considered here in a sociological sense. Many sociologists regard the self as a set of conscious and salient attitudes and "feelings" that ego holds toward himself as a social object.

It is commonly asserted that the relationship between the self and his others is very complex. This is indeed true. If self development is cast within the reference other orientation, it is clear that normative, comparative, and identification-object reference relationships affect the self. Although an explicit consideration of the relationship between self theory and reference other theory is not yet available, the tenor of these two areas suggests that the norms of certain reference others are incorporated into the self attitudes of the individual, reference other comparisons are reflected in the evaluative dimensions of the self, and identification-object reference others become involved in a number of the individual's self attitudes. (For one significant discussion of the self-other relationship, see the effort by Leonard S. Cottrell, Jr., in David A. Goslin [ed.], *Handbook of Socialization Theory and Research* [Chicago: Rand McNally and Co., 1969], pp. 543–70.)

In one of the few studies to explicitly relate the reference group approach to self theory, Mannheim investigated several hypotheses involving the identification reference group and various dimensions of the self (258). This study is of interest because Mannheim focused upon the identification reference group. She is one of the writers to have used this term. Mannheim employed the following definitions: "(a) The Real Self Image—as ego defines himself to himself; (b) The Looking Glass Self—as ego thinks others think of him; and (c) The Ideal Self—as ego would like to be" (258:266).

Mannheim tested her hypotheses among 103 male freshmen at the University of Illinois, who lived together in several university housing barracks. Each barrack was subdivided into four suites housing about four students each. The residents of each barrack knew each other well and interacted closely both physically and socially. The relevant information was gathered from these students during the third and twelfth weeks of the semester. Mannheim's summary indicates both the hypotheses and the conclusions of her study (258:279):

"(1) The extent of agreement between the self image of the individual and his reference group self was not affected by his actual membership relations to his reference group.

"(2) There was greater agreement between the self image and the membership group self for individuals who selected their membership group as a reference group than for individuals who did not select it as a reference group. . . .

"(3) An unstable reference group pattern was associated with greater changes in the self image than was a stable reference group pattern.

"Similarly, a change in the reference group pattern was associated with changes in the reference group self and ideal self descriptions.

"(4) Individuals tended to change their self image over time in the direction represented by their reference group self."

Mannheim's study is impressive for a variety of reasons. It contained a number of a priori hypotheses that were generally upheld. These hypotheses were tested within a natural situation, where dominant identification reference relationships could develop, and they were subjected to careful methodological scrutiny. For instance, the validity and reliability of the several operational definitions were considered, and appropriate statistical procedures were employed.

Physical Survival.—While there is not a substantial body of evidence regarding the effects of identification-object reference others upon the physical survival of individuals within concentration camps, and although the available evidence does not conform to rigorous scientific standards, this material must be considered as it suggests that reference others may influence the individual's physical survival within the concentration camp. To even hint that such a relationship exists is to attribute considerable support to the reality of the reference relationship.

One investigator to focus upon the role of group identification in the physical and psychological survival of the individual in the concentration camp is Norman Jackman (194). Jackman analyzed the existing literature on German concentration camps during World War II in his work, "Survival in the Concentration Camp," and concluded "that there was a relationship between the *kinds* of reference groups and survival" (194:24). While Jackman's effort involved several dimensions in our individual-other typology, the role of the identification-object reference relationship is clear.

Jackman observed that, if the individual's reference groups were within the concentration camp, his chances for physical survival (the avoidance of death) and psychological survival (the retention of sanity) were maximized. One evidence for this involved a "training camp" group of twenty boys and an adult leader who came as a unit to Buchenwald, the dreaded German concentration camp. This group decided that they were all going to leave the camp alive and sane, and they did

(194:24, my italics): "An amazing degree of group unity developed among these boys. They came into the camp with a background of association and the initial period of adjustment was eased through *personal identification with one another*. A solid in-group feeling developed; members never shared with outsiders, and the group acted as a unit to procure advantages for its members which would have been unattainable by the individual acting alone." On the other hand, if the individual's reference others were outside the camp, Jackman concluded that the individual's chances for physical survival were decreased as he had no membership group and complementary resisting reference group to help him survive. Jackman suggests that external nonmembership reference others helped the individual to maintain his sanity.

Jackman also indicated that certain kinds of reference others were dysfunctional for survival in the concentration camp. For example, the person who identified with the middle class experienced extreme stress in the concentration camp as this situation was contrary to everything he believed. The individual who identified with the Jehovah's Witnesses seldom physically survived the concentration camp experience because this identification encouraged passive resistance, but he usually maintained his sanity as he was secure in a feeling of superiority to the morally damned Gestapo. These and other results lend support to Jackman's thesis that a relationship existed between the kinds of reference others individuals had in the German concentration camps during World War II and their chances for survival.

Another illustration of the role of reference others within the World War II concentration camps comes from the work of Viktor Frankl, a psychiatrist, who actually endured the concentration camp experience (132). While Frankl's work must be regarded as a personal document, it is important to realize that these are the observations of a trained observer. It is of interest that Frankl's experiences were in the smaller and less well known German concentration camps where most of the actual exterminations took place.

A basic reference other theme that can be drawn from Frankl's work is that many prisoners desired to stay alive because of their identification-object reference relationships with certain others. Frankl notes in his discussion of the turmoil that occurred among the prisoners when it became known that some of them were soon destined to be sent to the ovens (132:6–7, my italics): "There was neither time nor desire to consider moral or ethical issues. Every man was controlled by one thought only: *to keep himself alive for the family waiting for him at home, and to save his friends*. With no hesitation, therefore, he would arrange for another prisoner, another "number," to take his place in the transport."

Frankl's discussion of the survival of prisoners in the concentration camp portrayed an explicit concern for the identification-object reference relationship while Jackman emphasized the perspective that was derived from the identification-object reference other. Additionally, it is evident from Frankl's writings that the prisoner's family functioned as a salient identification-object reference other. At one point Frankl observes (132:59): "In a position of utter desolation, when man cannot express himself in positive action, when his only achievement may consist in enduring his sufferings in the right way—an honorable way—in such a position man can, through loving contemplation of the image he carries of his beloved, achieve fulfillment."

We conclude our discussion of the effects of reference others by considering their consequences for society. This is a difficult task because there is not an extensive amount of empirical evidence focusing upon this subject, and—if one grants the generic character of the reference relationship as being at least minimally characteristic of all social situations—normative, comparative, and identification-object reference relationships are both subtly and directly involved in a large number of the social and cultural processes required for the functioning of the social system. *Individual characteristics* are necessary for the survival of a *structural* entity (191:79): "In stating what it is that any society must have in order to survive, in presenting what are called 'the functional requisites of any social system,' the sociologist is, in effect, specifying a series of adult characteristics which must presumably be acquired by a substantial proportion of the population during the process of socialization. Thus the requisites of any social system become the imperatives for any system of child socialization." Our discussion is limited to several selected functions of reference others that have been given more than passing consideration in the literature.

Scholars who have considered the functional requisites for the continued functioning of society have concluded that the culture must be transmitted from one generation to another (236). This presupposes that the socialization process is such that the individual acquires the attitudes, opinions, idea systems, and values of the society (189; 190).

Without pursuing the point further, it should be abundantly clear that one of the central functions of the reference other is to provide the individual with his attitudes and values. It was earlier emphasized that all institutional arrangements are ultimately mediated through the reference individual.

The survival of the social system presupposes that limitations are placed upon disruptive forms of social behavior (236). Although external modes of social control are employed to achieve this end, it is necessary for internal mechanisms of social control to be developed. Individuals must acquire moral orientations (189; 190). Reference others and reference relationships play an indispensable role in this process. [For one study explicitly indicating the relationship between reference others and conformity, see (282).]

Shibutani gives attention to this function of reference others in his article, "Reference Groups and Social Control" (371). Although Shibutani usually emphasizes reference groups as perspectives, he gives considerable attention to the role of salient reference others in this article. He indicates that being able to identify the audience for whom a man is performing is of great importance because audiences exercise social control. As Shibutani is arguing that individuals behave for audiences, this suggests the role of salient identification-object reference relationships as a social control mechanism. It should quickly be added that internalized normative reference relationships are also vital to this process. To the extent that the individual internalizes the norms of the society, he develops self-control.

The comparative reference relationship is also involved in the maintenance of the social order. We have previously indicated that relative deprivation may result in social unrest and various forms of deviance. A certain level of relative gratification must be maintained in social systems. Durkheim has made a rather harsh but striking observation in this regard in his consideration of the Saint-Simon doctrine of social peace and free economic appetites (111:200, my italics): "So it is inevitable that at the end of a short time the latter find their share meager compared with what goes to the others, and as a result new demands arise, for all levels of the social scale. . . . And they will call all the more imperiously for a new satisfaction, since those already secured will have given them more strength and vitality. This is why those at the very top of the hierarchy, who consequently would have nothing above them to stimulate their ambition, could nevertheless not be held at the point they had reached, but would continue to be plagued by the same restlessness that torments them today. *What is needed if social order is to reign is that the mass of men be content with their lot. But what is needed for them to be content, is not that they have more or less but that they be convinced that they have no right to more.*"

The survival of the social system also presupposes that role differentiation and role assignment occur (236). In both open and closed social structures individuals must be socialized into the role system, while the open type of society has the additional problem of recruiting individuals into its achieved positions. These processes presuppose that the individual develops a self-system and personal identity within the role context (189; 190). Reference others occupy a vital place in this process.

Our previous discussion of the effects of reference others upon the educational plans of individuals is evidence of the role recruitment function provided by reference others. The reference other directs ego's attention to designated social objects. The studies of Slocum (380), Hadley and Levy (155), and Simpson (378) demonstrate the effects of reference others upon the occupational aspirations of individuals. More generally, the reference group concept has been related to the development of motivation, (76), ambition (366:444–47), and task persistence (231).

One excellent example of the relevance of reference relationships for role socialization is provided by Wallace's study, "Reference Group Behavior in Occupational Role Socialization" (418). Wallace tested the hypothesis that *"if an individual manifests a desire to gain acceptance into a given group, then he will adopt the values related to that group in the process of gaining membership"* (418:370). His subjects were students at the University of Minnesota Law School. Some of these respondents intended to practice law and some did not, that is, some had the legal profession as a reference group and some had other reference groups. Wallace's hypothesis was confirmed.

This study is also an empirical example of the process of *anticipatory socialization,* an extremely important process that we have not sufficiently considered. The concept of anticipatory socialization was introduced by Merton and essentially indicates that, if a nonmembership other becomes a reference other for ego, he will begin to be influenced by it (264:359 n; 272:87–95). This is what happened in Wallace's study. Anticipatory socialization is important for individuals since, if they do develop a membership affiliation with the nonmembership other, their adjustment and mobility in the new context *may be* enhanced. This process facilitates role socialization for society. One study indicates, however, the possible dysfunctionality of anticipatory socialization for society. The author concluded that "furthermore, the study purports to explain this form of deviance by reference to anticipatory socialization, which is usually thought of as functional for social control, rather than for deviance" (264:364). Importantly, from a conformity perspective, anticipatory socialization may "incorrectly" prepare ego for his new positions.

The objective of this chapter was to illustrate and document the consequences of reference relationships for the individual and society. It was argued that reference relationships do exist and that they are not merely scientific constructs. Due to the post hoc criticism that is frequently made of the reference other area, studies were selected because of their methodological sophistication, the a priori character of their predictions, or the impressiveness of their results.

With regard to the effects of reference relationships for individuals, we saw that normative reference others may influence premarital sexual behavior, smoking habits, racial and authoritarian attitudes, and educational plans. Comparative reference others may affect crime rates, relative deprivation, and mental illness. The effects of identification-object reference others were suggested for pain tolerance, self attitudes, and physical survival. The range of the consequences that reference relationships have for individuals certainly lends support to their generic quality.

Unfortunately, it was necessary to limit our discussion of the effects of reference relationships for society to the transmission of culture, social control mechanisms, and the role socialization process. While these three areas represent requisites of social systems, the generic quality of reference relationships suggests that they are involved in many of the critical social processes of society. Perhaps the identification-object reference relationship has been slighted the most in our presentation. Parsons has indicated, for instance, in his discussion of the functional prerequisites of social systems that "it seems to be reasonably well established that there are minimum conditions of socialization with respect for instance to the relation between affectional support and security, without which a functioning personality cannot be built up" (293:28). We were also not able to give sufficient attention to the role of comparative reference relationships for the stability *of society.* Although this function of the comparative other for the total social system has not been given enough emphasis in the literature, it remains an important consequence. (For a recent and significant work in this regard, see Ted Robert Gurr, *Why Men Rebel* [Princeton: Princeton University Press, 1970].)

CHAPTER Seven

Theoretical Considerations

The reference other orientation offers quite important and varied implications for the theoretical advancement of the study of the reference other phenomenon. This chapter will provide the basis for improvement in this area by clarifying some of the erroneous perceptions of the reference group concept that have developed in the literature.

With respect to the latter point, the following statements are commonplace in the literature. (1) *The reference group concept is a concept and not a theory.* (2) *There is not yet a reference group theory.* While these statements merit attention, they are incomplete and misleading. One is left with the image of the reference group concept as having existed in a scientific vacuum never being utilized in an explanatory fashion. This view is not only inaccurate and oversimplified but also it has impeded the development of conceptual and theoretical insights into the reference other phenomenon.

Those writers who have stressed the fact that there is not yet a reference group theory are in effect saying that a reference group theory in a *strict* sense has not been developed. In other words, if one accepts the writings of Merton (271) and Homans (177) as indicative of the strict view of theory, they are suggesting that a set of logically interrelated empirical generalizations that provide a *deductive* explanation about the nature of reference groups does not exist. This conclusion must be reconsidered in light of the following observations.

1. This view implies that there can only be a *single* reference group theory, but this is simply not true. Although the pervaders of the above conclusion might argue that they were fully aware of this, and did not intend this meaning, their negative stance has left just this impression. One must infer that this connotation impeded creative efforts. It is anticipated that the reference other theorist will profit from the more encouraging and correct perspective that reference other *theories* can be developed about the determinants and the consequences of reference

others and that *in the process* some of those theories will pertain to designated substantive areas while others will be at higher levels of abstraction and not be limited to particular substantive domains.

2. Our extensive examination of the reference group literature revealed that there have been a number of *explanatory* efforts involving reference groups. Although these attempts do not usually meet the technical requirements of a theory in the strict sense, the preceding conclusion entirely ignores their existence. It must also be emphasized that several of these explanations (87; 89; 125) approximate the strict definition of theory.

3. The criticisms depicting the absence of a reference group theory and the conceptual nature of the reference group concept de-emphasize the role of concepts for theoretical developments. Concepts are the "building blocks" of theory, but attention was not directed to the fact that the reference group concept could be utilized within theories *precisely because it was a concept.* The stress given to the conceptual nature of the reference group concept may have also detracted from the realization that a cluster of interrelated concepts, or an orientation, is involved in the study of the reference other phenomenon. In this regard, there has been almost no appreciation of the role of orientations for theoretical advancements. Symbolic interactionism, for example, is often castigated for not being a theory, but seldom do its critics acknowledge the implications of this perspective for theoretical developments. From the scientist's point of view, this neglect of orientations is almost tragic because in a very literal way, *orientations are more valuable for broad theoretical construction than is any particular theory or even a set of theories.* This is because orientations are more basic than theories and can be utilized within a variety of theoretical efforts. Analogously, orientations bear the same relationship to theories as values do to norms. This statement does not imply that the scientist should not move beyond orientations to theory. Blumer has been criticized on these grounds for his emphasis on concept formation (276), but this evaluation is misplaced.

4. The rigid evaluation of the explanatory efforts within the reference group literature in terms of a strict interpretation of theory must be challenged on the grounds that *the developmental nature of a theory is completely overlooked.* The judgment should not be based simply on whether or not an ultimate state has been reached. One does not move directly from a concept to a theory. Much happens in the interim. An important theme of this chapter is that although the majority of the ex-

planatory efforts within the reference group literature are not theories from a technical standpoint, *they are explanations and they are moving toward theory in the ideal sense.*

The remainder of this chapter will largely concern itself with those published explanatory efforts that have involved the reference group concept. These illustrations will not only document certain of our previous statements; they will help to orient future theoretical works of the reference other theorist. But attention must first be given to the progressive nature of theories. This aspect of theory has been chosen for discussion because it has been ignored or misunderstood by the critics of the explanatory efforts in the reference group literature. It is also the single dimension of theory that needs to be understood most by the reference other theorist.

There was an earlier period during which modern sociologists focused upon the nature, logical consistency, and scope of theories. Merton (271) emphasized the fact that a theory is a set of logically interrelated empirical generalizations, Zetterberg (440) described axiomatic theory, and debates raged over the relative merits of Merton's middle range theory and Parsons's (293) more grandiose and inclusive theory. Implicit in some of the writings of this period was a concern with the deductive quality of theory. Most recently, a recognizable shift has occurred in the theoretical concerns of sociologists. Although Homans has stressed the deductive character of theory (177), the general trend involves the *construction and verification of theory.* The former and most pervasive emphasis is illustrated by the titles of some quite current and important books in sociology, such as Dubin's *Theory Building* (110), Blalock's *Theory Construction* (35), Stinchcombe's *Constructing Social Theories* (386), and especially Glaser's and Strauss's *The Discovery of Grounded Theory* (141). These books are also concerned with the verification of theory. It is of more than passing interest that writers are now able to integrate theory construction with theory verification in their discussions. We give some attention to the latter topic in our next chapter.

The change in focus has had two discernible effects upon sociologists. There is an increased awareness of the developmental nature of theory. DiRenzo has best captured the essence of this phenomenon with his statement that "to understand the structure of, and the requirements for, scientific explanation is to understand the basic nature of the scientific enterprise" (106:245). Kurt Wolff also exemplifies this position in his discussion of the sociology of knowledge and sociological theory and argues that it can be taken without negating the quest for generalities

(435:552–53, first italics mine): "There are some historical problems to which modern sociology specifically might address itself. Instead, it appears to be preoccupied, in America possibly more than elsewhere, with rather ahistorical formal 'structural' relations and processes and with improving itself as a specialty in such preoccupation. *To say this is not to suggest that sociology should not be a generalizing science. Rather it is to argue that sociology would facilitate its task of being a generalizing science if it recognized its need for an historical theory of society, no matter how crude it might be to begin with.* If sociology wants to be historically relevant, it cannot reject its commitment to historical realism and abide its psychological realism which no longer is historically adequate. For even a generalizing science, *if it is a social science,* starts with the historical situation; it may deny it but it cannot escape it. In this respect, social science cannot be entirely true to the pure type of science which 'brackets' the ontological quest."

It is of particular interest that some of the sociologists who are the most outspoken regarding the deductive quality of theory acknowledge the value in recognizing the cumulative nature of theory in the social sciences. Homans, for instance, observes (177:975): "But there is another strategy, and one that the history of science suggests is more likely to be successful in a new science like ours. . . . The strategy starts with the empirical findings themselves and seeks to invent the more general propositions from which these same findings, and, under different conditions, other findings may be derived. This is the strategy by which deductive systems are inductively arrived at." This is the aspect of social theory that the critics of the reference group literature have missed. The construction of deductive theory is *developmental* and presupposes a backlog of scientific efforts.

It must further be emphasized that not only has a conceptual realization occurred regarding the progressive aspect of social theory but also that this insight is being *incorporated* within the research process. The most explicit example of this is contained in Glaser's and Strauss's work, *The Discovery of Grounded Theory* (141). These authors convincingly argue that theory should always be *grounded in empirical data.* They recommend that the analyst attempt first to develop a grounded substantive theory. This is an explanation about a designated phenomenon that is based upon an empirical examination of that phenomenon. They suggest that the analyst next expand his efforts by continuing to develop his theory through the empirical examination of other distinct but conceptually similar substantive areas. This procedure should facilitate the emergence of a more abstract and formal theory about the conceptual similarities shared by the substantive areas that have been examined. This process allows the formal theory to be grounded in substantive theory that has been grounded in the empirical world. The interested reader is directed to Glaser's and Strauss's original work (141) and to their more recent publication in which a formal theory of status passage is developed (142). Denzin also provides an overview of their approach (97).

The remaining implication of the sociologists' more recent concern with theory construction is slightly more subtle in character. There is evidence that not only is the developmental nature of theory becoming a focal point but also that *the very nature of theory is being reevaluated.* For instance, it is not uncommon to find social scientists stressing the fact that there are different types of explanations (311:123–45). More specifically, Louch has argued the merits of ad hoc explanations in the study of human action (247). Brown has emphasized the fact that deductive theories in the social sciences are generally historical in character and should be recognized as such (56), and Scriven has elaborated upon the role of explanation and prediction within evolutionary theory and the implications of this for various disciplines, including several of the social sciences (347). The Scriven article as well contains a particularly compelling discussion of the value of nondeductive explanations.

The present concern of social scientists and others with the essence of explanation is a healthy sign. Although it is ironic that the social scientist must remain less than profound about the very end that he is trying to achieve, his increased awareness of these difficulties will facilitate his attainment of that goal. It is not within our capacity to resolve the issues surrounding explanation, but we can bring them to the attention of the reference other theorist. We would also urge the reference other theorist to be open to *any* avenue that might lead to demonstrable explanation and not be too quick to dismiss what could be the beginnings of promising explanations because some deem them "low level." Stinchcombe has recently reminded us that *"a little theory can go a long way"* (386:v) and the following quotation from the distinguished philosopher, Nicholas Rescher, indicates that even the professional student of science remains cautious as to the nature of theory (318:58, my italics): "The question of what can and cannot be 'explained' is not so easy as it only yesterday seemed to be—it ramifies into subtleties and distinctions. Where all looked simple and monolithic, the situation has become difficult and diversified. *No doubt a great deal of painstaking analysis remains to be done before a generally acceptable conception of the nature of scientific explanation is at hand;* one that is sufficiently comprehensive and versatile to accommodate the recent transformations of the scientific landscape. One thing at least can be said with reasonable assurance. Notwithstanding its erstwhile stature, and despite occasional flurries of nostalgia for its comfortable simplicities, *the deductive conception of explanation must yield up its claims to provide a comprehensive account of the nature of scientific explanation."*

A variety of substantive explanations (the word *explanation* signifying that our subsequent discussions are not limited to deductive arguments) involving the reference group concept will now be considered in order to portray the range of substantive areas to which this concept has been applied. It will become clear that the reference group concept and its cognate concepts have been employed both explicitly and implicitly within explanatory efforts.

Edwin H. Sutherland introduced his theory of "differential association" in 1939 (400), and in spite of various criticisms, it has been sustained and modified over the years. Many still regard it as the most satisfactory explanation for most criminal behavior. The essentials of Sutherland's 1947 nine-part version of his theory are that criminal behavior is learned through interaction in intimate personal groups and that a person becomes delinquent because of an excess of definitions favorable to violation of laws over definitions unfavorable to violation of laws.

The modification of Sutherland's theory that is of interest to us is Daniel Glaser's theory of "differential identification" (143). In reviewing the criticisms leveled against Sutherland's theory, Glaser notes that a recurring criticism concerned the notion of association in Sutherland's theory. Critics have asked, for instance, "Why doesn't the prison guard become a criminal, since his association is primarily with criminals?" (143:439 *n*). Glaser's elaboration contends that it is not association per se but identification that is the critical explanatory variable for criminal behavior. "The theory of differential identification, in essence, is that *a person pursues criminal behavior to the extent that he identifies himself with real or imaginary persons from whose perspective his criminal behavior seems acceptable"* (143:440). The fact that "Sutherland seems to have been dismayed by an assumption that 'association' is distinct from 'identification'" is stressed by Glaser (143:438–39).

While Glaser related his ideas most directly to role theory, they are in fact much more reflective of the reference other orientation. In our terminology, his theory revolves about the identification normative relationship. Glaser observes that "the choice of another, from whose perspective we view our own behavior, is the process of identification. It may be with the immediate others or distant and perhaps abstractly generalized others of our reference groups" (143:437). This statement, as well as numerous others in his article, also indicates Glaser's awareness of the importance of membership others, nonmembership others, and abstract or imaginary reference others for the explanation of criminal behavior.

Glaser's modification also reflects a concern for the nature of the reference relationship and the variety of reference others that influences the individual. The following quotation indicates his appreciation of the complexity of reference relationships (143:440): "Most persons in our society are believed to identify themselves with both criminal and non-criminal persons in the course of their lives. Criminal identification may occur, for example, during direct experience in delinquent membership groups, through positive reference to criminal roles portrayed in mass media, or as a negative reaction to forces opposed to crime. The family probably is the principal non-criminal reference group, even for criminals. It is supplemented by many other groups of anti-criminal 'generalized others.'" While more could be said regarding the nature and implications of Glaser's elaboration, this account illustrates and documents the fact that his explanation is rooted in the reference other orientation.

Martin Haskell (165) has developed an explanation of juvenile delinquency that is almost entirely rooted in the reference other orientation. The seven propositions in his explanation will be cited and briefly discussed.

"*Proposition One.—The family is the first personal reference group of the child.*"—The concept of a personal reference group is taken from Jennings's work (201) and refers to a group in which the individual receives sustenance, recognition, approval, and appreciation for just being himself. Haskell suggests that this group will remain a personal reference group as long as it meets these and other functions.

"*Proposition Two.—The family is a normative reference group.*"— Haskell describes the family as a normative reference group that provides the individual with the norms of the society. He suggests that this is true even in families with criminal parents.

"*Proposition Three.—Prior to his participation in a delinquent act, a street group has become a personal reference group of the delinquent boy.*"—The street group term is used rather than gang to emphasize that this group need not be committed to a delinquent subculture.

"*Proposition Four.—The street group that becomes the personal reference group of the lower class boy in New York City has a delinquent subculture.*" This proposition mainly emphasizes that the subjects in

Haskell's study were members of a group that did exhibit a delinquent subculture.

"*Proposition Five.—A boy, for whom a street group is a personal reference group, is likely, in the dynamic assessment preceding a delinquent act, to decide in favor of the delinquent act.*"—Haskell is emphasizing that once the street group, whether or not it has a delinquent subculture, becomes a personal reference group for the individual, it is very difficult for him not to engage in a delinquent act as he does not want to lose the approval of these reference others.

"*Proposition Six.—The individual tends as a member of a personal reference group to import its context attitudes and ways of behaving which he is currently holding in socio group life.*"—A socio group is one in which the individual's ideals and efforts are directed toward objectives which are not his alone. Jennings, who also coined this concept, observes that the socio group "tells" the individual what he can do to a much greater extent than the personal reference group.

Haskell draws upon Merton's means-end theory of anomie at this point and suggests that the school, a socio group, will provide ego with certain perspectives which will eventually have some effect on his attitudes and behaviors in his personal reference groups. For example, the lower class child due to training at school (a socio group) may come to resent his father (a personal reference group) because he has not obtained the cultural goals of the society.

"*Proposition Seven.—In a situation where the individual is a member of a normative personal reference group and of a delinquent personal reference group satisfying relationships in normative socio groups will exercise a decisive influence against participation in a delinquent act.*"— This concluding proposition represents a very important aspect of Haskell's theory. He is suggesting that if the individual has satisfying relationships in a normative socio group, such as a work group, he is less likely to engage in delinquent acts.

Merton, building on the work of Durkheim, was the first writer to present a structural functional explanation of anomie (271). The fundamental assumptions in Merton's explanation have been employed in what is usually described as a means-goals explanation of juvenile delinquency. Cohen is perhaps the leading proponent of this explanation. [For a discussion of the major explanations of delinquency and the standard references, see (107).]

Merton's explanation of anomie states that the American culture, and other similar cultures, tend to indoctrinate all groups with relatively high status aspirations. The possession of material goods is the major symbol of status and success in American society. All groups, however, are not provided with the same "institutionalized means" with which to achieve these "culture goals" of the society. This may result in a condition of anomie, or a breakdown of the regulative norms, in these segments of the society. Merton's theory predicts that the highest rates of crime and delinquency will prevail in these areas.

It must be emphasized that Merton's explanation did not reflect the concepts characteristic of the reference other orientation. Other writers have begun to modify and extend Merton's statement within this orientation. This is particularly true of the means-goals explanation of juvenile delinquency. These modifications are based on the premise that the social processes through which the individual comes to experience dissatisfaction and participate in deviant behavior are not contained in Merton's formulation. (It should be noted that Merton was attempting to develop a sociological explanation of anomie.)

The basic criticism of Merton's anomie explanation has concerned his failure to include systematically the role of reference others in his formulation. Lemert, for instance, has questioned the apparent freedom of choice allowed the individual in Merton's statement. He observes (232:68, my italics): "Instead of seeing the individual as a relatively free agent making adaptations pointed toward a consistent value order, it is far more realistic to visualize him as 'captured,' to a greater or lesser degree, *by the claims of various groups to which he has given his allegiance.* It is the fact that these claims are continually being preemptively asserted through group action at the expense of other claims, frequently in direct conflict, that we find the main source of 'pressures' on individuals in modern society, rather than in 'cultural emphasis on goals.' "

It has been suggested that Merton did not give enough attention to the role of the individual's reference others in influencing the underprivileged person's behavior in regard to the means-goals discrepancy (74; 75). Cohen has stressed the role of normative reference groups in this regard. He suggests that the underprivileged person may simply conform to the expectations, despite continued frustration, if his normative reference groups or moral convictions direct him to this alternative; break with normative reference groups that encourage conformity and literally "shop around" for other reference groups that encourage deviant solutions; or "go it alone," violating societal expectations without the validation that comes from reference group support (74:468–70).

We would add to the above observations that Merton's explanation implicitly emphasizes the role of the nonmembership reference other in the formation of deviant behavior. If this point were made more explicit in Merton's formulation, it would provide additional insights. Merton stresses that it is the cultural goals, or reference objects in our terminology, for which the underprivileged groups lack the means. But it would be incredible if at some point the underprivileged individuals did not also focus upon the nonmembership reference individuals and groups who possessed the desired reference objects developing either a positive or negative orientation towards them. In fact, this view suggests the possibility that the nonmembership other is by definition a comparison reference other. The nature of the identification-object reference relationship that the individual develops with nonmembership reference others possessing desired reference objects is a variable that students of deviant behavior should give additional consideration. There is the possibility of some type of synthesis between Merton's explanation of anomie and that part of the reference other orientation that pertains to the comparative reference other.

Although Merton's anomie explanation is not, and was not intended to be, cast within the reference other orientation, the preceding discussion suggests that this framework is in some respects implicit within it. To the extent that this is true, additional evidence is provided for the explanatory power of the reference other orientation. Perhaps delinquency should be regarded as a formal rather than a substantive area. The broad usage of Merton's anomie statements supports such a view.

As with many topics in the field of sociology, voting behavior was initially examined from an ecological perspective. Rice's pioneering study of voting employed this frame of reference (320). Gradually, however, a shift away from the use of aggregate data as a basis of empirical inquiry occurred. It is important for our purposes that a number of reference group cognate concepts have been utilized in these approaches.

In one of the earlier nonecological and classic studies of voting behavior, *The People's Choice*, considerable attention was given to the two-step process of communication hypothesis (230). In summary form this hypothesis states that "first, information moved from the media to relatively well-informed individuals who attended to mass communications firsthand. Second, it moved from those persons through interpersonal channels to individuals who had less direct exposure to the media and who depended upon others for their information" (92:127). This hypothesis reflected a general concern for the effects of the role of the mass media upon voting attitudes and behavior.

Although the "opinion leaders" who act as the filter for the mass media under the two-step flow of communication hypothesis are not often described in reference group terminology, this could be done. It seems clear that the "opinion leader" is a normative reference individual. In a later and also-classic study of the effects of the mass media, *Personal Influence,* the two-step flow of communication hypothesis is further considered (211). Explicit attention is given to the relevance of the nature of the "opinion leader." Katz and Lazarsfeld note that "which kinds of 'others' are significant, is a problem we shall attempt to tackle from time to time, although not in a systematic way" (211:64–65). (These authors gave consideration to these "others" on pages 49, 64, 68, and 96). Humke has also raised the question as to whether the "opinion leader" might be a role-related reference individual (181:166).

Kaplan conducted a more explicit examination of the relationship between reference groups and voting (210). His basic objective was to examine the popular explanation of the day that people voted according to their interests. Kaplan's analysis utilized many aspects of the reference other orientation. The concepts of the nonmembership group, the reference group, conflicting reference groups, socially structured reference groups, reference and membership categories, and various other aspects of the reference other orientation as it had developed up to that time were employed.

It is evident that the reference group approach provided Kaplan with a useful explanatory scheme with which to study voting behavior. He stressed the importance of ego's awareness of the reference other and the role of the primary group for voting behavior.

Hyman also employed a reference group approach to some extent in his pioneering consideration of political socialization (183). Previous investigators had not focused upon the relationship between political behavior and the socialization process. Hyman concluded that the family, a membership and reference group for the individual, was the most important agency of political socialization. He also observed that the political views of the child could change as he grew older, experienced social or geographical mobility, increased his exposure to additional reference others, or came to perceive his family as a negative reference group.

An interesting illustration of a substantive reference group explanation is the attempt by Benson, an historian, to explain certain voting behavior patterns in America during the Jacksonian period, 1816 to 1826. While Benson notes that his explanation is not a theory, he rejects "the notion that historians must choose between 'integrated theory construction' and no theory" (28:271). Benson's explanation involves the assumption that there are three basic determinants of voting behavior. He then proceeds to analyze the voting patterns of various groups of New Yorkers during the Jacksonian period on the basis of these variables. These factors are of interest to us as two of them pertain to the reference other orientation.

The first variable in Benson's explanation is the pursuit of political goals by individuals or groups. This is not a reference other factor and refers to the fact that an individual may vote yes or no on an issue because he is for or against it. Benson's second variable is fulfillment of political roles by individuals or groups. Although Benson describes this variable in terms of the positions that people occupy, he is also referring to the fact that the votes of some individuals on certain issues are influenced by those positive reference groups to which they belong. Benson observes (28:283–84): "Men may vote in a particular fashion because they are their fathers' sons, because they are members of certain ethnic, religious or socioeconomic groups, because they reside in certain areas or political units, because they belong to and are loyal to a certain political party." Benson's final factor refers to a negative or positive orientation to nonmembership reference individuals or groups. He draws from Merton at this point and indicates that the voting patterns of individuals may be influenced by *"groups to which they do not belong, or by certain individuals whose patterns influence them in determining their own"* (28:284).

Lipset and Trow have developed a reference group theory of trade union wage policy (243). This explanation is of particular interest as it involves an explicit and rather complete reference group substantive explanation, is sociological in character, and contains formal as well as substantive dimensions. Formal theories are at a higher level of abstraction than substantive theories, but each type can shade into the other (141:33). While only part of Lipset's and Trow's theory can be presented here, their entire framework was concerned with four major sociological questions: the social structure as a reference group determinant, institutional definitions of reference groups, the "legitimacy" of the social structure and the choice of reference groups, and the effects of the manipulation of reference groups.

The portion of their theory that pertains to the determinants of reference groups involves the following propositions (243:396):

"1. Individuals or groups who are subordinate to the *same* authority are more likely to use each other as reference groups, than if the reverse were true.

"2. Workers in a large 'membership' structure are likely to use abstract status reference groups, such as class and steel workers. Workers in small membership structures are more likely to use face to face relationships such as bench-mates and neighbors as their reference groups.

"3. Workers who *see structural elements as general status categories* are likely to use these categories as reference groups. For example, workers are more likely to become incensed over wage differentials between the plants of one company than they are over the same differentials between different companies."

It can be seen that the first proposition does not pertain to wage policy per se and is a formal statement, whereas the last two predictions involve workers and are substantive in character.

Although the previous discussions of Glaser's "differential identification" theory of criminal behavior, Haskell's explanation of juvenile delinquency, the means-end theory of juvenile delinquency, voting behavior, and trade union wage policy are representative of those substantive explanations that most extensively involved the reference group approach, there have been other instances in which the reference group concept and its cognates have been employed in explanations of this type. Some of the more important of these include Reiss's attempt to explain sexual attitude formation partly through the individual's reference individuals (317), Clark's extended treatment of reference groups and juvenile delinquency (72), Parker's and Kleiner's effort to relate mental disorders to reference groups (292), Wilensky's discussion of "moonlighting" as a product of relative deprivation (430), Fendrich's explanation of racial attitude formation (124), Caplow's discussion of organizational behavior as a function of organization sets (67:201–28), Sherman's implicit usage of the comparative reference group concept in the explanation of status revolution (367), Wheeler's (428) and Garabedian's (136) explanations of some aspects of prison behavior through an anticipatory socialization framework, and Henry's and Short's view of the relationship between suicide and homicide and comparative reference groups (168:54–65). (Caplow's contribution is of particular importance because it provides the foundation for a merger of the reference other orientation with the study of organizational behavior.)

A number of formal explanations involving the reference group phenomenon have also been developed. It will be recalled that a formal theory is not limited to a specific area. Kemper has proposed an explanation of achievement that is based primarily upon a reference group framework. His basic concern is with "a microanalytic level of factors which comprise the social psychological basis for achievement" (217:31). The major contention of his explanation is that "in order for ipsative achievement to take place, not only must the socialization process provide normative groups and role models, but audience groups must be available as well" (217:36). [Ipsative achievement involves the individual or self aspects of achievement, "i.e., the realization of individual potential" (217:36).]

The concepts of the normative, comparative, and audience reference groups are employed in the following manner by Kemper. The normative group provides ego with norms and values. The comparison group is one that provides ego with a frame of reference for judging the equity of his fate, the legitimacy of his actions and attitudes, the adequacy of his performance (the role model), or the accommodation of his acts to the acts of others. The audience reference group is one that rewards ego's behavior, and, while ego imputes values to it, the audience reference group does not provide ego with norms and values nor does it negatively sanction behavior.

Kemper's thesis is that all three types of reference groups are needed to promote maximum utilization of ego's ability and it involves three basic assumptions. (1) Normative reference groups serve a vital societal function in that they provide individuals with behavioral and attitudinal expectations, and consequently account for conformity. (2) It is not enough that ego be taught *what* he should do, he must be taught *how* to do it. In this regard, comparison reference groups are needed, especially role models. "The more complex the task, the more pressing the need for a concrete model" (217:35). (3) Since normative reference groups employ only negative sanctions, audience reference groups are needed in order to provide ego with rewards. The essential logic here is that punishment is deficient in that ego is simply told to stop it! He is not provided with any directions for behavior. "Without the prospect of positive reinforcement for his efforts, the actor's exertions lack motive force" (217:37). Kemper's explanation must, of course, be regarded as tentative. Nevertheless, his significant effort is an excellent example of a formal reference group explanation.

Jackson conducted an empirical examination of reference group processes in a formal organization (196). He believed that the existing evidence supported the contention that a person's attraction to membership in a group or organization is a major determinant of his behavior, but the processes and conditions under which this attraction—or identification in our terminology—occurs are not yet understood. Jackson's explanation contains a formal element in that he extends it to all types of groups.

Jackson assumed that individuals attempt to maximize their personal gratifications, organizations have informal and formal prestige systems, and obtained organizational rewards are related to the individual's degree of personal satisfaction. On the basis of these assumptions, Jackson hypothesized (196:309):

"1. *In any group or organization a person's attraction to membership will be directly related to the magnitude of his social worth.*

"2. *The magnitude of the positive relationship hypothesized in (1) will vary directly with the volume of interaction the person has with other members of the group or organization under consideration.*

"3. *Where alternative group orientations are possible for a person, his relative attraction to membership in one or another group will be directly related to his relative social worth in the groups considered.*

"4. *The magnitude of the positive relationship hypothesized in (3) will vary directly with the volume of interaction the person has with other members of the groups under consideration.*"

Jackson's study lent support to his assumptions and hypotheses and provided him with further insights into the processes under which the individual identifies with the organization.

Fishbein (130) derived and tested five formal hypotheses about the perception of nonmembers from Merton's initial discussion of membership and nonmembership groups. These hypotheses are largely based on Fishbein's elaboration of three variables in Merton's work. "Briefly, these variables are as follows: (1) whether the nonmember is eligible or ineligible for group membership (*eligibility*); (2) whether the nonmember is positively, negatively or neutrally oriented toward the group, i.e., is he motivated to (a) become a member, (b) avoid membership, or (c) doesn't he care? (*orientation*); (3) whether or not the nonmember was a member of the group at a previous point in time, i.e., is he a continued nonmember of an ex-member (*membership*)?" (130:272).

The hypotheses derived by Fishbein were (130:275–76):

"1. The more the members of an open group perceive a non-member as a threat to their group, the more negative will be their attitudes toward him;

"2. Members of an open group will perceive eligible non-members as more of a threat than ineligible non-members;

"2a. Members of an open group will perceive ineligible non-members more favorably than eligible non-members;

"3. Members of an open group will perceive ex-members as more of a threat than 'continued non-members';

"3a. Members of an open group will have a more favorable attitude toward continued non-members than toward ex-members;

"4. Members of an open group will perceive negatively oriented non-members as a greater threat than neutrally oriented non-members, who in turn will be perceived as a greater threat than positively oriented non-members;

"4a. Members of an open group will be most favorable toward positively oriented non-members, and least favorable toward negatively oriented non-members;

"5. With respect to both perceived 'threat' and 'attitude,' there will be a significant interaction between orientation and eligibility."

Fishbein's basic conclusions were that the variables of eligibility and orientation are important determinants of attitude and perceived threat but that the variable of membership is not.

Festinger developed a "theory" of social comparison processes with respect to opinions and abilities (125). His work has now been extended to the study of affiliation (342) and the labeling of emotions (343). "Festinger's 'Theory of Social Comparison Processes' grew out of a considerable body of experimental work on opinion formation and influence processes in small groups" (186:115). His theory consisted of nine hypotheses and a number of corollaries and derivations.

The essentials of Festinger's theory were expressed in his first three hypotheses (125:117–20):

"*Hypothesis I* There exists, in the human organism, a drive to evaluate his opinions and his abilities. . . .

"*Hypothesis II* To the extent that objective, non-social means are not available, people evaluate their opinions and abilities by comparison respectively with the opinions and abilities of others. . . .

"*Hypothesis III* The tendency to compare oneself with some other specific person decreases as the difference between his opinion or ability and one's own increases."

The remainder of Festinger's theory is, of course, also important. It should be noted that Festinger's predictions occasionally varied depending on whether opinions or abilities were involved.

Although Festinger's theory is regarded as internally consistent and amenable to empirical investigation (358:283), there have until recently only been a few empirical studies of it. Festinger's theory did, however, facilitate the development of social comparison theory in psychology. Singer (379) in reviewing the nine articles presented in the special issue of the *Journal of Experimental Social Psychology* on this subject raises some significant questions regarding Festinger's theory. He makes the important observation that individuals may compare themselves with others not only to evaluate one opinion or ability but also to evaluate their opinion *of themselves!* Singer also queried whether or not similar others are always used for social comparisons and suggested that the social comparison process may vary with the level of precision desired.

Although the number of formal reference group explanations in the literature is limited, three other efforts merit our attention. These include Davis's explanation of relative deprivation (87), Patchen's theory of social reward comparisons (296), and Cain's explanation of role conflict resolution (62). These works are among the more important formal attempts in this area but, due to their detailed and elaborate character, we will only be able to sketch their basic themes.

Davis has developed a *truly deductive* explanation of relative deprivation in an attempt to systematize and extend the ideas of other writers in this area. His theory consists of sixteen assumptions and a variety of deductive propositions. Davis contends that his "system of propositions is logically consistent, has an empirical reference, and can generate hypotheses for testing" (87:280). This work is of special sociological interest because Davis offers suggestions on the relevance of his theory for subgroup formation and he employs a number of sociological variables, such as consensus, rates of deprivation and gratification, and in-group and out-group comparisons.

Patchen developed a conceptual scheme regarding comparisons of social rewards (296). He attempted to extend Davis's work by focusing upon the character of the reference others with whom the individual compared himself, by assuming that ego compared himself with the reference other on a set of related dimensions, and by allowing for motivated choices in the individual's selection of reference others. (Davis assumed that choices of comparative reference others were random.) Patchen's explanation is particularly noteworthy in that it is explicitly concerned with the comparative reference relationship, extends Davis's work, is subject to empirical test, and related the reference group approach to dissonance theory.

Cain (62) has generated a sophisticated and unique reference group explanation of role conflict resolution. The essential hypothesis in Cain's theory is "that for any individual, action would be in the direction desired by the group with which the interdependence was highest (major identification group) in the majority of situations" (62:202). Her explanation then elaborates on those situations in which this basic hypothesis would not be expected to hold. Cain's explanation merits attention by students of role conflict because of its sophisticated presentation of role conflict within a reference group framework. The few sources that have explicitly related reference group theory to role theory include (45; 62; 95; 113; 222; 271:368–84; 278; 303; 307; 353; 401). A number of less direct statements regarding relationships between these two areas may be found throughout (73; 167).

This chapter has important implications for the reference other theorist! It should now be clear that the reference group concept has been employed in a variety of substantive and formal explanations. We have shown that the statement "There is not a reference group theory" is incomplete and misleading. The systematic insights that this book has provided into the conceptual and empirical dimensions of the reference other phenomenon will help to generate additional explanatory efforts.

The reference other theorist should also profit from the changing perspectives in regard to the nature of social theory. The greater receptiveness to explanations of different types, the realization that theory in the social sciences can be grounded in empirical data through the comparative method, and the general concern with theory construction in sociology offer a set of circumstances in which the utilization of the reference other orientation for theoretical advances can be maximized.

Finally it should be added that, although the stress upon deductive theory by the reference group critics has been questioned in this chapter, the value of this approach as a predictive and methodological tool is not at issue. *Generalizable knowledge is always preferable to particularistic knowledge,* and the methodological implications of deductive theory should be emphasized. Our intention has been to indicate that induction is always a necessary complement to deduction within the social sciences. In fact, Wallace has recently reminded us that induction and deduction are always *reciprocally* related in the scientific process (419: ix). It is this stance that the reference other theorist is encouraged to appreciate.

CHAPTER Eight

Methodological Considerations

The methodological aspects of investigations into the reference other phenomenon are the focus of this chapter. This is a subject of immense importance as knowledge in this area is ultimately dependent upon our ability to observe validly and reliably the appropriate portions of the social world and determine the causal sequences that characterize them. Parenthetically it should be added that, since research and theory are interrelated, the reader's insights into reference others should be enhanced through an examination of the material on the following pages.

Our observations are based upon a review of the methodological status of the reference group writings, the unique dimensions of the reference other phenomenon, and the recent methodological literature within the social sciences. Although our discussion contains guidelines intended to facilitate the future study of the reference other phenomenon, rigid recommendations are not included. The fadlike character of many methodological techniques, variations in the objectives of researchers, the tentative nature of science, and the very complexity of the reference other phenomenon, demand that we proceed with caution, flexibility, and circumspection in our study of the social world.

The reference group literature is characterized by several methodological problems. These areas will be detailed with the full anticipation that future researchers will negate them. Our objective is not to berate past authors. Indeed, in other contexts, we would applaud their insights. It is also probable that works in this area have matured in about the same manner as other efforts in sociology and social psychology.

The most fundamental and negative methodological feature of the reference group literature has been what might be regarded as a lack of *intensiveness*. This characteristic has pervaded all aspects of the research endeavors in this area and is reflected in the problem formation stage, the research designs, the data gathering procedures, the measurement operations, and in the interpretations at the cause and effect level. The incompleteness of many of these studies is illustrated by

Woelfel's and Haller's recent review of certain literature involving the significant other. They concluded that (434:75, my italics): *"In no instance* has a study (1) detected the exact significant others of a sample of individuals with an instrument of known validity and reliability, (2) measured the expectations of those others for the individuals in question, and (3) compared the effect of the expectation of others with other variables of known effect on the attitudes of individuals." (Woelfel and Haller based their study upon Kelley's normative definition of the reference group, that is, reference groups set and enforce norms.)

While the inadequacies of the reference group literature will be detailed subsequently, let us now consider some reasons for their existence. There are two factors that merit discussion. First, the complexity of the reference other phenomenon has not been appreciated! This is particularly evidenced by the lack of integration of our conceptual and theoretical insights into empirical research. For instance, when the social psychological character of reference relationships is visualized, it becomes clear that different sources and levels of data are required. The individual, the reference relationship, and the reference other have to be considered; and if one is at all interested in the sociological dimensions of reference others, variables of this type must be incorporated into research designs. Attention has to be given to the scope of influence, the salience, the empirical and membership statuses, and the conflicting and sustaining character of the individual's reference others. Some investigations must delimit ego's reference set and demonstrate the *relative* importance of different reference others as well as the conditions under which their influence is most pervasive. Unfortunately, reference group studies have not generally been characterized by the breadth presupposed by insights of this type.

Some critics may suggest that these observations imply too much as knowledge possesses a cumulative dimension and the scientist is seldom able to study the phenomenon of interest to him in its entirety. Nevertheless, the intrinsic nature of the reference other phenomenon dictates that more intensive and comprehensive research should be conducted. The following quotation from the Woelfel and Haller study not only indicates the number and types of variables that these investigators found it necessary to operationalize but it also illustrates the fact that the present methodological level within the social sciences is generally able to accommodate our conceptual insights into the reference other phenomenon (343:77): "Thus, the theory delimits five critical variables: (1) the dependent attitude; (2) the information provided by significant others; (3) those elements of phenomenal reality relevant to the dependent attitude which ego directly observes as self-reflexive activity; (4) the prior attitudes of the individual; (5) the individual's position in the social structure." Other views have sometimes been offered in regard to the testability of reference group type explanations. For instance, control theorists have stated that Sutherland's theory of "differential association" cannot be subjected to empirical validation, but there is representative research (316) on this topic.

The other factor that has impeded methodological advances is the quantitative emphasis that has reigned within the field of sociology. This analytical bias is aptly described by Blumer (42:24): "To my mind a recognition that methodology applies to and covers all parts of the scientific act should be self-evident. The point needs to be asserted only because of an astonishing disposition in current social science to identify methodology with some limited portion of the act of scientific inquiry, and further, to give that portion a gratuitous parochial cast. Today 'methodology' in the social sciences is regarded with depressing frequency as synonymous with the study of advanced quantitative procedures, and a 'methodologist' is one who is expertly versed in the knowledge and use of such procedures. He is generally viewed as someone who casts study in terms of quantifiable variables, who seeks to establish relations between such variables by the use of sophisticated statistical and mathematical techniques, and who guides such study by elegant logical models conforming to special canons of 'research design.'" It is probable that this quantitative emphasis has been peculiarly disadvantageous for reference group researchers due to the complexity of the reference other phenomenon. *Its most fruitful study presupposes methodological advances at all stages of the research process.*

Future researchers of the reference other phenomenon will not have to face this quantitative bias to the same extent. There is a present trend toward an expanded view of methodology within sociology. More consideration is being given to the philosophical foundations of research in the social sciences (56; 106; 209). Qualitative methodology is becoming recognized as a distinct specialty within sociology (99; 129). "Soft" data gathering techniques are gaining respectability. For instance, participant observation (251), field research (305:109–43), and content analysis (175) are becoming the objects of specialized attention. Unobtrusive measures have been "discovered" in sociology (424). More emphasis is being given to theoretical sampling (141) and even the symbolic character of *the research act* is being popularized (97). These changes insure that the reference other phenomenon can now be more effectively studied.

However it must be *quickly stressed* that the quantitative bias in sociology has aided the reference group theorist in numerous ways. We would also underscore the fact that the quantitative bias had both positive and negative consequences for reference group study. Some researchers have been able to quantify the relative influence of significant others. Several studies of this type are noted in (434:75). Causal sequences involving reference group variables have been supported in some instances (377) and suggested in others (124). Acceptable scales have been developed to measure attitudes *toward* significant others (359:415–500). The scales cited by Shaw and Wright seem to be attempting to measure several aspects of reference relationships, including degree of identification and scope of influence. Only recently the first operational measure designed to determine the normative influence of significant others that has any substantial evidence of validity and reliability was introduced into the literature. The Woelfel and Haller study contains an excellent example of an operational measure that is not dependent upon ego's awareness of the reference other. The authors stress that "thus, the individual is *never* asked who influenced him or whom he likes, or to whom he refers himself for definitions, etc." (434:79). These authors, however, employed an exploratory interview approach to determine those others that might be influencing ego. This suggests, using our terminology, that they were reference others whom the subjects had at least a "taking into account" awareness. The experimental method has been effectively employed in the field to examine the effects of membership and nonmembership groups upon attitude change (372). The implications of these advances are of enormous importance and suggest that, if the sociologist's quantitative abilities are integrated with his developing qualitative skills, our knowledge of the reference other phenomenon can be significantly extended.

Reference group studies have typically been cross-sectional in design and have relied heavily upon questionnaire data obtained in either a self-administering or a brief interview situation. There are a number of reasons why this bias is undesirable, and it is recommended that greater emphasis be assigned to longitudinal designs and other data-gathering procedures.

The basic reason for the dysfunctional character of the cross-sectional and questionnaire bias is that it does not permit a *complete* study of the reference other phenomenon. Although it is possible that the current stress in sociology upon process is to some extent a temporary fixation, studies of the reference other phenomenon must include a consideration of the dynamic. Many quite fundamental questions about the formation, development, and termination of reference relationships are not solvable through the brief exposure of the investigator to his subjects through the cross-sectional and questionnaire approach. Similarly, it is questionable if the interpretive qualities of the socialized individual are accommodated by this method. In general, this research strategy does not correspond with *the model of man* that is provided by our present insights into the reference other phenomenon. (The failure of reference group writers to center their efforts around a model of man is discussed in the final chapter.) The following quotation, depicting an inherent problem encountered in cross-sectional studies of normative reference relationship conflict, further illustrates the negative consequences of the bias being discussed here (78:106): "To us, then, choosing among alternative reference groups is a dynamic process involving conflict and its resolution. It is not enough to examine an individual's behavior at a point in time to determine his reference group unless that point in time represents an equilibrium state; insofar as an individual is switching back and forth we would not want to argue that he has selected or rejected a given reference group. A key feature of our experimental situation is that it enables us to detect equilibrium states."

Some have also stressed that the quantitative trend in sociology, which has fostered the cross-sectional and questionnaire bias, prohibits the modifications of the researcher's images of reality since this emphasis is "not designed to develop a close and reasonably full familiarity with the area of life under study" (42:37). Even if this observation were only partially true, it is an important one for the student of the reference other phenomenon. We cannot assume that the totality of relevant variables in this area has been identified. In a more general manner, Jones (203) has argued that all sciences are characterized by some *and different* biases, and that these biases influence the type of problem studied, the research designs employed, and ultimately the scientist's view of the phenomenon under study. The implications of observations of this type are toward a diversification rather than a standardization of method.

The inadequacies of the cross-sectional and questionnaire bias for the study of the reference other phenomenon may be illustrated in yet another manner. Recent writers in sociology have begun to emphasize that all research approaches are inept in some respects (424). For instance, the survey approach will enable the researcher to gain insight into the structural properties of organizations but indicate little of the historical origins of these characteristics. Consequently, it has been recommended that research methods be *triangulated* within the same study so that the assets of one approach may supplement the deficiencies of another approach.

This suggestion has obvious and critical implications for the reference other theorist and is described in the following quotation from Denzin's work (98:452). "However, we do raise one final point of consideration, and this is the fact that, because no single method adequately handles the problems of internal and external validity, it is necessary for the sociologist to *triangulate* his research methods whenever possible. That is, more than one method should be brought to bear upon any research problem. Thus, we will show that participant observation is best viewed as a method that combines survey data and quasi-experimental variations with document analysis and direct observation. Our last criterion under the category of validity is the *triangulation of methodologies*. This, of course, proposes a new line of action as well as a new set of symbolic meanings for the research process generally. We concur with Webb, *et al.*, who argue that in the contemporary age of social research it is no longer appropriate to conceive of *single method investigations*."

It should be added that there is sufficient evidence within the reference group literature itself to support more varied and integrated research strategies in the study of the reference other phenomenon. In fact some of the more interesting material includes content analyses (108; 156), anthropological field studies (33), observational studies (8), laboratory studies (71), experimental field studies (372), longitudinal studies (64), surveys (46), and other questionnaire type studies (394). The number of efforts, however, that have not reflected the cross-sectional and questionnaire bias is limited, and triangulation is not at all characteristic of the reference group literature.

Another aspect of the reference group literature that requires modification is the emphasis that has been assigned to the individual and his perceptual characteristics. Most reference group studies have been based upon the perceptual data obtained from individuals. Although the nature of the reference other phenomenon dictates that this type of information be obtained in order to determine the reference others that are orienting the individual's behavior, it is the *extreme* concern of the reference group theorist with the individual and his perceptions that is at issue. Even though our typology allows for the consideration of others that do not fall within ego's awareness, the study of the reference other will, of course, typically necessitate an awareness perspective!

One dysfunctional consequence of the focus upon the individual's perceptual qualities is that little has been learned about the effects of reference others upon overt behavior. This is unfortunate because our knowledge of the reference other phenomenon must remain incomplete until this void is filled. This perceptual trend is partially a function of the state of knowledge in sociology and may not be easily corrected. Coleman has recently concluded that most of the evidence in sociology involves reported rather than observed data (80:109), and Deutscher, who perhaps more than anyone else has stressed the urgency of examining the relationship between attitudes and behaviors, has made the following observation (102:35): "It is important that my comments not be misunderstood as a plea for the simple study of simple behavioral items. This would be a duplication of the same kinds of mistakes we have made in the simple study of simple attitudinal items. Overt action can be understood and interpreted only within the context of its meaning to the actors, just as verbal reports can be understood and interpreted only within the context of their meaning to the respondents. And in large part, the context of each is the other. But the fact remains that one of the methodological consequences of our recent history is that we have not developed a technology for observing, ordering, analyzing, and interpreting *overt behavior*—especially as it relates to attitudes, norms, opinions, and values."

Another unfortunate consequence of the perceptual bias is that the complexity of the influence processes involved in reference relationships has been significantly oversimplified. As we indicated earlier, it has traditionally been assumed that ego is in some way aware of his reference others, but this does not mean that ego will necessarily be knowledgeable of the nature, intensity, or scope of their influence over him. Rosen is one of the few writers who has made this position explicit (333:143-44, my italics): "It is in this area that the need for more precise techniques for locating reference groups and evaluating their relative influence becomes urgent. Too much reliance upon the questionnaire, with its tendency to depend upon the subject's perception of his referents, for the location of reference groups, *can obscure the fact that there may be referents whose importance he does not perceive or cannot verbalize.*" It remains a moot question at this time as to exactly what methodological strategies and techniques should be employed to remedy this deficiency, but it is apparent that objective information must be obtained *about ego's reference others* when this is possible if our insights into the dynamics of reference relationships are to be extended.

The tendency of the reference group theorist to concentrate upon data provided by the individuals whose reference others are being determined has still further implications. In general, the reference group theorist has not assigned much direct attention to ego's reference others nor to the sociocultural context in which reference relationships are formed. Consequently, very little has been learned about such vital questions as the conditions under which objective perception is most likely to occur or the factors that impede the development of reference relationships between ego and his potential reference others. (This is an important point. The tendency to focus upon information provided by ego has precluded the study of those others who do not become reference others for ego. It is imperative that we learn about the factors and processes that *prevent* the formation of reference relationships if our knowledge about the reference other phenomenon is to be complete.) The reference other theorist will do well to heed Denzin's recent recommendations concerning the methodological assumptions of interactionism. He has stressed that "the researcher must link his subjects' symbols and meanings to the social circles and relationships that furnish those perspectives" and "consider the 'situated aspects' of human conduct" (96:926).

Another and somewhat latent consequence of the tendency of the reference group theorist to focus upon the individual is that the reference other has typically been treated as an independent variable. The usual approach is to consider the effects of reference others upon designated aspects of the individual. This is an undesirable pattern from a sociological perspective because the determinants of reference relationships are at least as important as the consequences of reference relationships. To the extent, however, that the reference other theorist finds this suggestion attractive, he should be warned that *different patterns of conceptualization and methodologies may be necessitated.* Peter M. Blau made a similar observation in his consideration of the field of sociology: "But it is only in reconceptualized form that patterns of conduct clearly refer to attributes of collectivities rather than those of individuals; differentiation and homogeneity, rather than the various individual activities used in defining them, are distinctive structural attributes. Different approaches are required in studies that take such structural conditions as given and examine the constraints they exert on human behavior and in those that endeavor to explain why social structures develop these attributes." Blau made this observation in his discussion of the "objectives of sociology," which is part of the recent monograph that contains the Coleman article on the "methods of sociology" (80).

The reference group theorist has not given much attention to the time sequences between variables nor to the control of extraneous variables. These methodological inadequacies are especially damaging because the establishment of a causal relationship between an independent variable, X, and a dependent variable, Y, not only presupposes that an association must be demonstrated between X and Y but also that it must be shown that X did not occur after Y and that Y is not a consequence of variables other than X. A causal perspective also assumes an explanatory link between X and Y. While the topic of social causation is still debated, there is agreement among those scientists who present guidelines for the establishment of causal relationships regarding the importance of time sequences and extraneous variables. It is for this reason that the reference other theorist must incorporate these two dimensions into his research designs. [A good discussion of the requirements for the demonstration of causality is presented in (354).]

Although the assumptions about time sequences and extraneous variables are always critical from a causal perspective, they are peculiarly important for our understanding of the reference other phenomenon. For instance, we have already emphasized that a given reference other (1) may have been the source of certain of ego's values and continues to reinforce them, (2) may have been the source of certain of ego's values but does not continue to reinforce them, or (3) may reinforce certain of ego's values but was not the source of them. These possibilities are further complicated by the fact that ego may bear a membership affiliation with a *nonreference* other who happens to possess certain values similar to his but who is not a source or a reinforcer of them. In other words, the nonreference other, who appears to be a reference other, functions as an extraneous variable for the analyst. *The reference other theorist will not be able to distinguish between these alternatives in any specific instance unless he has some defensible insight into the time order among his variables.* Perhaps if more attention is assigned to Merton's concept of "sustaining reference groups," our ability to distinguish between these options would be enhanced.

Unfortunately there are not any simple techniques available to the reference other theorist to facilitate the examination of time sequences and extraneous variables. In regard to the former factor, longitudinal designs will have to be employed when possible so that some assurance can be had that Y did not precede X. Although recall questions have been successfully employed in the social sciences to gain insights into time sequences, the complexity of the reference other phenomenon generally precludes this possibility. It must be pointed out that some of the questions of interest to the reference other theorist are more amenable to a longitudinal approach than others. For instance, we can visualize manipulated and nonmanipulated situations where ego is exposed to reference individuals before any normative influence could have possibly occurred. On the other hand, the researcher who is attempting to study the influence of imaginary reference others will have greater difficulty in locating or creating situations where it can be documented that the reference relationship between ego and the imaginary reference other occurred prior to the influence of the imaginary reference other. Most likely the researcher will have to resort to a cross-sectional design in this instance, but, while this strategy will result in a statistical correlation, documentation of the time sequence under consideration is impossible. Although solutions to problems of this type are not readily found within the social sciences, it must be reaffirmed that the canons of science are not lifted because of the difficulties of investigation. However, there are numerous questions within the reference other orientation that are amenable to a longitudinal approach. While practical problems always hinder the longitudinal effort, there are no theoretical reasons why more of these studies could not be conducted!

Regarding the control of extraneous variables, the reference other theorist only has those avenues open to him that are in general usage within the social sciences, namely the experimental method and a number of nonexperimental procedures, including quasi-experimental research designs, multivariate statistical techniques, and analytical induction. Before considering these approaches further, it should be reemphasized that a concern for extraneous variables is not a characteristic of the reference group literature, and any type of progress by the reference other theorist in this area would represent a significant advancement.

There is evidence that the experimental method has fallen into disrepute in some of the social sciences (80:99). (We regard an experimental design as being characterized by the principle of randomization, at least one control group and the experimental group, and the introduction of the stimulus by the investigator.) This appears to be a function both of the infrequent usage of this method in the "real world" and the recent literature that emphasizes that the experimental method is not void of errors of various kinds. Nevertheless, as Hauser has recently observed, this method "represents the most powerful means which man has yet devised to test an hypothesis and to establish causality" (166:125). We can only encourage the reference other theorist to employ this method whenever possible. Small group laboratory experiments continue to offer considerable potential for the study of reference relationships. Significant laboratory studies in the reference group literature include (11; 61; 71; 212; 427). In spite of the "artificiality" of these studies, there has never been any doubt that laboratory results may provide hypotheses about the external social world, and writers are increasingly noting that meaning can be put into the laboratory situation (109; 345). Furthermore, there are various suggestions in the literature regarding the drawing of systematic inferences about the actual social world from laboratory results that have not been fully utilized (415:244–49). In a broader context, experimental field studies also offer promise for the development of causal propositions within the reference other orientation. They are directly concerned with the external social world, and reference group theorists have both successfully employed this method in their work (372) and recommended its increased usage (434:86).

The reference other theorist, however, will generally have to depend upon nonexperimental approaches. This is due both to those factors that prohibit him from manipulating variables and creating situations and the need to reexamine experimental results within the context of the external and uncontrolled social world. It is not often enough emphasized that while the principle of randomization allows the researcher to equate his experimental and control groups with respect to both known and unknown variables, "the removal of the effects of these other variables may sometimes eliminate the very conditions which, *outside* of the experiment determine Y—or the XY relationships" (322: 637–38). Factorial designs within experimental settings and replications under varied experimental conditions help to reduce this problem, but experimental results have to be tested eventually within uncontrolled social situations if valid generalizations are to be made about the social world. It is at this juncture that the reference other theorist must turn to quasi-experimental research designs, multivariate statistical techniques, and the method of analytical induction.

Quasi-experimental research designs include various procedures, such as the multiple time-series design, counterbalanced designs, and the nonequivalent control group design, that enable the researcher to approximate the "true experiment." Since these designs involve "methods of *securing* adequate and proper data to which to apply statistical procedure" (63:1, my italics) and as they only are approximations to the "true experiment," they are depicted as *quasi-experimental designs*. Campbell and Stanley, who have recently detailed these designs and encouraged their usage in educational research, have described them as follows (63:53): "It is in the spirit of this chapter to encourage 'patched-up' designs, in which features are added to control specific factors, more or less one at a time (in contrast with the neater 'true' experiments, in which a single control group controls for all of the threats to internal validity)." While we will not review these designs, it must be emphasized that quasi-experimental designs—which are discussed in (63:34–71)—are especially valuable to the reference other theorist because they facilitate his attempts to arrive at cause and effect statements in that the specific limitations of each design are recognizable.

Extraneous variables can also be controlled through the use of multivariate statistical techniques. This approach involves the statistical manipulation of data after it has been obtained rather than the experimental or quasi-experimental control of extraneous variables during the data-gathering process. The set of statistical procedures available to the reference other theorist is becoming increasingly varied and elaborate and includes the traditional correlational, regression, and analysis of variance and covariance methods, the analysis of contingency tables through partialing and direct standardization, certain nonparametric statistics, path analysis, and other more advanced modes of analysis, including various econometric techniques. The reference other theorist should be cautioned, however, that statistical manipulation is only a substitute for the experimental method. Only a finite number of selected and known extraneous variables can be statistically controlled. On the other hand, this approach provides insights into the causal patterns among combinations of variables. Some multivariate statistical techniques enable the investigator to infer causal "chains" among three or more variables. For an illustration of this in the reference group literature, see (124).

Analytical induction can also be used to facilitate causal inference. This approach assumes the existence of universal laws and attempts to uncover negative cases through theoretical sampling. Although this procedure has been subject to various types of criticisms, it has resulted in several important social theories, and is characterized by both advantages and disadvantages (97:194–99). Given the difficulty of establishing causal relationships in the social world, the reference other theorist should certainly not discount this alternative. Robinson has systematized the steps in the analytical induction method (323:813): " '(1) A rough definition of the phenomenon to be explained is formulated. (2) An hypothetical explanation of that phenomenon is formulated. (3) One case is studied in the light of the hypothesis with the object of determining whether the hypothesis fits the facts in that case. (4) If the hypothesis does not fit the facts, either the hypothesis is re-formulated or the phenomenon to be explained is re-defined, so that the case is excluded. (5) Practical certainty may be attained after a small number of cases has been examined, but the discovery by the investigator or any other investigator of a single negative case disproves the explanation and requires a re-formulation. (6) This procedure of examining cases, re-defining the phenomenon and re-formulating the hypothesis is continued until a universal relationship is established, each negative case calling for a re-definition or a re-formulation.' "

Various writers have indicated that the two most difficult problems facing the social scientist are the establishment of cause and effect relationships and the adequate measurement of variables. It is for this reason that the reference other theorist must assign considerable attention to the measurement process. While there are a variety of reasons for the importance of measurement, the most fundamental premise is that the scientist is not able to measure his concepts directly and hence must employ operational measures as indexes. If the operational measures are "questionable," the scientist is in a dilemma. He will be unable to determine if his results are a reflection of the state of the "real world" or a function of unacceptable operational measures.

An attractive feature of the measurement efforts in the reference group literature is the diversity and imaginative character of the operational measures that have been employed. Sensitizing concepts must be amenable to multiple operations. The examples cited in this paragraph are especially worthy of consideration since they were carefully selected to illustrate a variety of operational measures. These measures include the single forced-choice question (328; 332), the single open-end question (54:71; 95; 328), the index (264; 315), the scale (124; 394), projective-type measures (64; 408), observational-type operational measures (8; 33), operational measures based upon available data (108; 112; 156), experimental-type operational measures (144; 205), and unobtrusive measures (205; 436). Sociometric techniques have also been employed to measure the positive and negative bonds between individuals.

The open-end question is particularly useful to the investigator who desires to determine the reference sets or the salient reference others of individuals. The open-end question has also been employed in the study of the negative reference other (383:21), and Hyman (182) and Runciman (337) have utilized series of open-end questions to study the comparative reference other. The researcher who uses the open-end question must, however, carefully consider if *the type of influence* extended by the reference other has been effectively operationalized.

The imaginative character of the various operational measures is well illustrated by the studies of Kagan and Phillips (205) which tested several hypotheses involving identification by measuring on a series of prearranged laboratory trials the degree of cardiac rate and acceleration experienced by sixteen children following parent success and stranger failure. The Kagan and Phillips study also contains a good example of an unobtrusive measure of ego's identification with a reference individual. The authors employed the smiles of children as an index to this variable.

Campbell employed the following projective-type story question in a study of the internalization of moral norms (64:399–400): "Mike went out one Friday evening with his buddies with nothing special to do. They drove around for a while and someone suggested that they see what it's like to take a drink. Each had several drinks, and they seemed to have a real good time. A little before midnight, Mike went home and went to bed. When he woke up next morning, what were his feelings about the evening? Give the reasons why he felt this way." Campbell administered this question to a sample of high school students in a dry county and was attempting to describe the reference others that characterized the students who felt guilty about their behavior.

Unfortunately, the operational measures that have been employed in the reference group literature are also characterized by other less desirable features. The most obvious of these is that there is very little evidence for the validity and reliability of these operational measures. Our review of the literature, and that of other writers (121), indicates that only a few studies (94; 434) have given explicit attention to these dimensions, and the majority of the substantive studies of reference groups have relied upon "face validity." Although this form of validation has merit, it does not involve empirical validation. The operational measures employed by the reference group researchers may be consistently measuring what they purport to measure, *but we cannot be sure* unless more rigorous checks are made. Techniques for determining the validity and reliability of operational measures are presented in many methods texts. A good discussion of these procedures for the content analysis approach may be found in (175).

A less general but related negative dimension of some reference group studies is that reference others have occasionally been ascribed to individuals (216; 299). The validity of this procedure has been questioned (434:75) and should generally be avoided because it conflicts with certain of the fundamental tenets of the reference other orientation. For instance, the salience, the scope of influence, and the membership status of reference others cannot be treated as variables when this approach is employed. At least one researcher has concluded that his failure to support the hypotheses of his study may have been due to the fact that he incorrectly assumed the reference others of his sample (299).

Perhaps, however, *the fundamental strategy* that the reference other theorist should follow in his pursuit of valid and reliable operational measures *is to specify more carefully the conceptual aspects of the reference other phenomenon that he is attempting to measure*. In this regard, an observation of Stratton's is of interest (394:258): "To have meaning as an independent variable for explaining behavior, this concept should be used only when an individual: (1) is aware of the existence of the group; (2) knows the values and beliefs that characterize it; and, (3) is concerned with maintaining consistency with them. This is not meant to imply that the individual must be fully conscious or able to articulate that he has the group's standpoint, but it does imply that he must have some minimal knowledge of the group's standpoint and that he must, in some way, be governed by it."

Although Stratton's statement is limited to "role-taking" or "taking into account" awareness situations, it has *extremely important implications* for measurement efforts in this area. Measurement procedures must always reflect the conceptual aspects of the phenomenon being measured. The lack of intensiveness of the reference group studies has usually precluded this. The reference other theorist should more carefully specify the parameters of the reference other phenomenon that he is attempting to measure before developing operational measures to gather data. In other words, the researcher must, among other things, decide upon the type of awareness he desires to attribute to ego in regard to the reference other–"role-taking" awareness, "taking into account" awareness, or non-awareness.

Our overview of the operational measures utilized in the reference group literature, then, presents a contrasting result. From a positive perspective, they are imaginative and diverse enough to be accommodated to a variety of data gathering procedures. For instance, further evidence that unobtrusive measures can be utilized in the study of the reference other phenomenon has been provided by Wood (436: 145): "The wearing of clothing indicative of a certain social group in situations other than those formally prescribed, may be seen as a measure of the degree to which the values of that group are internalized, that is, the degree to which that group acts as a reference-group guiding the individual's behaviour in a wide range of situations."

Some of these operational measures also reflect considerable insight into the nature of the reference other phenomenon. Kuhn (228; 229), for example, has urged the utilization of open-end questions to detect the salient reference others of individuals. And writers have quantified the relative influence of reference others and offered important guides for the operationalization of the scope of the influence of others. In regard to the latter point, Woelfel and Haller suggest that the researcher should attempt to document the fact that reference individuals are related to the formation of *particular* attitudes (434:75). They argue that this approach will enable the investigator eventually to locate reference individuals who influence one or numerous attitudes. The opposite strategy, however, would not as easily allow the identification of reference individuals who are only segmentally important. One may also argue that our progressing conceptual insights into the reference other phenomenon and the general methodological advancements within the social sciences should facilitate the attainment of adequate operational measures of the reference other phenomenon. From a negative perspective, the existing operational measures are characterized by a number of deficiencies; most importantly, there is generally little evidence for their reliability and validity.

Our goal in this chapter has been to consider the methodological status of the reference group literature in light of our developing insights into the reference other phenomenon and the current state of methodology within the social sciences in order that some functional guidelines could be provided for the future efforts of the reference other theorist. While we feel that this objective has been reasonably met, the necessary inadequacy of our task must be emphasized.

A mastery of the research process in the social world is indeed a difficult if not literally an impossible task. Some have argued that the expert in methodology can become competent in but a few areas (99:18). It is unfortunately not enough to ask the creative question! The researcher must bring a host of skills to the research situation, including insights into philosophy, science, logic, qualitative and quantitative research methods and techniques, a general knowledge of the social sciences, and a detailed understanding of the literature that pertains to the problem. Only then can the research be designed, executed, interpreted, and reported. These procedures demand still other abilities of the researcher, including entrepreneurship, practicality, communicative skills, objectivity, and flexibility. It should be evident consequently that we have related but a few selected methodological ideas to the reference other orientation. Although those points were stressed that promised to have the most meaningful and general usefulness for the reference other theorist, there are obviously additional and more specific aspects of the research process that need to be examined. For a discussion of the more specific problems facing the reference other theorist in the study of comparative reference others, see (338).

Our discussion of the breadth of the research process has one other possible implication for the reference other theorist. It is conceivable that certain of the limitations that have characterized the reference group literature are an additive function of the complexity of the reference other phenomenon and the intrinsic difficulty of social research. A greater synthesis of theory and research in this area may have been hindered by the very complexity of the task. The investigator of the reference other phenomenon should be knowledgeable of several of the social sciences, understand and be willing to employ qualitative and quantitative research methods and techniques, be empathetic but yet objective about human behavior, be intuitive but yet procedural, and, not unimportantly, have the opportunity to utilize his skills. The accumulation of these experiences within a single person, however, does not occur often, and indeed is a rare event.

CHAPTER Nine

The Reference Other Orientation in Perspective

The historical development of the reference group concept has been examined from its early inception to its most recent characterization. This has involved an integration of concepts, empirical findings, and diverse views. In this regard, it is anticipated that many readers may have reservations concerning certain of our conclusions. This is inevitable given the nature of the endeavor. The reference group literature had not been previously synthesized.

One fact cannot be denied however; namely, the existence and importance of the reference other orientation. In spite of the numerous instances in which the reference group concept is referred to in the social science literature, it has not received *the systematic and intensive utilization* that it merits. From a theoretical perspective, symbolic interactionism, role theory, self theory, and other social psychological orientations have been more routinely and thoroughly employed in the social sciences.

Our point is obviously not that the reference group concept has been infrequently employed in the social sciences but rather that its usage has not been *systematized.* The primary group literature, the materials involving identification processes and role models, the references on peer groups, the reinforcement theories, the writings of the symbolic interactionists, and a host of other sources in one way or another pertain to reference others; but unfortunately the common denominators in this literature have not crystallized to the point where the reference group concept is conceived of as having the same explanatory and predictive potential as other no more deserving concepts and orientations.

This identical observation concerning lack of systematic and intensive utilizations must also be made with respect to applied areas. Although the reference group concept has been successfully adapted to a variety of problematic situations (see chapter one), its relevance for control purposes has not been generally recognized. Herriott's conclusions depicting the social determinants of educational aspirations are of special interest here (170:171, my italics): "Those concerned with the development of national policies for increasing the educational aspiration of talented adolescents may attach special importance to our finding that *significant others in an adolescent's environment* can have considerable influence over his educational plans. What should be particularly noted is the finding that the strongest independent relationship with level of educational aspiration observed in these data was with the expectation perceived from a 'friend of the same age.' *This variable has been greatly neglected in most formulations for national or regional action.*"

This lack of a methodical usage of the reference group concept in theoretical and applied domains may be due to the varied criticism leveled against it, the negative stance taken by many towards the concept because it is not a theory, its social psychological character, or the lack of systematization of the reference group writings. It seems likely that the varied and complex dimensions of the reference group concept were not generally appreciated; a reference other orientation was not visualized.

In any event, this book marks a beginning in the alleviation of these obstacles, and the reference other orientation should now receive a more complete incorporation into the scientific enterprise. There is evidence that this is already beginning to occur. Anderson oriented much of the first chapter of his recent book, *New Sociology: A Critical View* (9), around the reference group concept, and the Sherifs alloted two chapters of their 1969 social psychology text (366) to this concept. Others have emphasized that the reference group concept is not a panacea, and while we would tender the same caution about the reference other orientation, our stress is upon the potential of the reference other orientation. There are no panaceas in science, but the positive functions of the reference group concept have not been adequately realized. If the reference other orientation matures in a scientific manner against the backdrop of alternative concepts, orientations, and theories, there is the reasonable expectation that our present insights into individual-other relationships will be significantly extended.

Numerous aspects of the reference other orientation have been considered. The basic themes contained in this material will now be elaborated. This procedure will not only reaffirm many central ideas but the reader should now be in a better intellectual position to appreciate them.

We have continually stressed that the reference other orientation involves three components—the reference other, the reference relationship, and the individual. Nevertheless, as the title of this book suggests, it is the reference other that occupies the position of priority. In retrospect, the reference other is the trademark of the reference other orientation. It is the reference other from whom the individual takes his norms, values, and perspectives; it is the reference other with whom the individual identifies, and it is the reference other to whom the individual compares himself.

It must be understood that the reference other may or may not have an empirical status. *The reference individual is the only reference other capable of directly influencing the individual;* critically, the reference individual also provides ego with his social object reference others. At the same time, it must be emphasized that once reference others are "established" within the phenomenological world of the individual, they function as reference others irrespective of their empirical status. *Reference others share a commonality in the symbolic world of the individual.* It is precisely for this reason that individuals may be oriented to persons, groups, social categories, subcultures, imaginary or semi-imaginary reference others, and even physical objects. Whatever is capable of being perceived or imagined by the individual may come to function as a reference other for him. One must, however, not lose sight of the importance of the empirical attributes of reference others. Only reference individuals, and perhaps groups, are capable of exerting external social control over the individual. The social control mechanisms associated with imaginary reference others, and the typical reference individuals and quasi-empirical reference others with whom ego has a nonmembership affiliation, must be internally generated by the individual.

A major theme of this book has concerned itself with the intricacies of the reference other phenomenon. Individual-other relationships not only consist of a reference other, a reference relationship, and the individual but also each of these components involves additional characteristics. This situation is a reflection of reality and portrays the basis for an individual-other typology.

Reference others may be depicted in terms of their empirical status and membership affiliation vis-à-vis the individual. Empirical reference others only involve reference individuals. Quasi-empirical reference others include reference groups, reference categories, reference norms, reference objects, and the reference self. Reference others may also be entirely imaginary or a composite of reality and fiction. The individual has a membership or nonmembership affiliation with his reference individuals, reference groups, and reference categories.

There are three types of reference relationships; the normative, comparative, and identification-object. Each of these reference relationships may vary in the scope of its influence over the individual. In this regard, normative reference relationships are compliant, identification, and internalized. The scope of influence of the comparative reference relationship involves the number of dimensions over which ego compares himself to the reference other and the degree of relative deprivation or gratification that he receives from these comparisons, as well as the range of behaviors that flow from the comparisons. The identification-object reference relationship varies in terms of the intensity of its positive or negative sentiments and in the scope of the behaviors that ego directs toward the reference other. The identification normative reference relationship as well varies in terms of the intensity of its positive or negative sentiments and in the scope of its normative influence. If the reference other is an individual, the reference relationship may be role-specific or person-centered.

The reference other may also be more or less salient for the individual; ego may or may not "take the role" of the reference other, and the various characteristics of the reference other appropriate to each reference relationship may be objectively or subjectively perceived by the individual.

The complexity of the reference other phenomenon becomes apparent when the *multiple and changing* nature of reference sets is considered. While the diversity of social situations varies cross-culturally, most socialized individuals encounter a multitude of reference others. These reference others are both sustaining and conflicting in character. Reference sets are subjected to modification as individuals experience position changes and are exposed to new reference individuals and directed to additional social object reference others. During the process, reference sets both gain and lose reference others. Our knowledge of the dynamics of changes in reference sets, however, is severely curtailed by the fact that individuals often retain symbolic attachments to selected reference others with whom their actual role or person relationships have been terminated.

Although this overview of the reference other orientation illustrates the complexity of the reference other phenomenon, it should not be concluded that the reference other orientation has been described in its entirety. We have only circumscribed a small segment of it. All social concepts are sensitizing. The real world is a labyrinth, consisting of particularistic combinations of variables. This effort is but an *initial step* in the unraveling of its perplexity.

A fundamental focus of the reference other orientation concerns the nature of the influence associated with reference others. In essence, a reference other is an other that is having an influence over an individual. For this reason, and because the nature of this influence has been described in *a broader and more involved* manner in this book than in prior reference group writings, our views in this area will be delineated.

Many writers have limited their usage of the reference group concept to a normative dimension. The reference other is perceived as influencing ego's attitudes, values, and perspectives as well as the overt behaviors corresponding to these psychological effects. We have not only retained but also extended this normative view. Normative reference relationships are depicted as compliant, identification, and internalized. The concept of compliant influence runs counter to the traditional conception of the reference group which focused upon ego's psychological orientation to reference groups. This concept, however, underscores the overt function of membership others with whom ego has a minimum psychological commitment, and it draws attention to a relationship that could evolve into one that reflects something more than just overt conformity. The identification normative reference relationship is the relationship that has been traditionally stressed in the reference group literature. The normative influence of the reference other is recognized and the identification mechanism is presupposed. The internalized normative reference relationship describes a situation where the normative influence of the reference other is maximized as the normative attributes of the reference other literally become a part of the individual. Ironically, this is exactly when the influence of the reference other is minimized since ego now follows the appropriate normative patterns because he has accepted them and not because of his identification with the reference other.

The comparative reference relationship is one in which the individual compares himself on some dimension to a reference other. Perhaps, if ego did not evaluate and react to his standing relative to the reference other, it would be incorrect to define this situation as an influential one as no type of effect would have occurred. We have limited our usage of this concept to those typical relationships where ego does evaluate his relative standing and experiences some degree of relative gratification or deprivation from the comparison. This psychological reaction may in turn trigger some type of motivating response which could ultimately display itself in ego's overt behavior. The individual's psychological reaction to his comparative standing and any corresponding psychological or behavioral motivating responses are indicators of the influence of the comparative reference other.

The reference other with whom ego has an identification-object reference relationship is regarded by us as a *distinctive* other. While identification has been traditionally considered a mechanism for normative influence, the reference other with whom ego is positively or negatively identified has not been emphasized. Our position is that the identification-object reference other is important for ego *as an object*. The individual orients a significant part of his symbolic and overt behavior towards the reference other with whom he has an intense identification-object relationship. It is in this sense that the reference other "extends" its influence. This reference other is not a source of attitudes as he is in a normative reference relationship. Ego may, of course, have an identification-object reference relationship and an identification normative reference relationship with the same reference other.

One final comment must be made in regard to a fundamental conception of influence employed in this study. Influence has been conceived of as a continuous variable. Other writers have generally written as though it were discrete. Identification-object and identification normative reference relationships, for instance, may be positive or negative, vary in terms of their intensity, and reflect differing kinds of influence. Similarly, comparative reference relationships do not encompass the same scope of influence, and they generate varying degrees of relative gratification and deprivation. While this view may be difficult to operationalize, it represents a more realistic image of individual-other relationships. The internalized normative reference relationship may not be a continuous variable. Norms are possibly either internalized or not. But this remains a vexing question.

An underlying theme of this book has been the fact that ego is capable of being influenced by reference individuals and quasi-empirical and imaginary reference others. This is an important view as it reflects reality, facilitates the recognition of the distinctive functions of reference others of differing empirical referents, and underscores the necessity of employing both a phenomenological and a nonphenomenological approach in the study of the reference other phenomenon.

From a phenomenological perspective, reference others need not have an empirical existence. It is for this reason that ego may orient his behavior toward deceased relatives, mythical entities, and the like. The fact that ego can symbolize the reference other is all that matters given this framework.

An understanding of the processes involved in the formation of reference relationships also presupposes a nonphenomenological perspective. The analyst cannot just be concerned with ego's perception of his reference others. Most importantly, the reference individual must be considered as it is this other that provides ego with his quasi-empirical and imaginary reference others. We have also emphasized the fact that ego will not necessarily be knowledgeable of the influence extended by those reference others of whom he has an awareness, and that he may even be influenced by some others with which he does not have a "role-taking" or a "taking into account" awareness.

The realization of the necessity for this dual approach to the reference other phenomenon tends to negate certain of the conflicting emphases in the reference group literature. Reference categories, for instance, may serve as reference others, but they are not initial sources of normative influence. Normative characteristics must be attributed to them. This twin perspective also emphasizes the need for combined studies of the structural qualities of groups and the corresponding dimensions of ego's perception if such viable processes as cultural transmission and socialization are to be understood.

Although a model of man has not been explicated in this book, our review of the reference group literature leads us to certain conclusions. Many authors have implicitly taken a dichotomous view of the deterministic quality of the socialized organism writing as though it were completely circumscribed or entirely free from the social system. A few others have argued that man is both a creature and a creator of his culture. While our view is reflective of the latter position, it extends this perspective in several important respects.

We would emphasize that ego cannot be considered apart from the sociocultural system, that he is considerably influenced by it, that he reacts to it, that he is simultaneously a creator and a creature of it, and that the degree to which he is determined by the sociocultural system is a variable, depending upon the peculiar nature of the sociocultural system, the individual's position within it, and the character of the influence being considered. Individuals within different sociocultural systems, individuals within the same sociocultural system, and the same individual within the identical sociocultural system at varying points in time, may be subject to differential degrees of influence.

The impinging character of the sociocultural system upon the individual's reference set was portrayed in a variety of ways in our review of the reference group literature. The very nature of the ongoing sociocultural system into which the individual is placed at birth, and the particular set of ascribed positions and roles that are thrust upon him at this time, place inescapable parameters upon his initial reference set. The institutional arrangement of the society, the openness of the social stratification system, the value structure, and other societal factors continue to place unavoidable conditions upon the changing aspects of ego's reference set. To a significant degree, the reference sets of individuals can be predicted through a knowledge of the sociocultural system and a history of the individuals' positions within it.

But the individual is not entirely determined by the sociocultural system. The system itself provides ego with some flexibility in the development of his reference relationships, and its very complexity places ego in a variety of conflicting situations. Paradoxically, this conflict provides ego some choice. Certain alternatives are created within the boundaries of the system. The individual also has the capacity to respond to social systems in a creative manner. Ego is consequently able to control his own destiny to some extent. These and other factors tend to mediate the impact of the sociocultural system upon the development of reference relationships. The reader should realize that there has been considerable debate regarding the relationship between choice and determinism. The former may not negate the latter.

Unfortunately reference group theorists have not systematically incorporated this reacting view of the organism into their work. The most apparent example of this is the unalterable link perceived between identification and normative influence. Positive identification is regarded as tantamount to normative influence. Negative identification is similarly associated with the rejection of norms and perspectives, and the possibility of normative influence without identification is virtually ignored. Any capacity on the part of the organism to appraise the normative qualities of the reference other has not been seriously considered in the literature. [Some important exceptions include (31; 48; 160).] It is clear that a deterministic framework has been adapted in this regard. If our view of the socialized individual is correct, it is necessary to take this perspective at certain junctures in the study of the reference other, but it must be *integrated* with a nondeterministic or reacting view of the organism. Kuhn perceived a contradiction between the indeterminate assumptions of reference group theory and the determinate assumptions of reference group research (228:70).

An attractive feature of the reference other orientation is its potential for elaboration. We shall proceed to discuss a few of these extensions. There has been occasional reference in this book to self theory, role theory, and symbolic interactionism. The impression has probably been left that these orientations are distinctive from one another and from the reference other orientation. While this is not an improper inference, one must query if the similarities between these orientations have not been overlooked. It is important to realize that they are all *sociological social psychological orientations* and that any distinctions among these subdivisions will become irrelevant in the final analysis.

We regard symbolic interactionism as having the potential to *encompass* role theory, self theory, and the reference other orientation. This would be a most functional merger as symbolic interactionism is the most sociological of all social psychological orientations, and it is based upon a sociocultural set of principles regarding social behavior. It is also beginning to achieve the diversity that is necessary for a social psychological examination of the reference other phenomenon. [The broadening dimensions of symbolic interactionism are discussed in (384; 422).] Role theory focuses upon the social structure, self theory concentrates upon the individual, and the reference other orientation emphasizes the social psychological linkages between the sociocultural system and the individual. While it has been necessary for the sociologist to segment his efforts in these areas, an integration of the role, self, and reference group writings within a common framework is an indispensable endeavor. One symbolic interactionist, who has made this argument for the latter two areas, observed that (157:105): "The foundation for this contention lies in the postulate that the self and society represent different aspects of similar social experiences. Therefore, research in social psychology, in my opinion, must be directed toward bridging the gap between the existence of 'internalized audiences' and self-attitudes. Ideally, the respondent-produced meanings of self-attitudes should have some relationship to the *perceived* states of mind of others." A need to expand role theory is noted in (307).

Unfortunately, symbolic interactionism has never centered upon the reference other. In fact, the reference group writings have generally been eschewed by the symbolic interactionist. This has not only been dysfunctional from a scientific perspective but it is also ironic. The very essence of the symbolic *inter*actional approach presupposes that the reference other play a pivotal role in this orientation, and the writings of those symbolic interactionists who have given attention to the reference other attests to the relevance of these areas for one another. A consideration of the factors that have inhibited a merging of the reference group perspective within symbolic interactionism will facilitate this synthesis in the future.

We have previously considered the influence of the early symbolic interactionists upon the reference group concept. Since then the various editions of the Lindesmith and Strauss text have acknowledged the reference group concept (239) and Shibutani has explicated the role of the reference group concept in the symbolic interactional approach (370). There is also evidence that the symbolic interactionist is beginning to give more attention to the reference other. This observation has not only been made by others (267; 384) but also the importance of the reference other is being noted in both the empirical works (43) and the theoretical efforts (96; 397) of the symbolic interactionists. Nevertheless, the vast majority of reference group studies are not conducted within a symbolic interactional framework, and the symbolic interactionists have not only failed to focus upon the reference other but also are usually critical of the reference group literature.

As we suggested earlier, the lack of interest of recent symbolic interactionists in the reference other has an historical precedent. While the other played an important role in the early writings of the symbolic interactionists, *"the other* is never attended to with the discerning and analytic interest which they give to the actor" (229:6). Beyond this, however, the emphasis attributed by the symbolic interactionist to perception negated any detailed study of empirical reference others or the "objective" qualities of the social structure. There is no objective reality for the symbolic interactionist. In a related context, the symbolic interactionist has emphasized symbolic membership rather than "actual" membership. This is what prompted Strauss to question the very value of the membership group concept (395:148–53) and to state (395:152): "'Multiple group membership,' 'reference group membership,' judgments 'anchored in group standards and frames of reference'—such terms come close to but do not directly focus on what, I would maintain, is the heart of membership: that is, its symbolic character."

The most negative feature of the reference group literature for the symbolic interactionist has revolved about the reference category. Symbolic interactionists do not attribute any substantial role to reference categories in the self-development process, and they emphasize that reference individuals rather than reference categories are the sources of norms. The association of many reference group studies with the survey method has also provoked criticism among the symbolic interactionists since they perceive this approach as incapable of unraveling the complexities of the self-other process. From a similar perspective, some symbolic interactionists have implied that the reference group writers have added nothing of substance to the insights of the early symbolic interactionists concerning our understanding of the other. For an elaboration of these criticisms, see (229).

Merton also played an important role in the emergence of the gulf between the reference group theorists and the symbolic interactionists. He has championed both reference group theory and the functional approach in sociology. Many symbolic interactionists view certain of the basic tenets of functionalism as inconsistent with those of their own perspective [see the section on functionalism in (263)], and this rejection of functionalism seems to have carried over to Merton's reference group writings. Merton's castigation of the early symbolic interactionists for their lack of empirical research did not facilitate a more positive acceptance of his views on reference groups among symbolic interactionists.

This review of the factors that have prevented the assimilation of the reference group perspective within symbolic interactionism indicates that there are no valid reasons for this chasm to exist. The convictions of the symbolic interactionist regarding the critical role of perception in social relationships, the sociocultural character of all social behavior, the importance of language and symbols, the lack of an objective reality, the derivative character of reference categories, the normative functions of reference individuals, the reality of internalized audiences and the role-taking process, the complexity of self-other relationships, and the potentially changeable character of the socialized individual are not inconsistent with the views of the reference other presented in this book. In fact, *these very thoughts pervaded our discussion* and now need to be further incorporated into the study of the reference other. The basic sin attributable to the symbolic interactionists is that they have not brought their theoretical and conceptual apparatus to bear upon the reference other. It is irrelevant as to what person or school has provided the greatest insight into the other. What is important is that the social scientist must now bring the best of what is available to this area.

However, the symbolic interactionists must be willing to integrate their views with: (1) the social fact of a "consensual reality" that confronts all socialized individuals, (2) the possibility that reference categories may function as reference others under some circumstances, (3) the importance of actual membership in groups due to the mechanism of external social control and the possible development of symbolic membership under certain conditions, (4) some determinism in human affairs, (5) a recognition of stability and change in the self, and (6) a greater emphasis on the structural properties of social systems. The last point needs to be emphasized! Only a few symbolic interactionists have really appreciated the role of the social structure in human affairs (e.g., 157; 171). Apparently, and optimistically, the neo-symbolic interactionists and the social interactionists will be able to adjust their ideas *without sacrificing the fundamental and important principles of their perspective.*

A critical concern of the reference other orientation is with the three relationships. Additional systematic research into each of these would improve our understanding of the reference other phenomenon.

Although the most significant insights have occurred in regard to normative influence, this is only a relative evaluation. Our knowledge could be enlarged through (1) the conduct of more intensive and theoretically oriented studies exploring the relationships among sociocultural systems, reference sets, and normative influence, (2) longitudinal designs focusing upon the varying influences of reference others across time, (3) the generation and testing of middle-range and formal theories of reference others and their normative influence, (4) investigations of the conditions under which normative influence occurs in the absence of identification mechanisms, and (5) concentrated sociological studies of the internalization process. In general, each of the reference relationships should be treated both as independent and as dependent variables.

The area of the reference other orientation that is most in need of restructuring involves the comparative reference relationship. Although this dimension is receiving fruitful study in psychology from a social comparison perspective, it has seldom been considered from a sociological viewpoint. A basic change in strategy is needed. The processes and conditions under which comparative reference relationships are structured by the social system have been ignored. Similarly, very little is known about the interrelationships between the comparative, normative, and identification-object reference relationships. It would be revealing to determine something as simple as whether or not ego compares himself to his positive and negative identification-object reference others. The examination of these interrelationships should be of particular interest to the symbolic interactionist in his study of the self. Additional insights would be provided by more focused examinations of the *relative* influences of comparative, identification-object, and normative reference others upon the self development process.

The identification-object reference relationship has also not been often studied by the reference group theorist. Since identification was regarded as a mechanism for normative influence, it has generally been simply designated as present or absent. Also, the identification-object reference other was not perceived as an object of influence. More attention needs to be given to the formation and dissolutionment of both positive and negative identification-object reference relationships. Sociological determinants in particular require more emphasis. Special priority should be assigned to the negative reference relationship. Various writers have occasionally indicated that the negative reference group should be given more stress (186:26, 430–42; 260; 264; 271:300), but very little empirical research has been generated in this area. There is even some evidence (33) that the negative reference other concept should be more fully incorporated into research on alienation, a relational concept. Other studies that have considered the negative reference other include (28; 130; 183; 287; 312; 346). For a discussion of negative referent power, see (133). Other approaches that are apparently concerned with negative reference others include balance theory, labeling theory, the developing stereotype literature, and, to some extent, the writings on self-disclosure.

Another sphere needing further research concerns itself with the forms of symbolic and overt behaviors over which identification-object reference others have an influence. Perhaps most crucially, the reference other theorist should concentrate upon the role of *ambivalence* in the development and termination of the identification-object reference relationship. Reference others have been typically perceived simply as positive or negative. This is, however, a falsification of reality. Although the process of ambivalence has been considered more often in regard to normative reference relationships, even here the concept has only been researched in a very preliminary manner. The literature describing normative reference relationship conflict has been concerned with the individual's ambivalence resulting from his relationships with two or more reference others. Our suggestion directs attention to ego's ambivalence involving a *single* reference other.

Reference relationships should not be studied in isolation. The nature of the reference other phenomenon requires that the reference other and the individual also be considered. In regard to the reference other, more information is needed detailing the empirical and membership statuses of the totality of the reference others within reference sets. Descriptive and cross-cultural studies are particularly needed in this area. Very little is known about the composition of reference sets and how they vary from one society to another. The present literature on adolescents in America, for instance, leads one to the conclusion that only reference individuals function as reference others, but even a puerile knowledge of anthropology indicates that this is not true. A concerted effort should also be made to determine the functions and the relative importance of the reference others within reference sets. This would provide needed insights into the processes whereby individuals come to be influenced by specific reference others at given points in time. Nonmembership others must also be emphasized more!

The awareness dimension of the individual must be given much more study. We need to know more about the conditions under which ego is symbolically directed by his reference others as opposed to the circumstances where the effects of ego's reference others are not dependent upon his symbolic awareness of them. Study in this area would also enable us to determine the extent to which ego is influenced by others of which he is not aware. In spite of the emphasis given to the role-taking process by sociologists, its nature and correlates remain an enigma. Its intelligent study could provide clues to the conditions under which individuals move away from the influence of their reference others. The salience variable has been given some attention in the reference group literature but, as it may represent the decisive explanatory and predictor variable within the reference other orientation, more research is presupposed in this area. Finally, the relationship between the perceptual world of individuals and the realities of their reference others demands closer scrutiny. One may only now surmise the extent to which individuals fallaciously follow the dictates of their reference others. The reference other theorist should give particular attention to the individual. In many respects, this component of the reference other phenomenon was given the least study by the reference group writers.

A variety of sociologists have employed selected aspects of the reference other orientation in their writings, but this has often been done in an *implicit or preliminary* manner. An increased recognition of the reference other dimensions contained in this work would facilitate a more intensive examination of the phenomenon being considered within the framework of the reference other orientation and provide for a more systematic accumulation of knowledge.

Some of the more important instances of this include the writings of Centers, Gouldner, Matza, Becker, Toby, Seeman, Riesman, and Lenski. Centers's classic study of the psychological aspects of social classes (69) is clearly an example of a focused interest in membership and nonmembership reference categories. Gouldner's concern with organizational perspectives (148) is an excellent illustration of Shibutani's view of reference groups as perspectives. Becker's work on marihuana socialization (25), and Matza's important writing on delinquency and drift (261) portray the critical role of *the reference individual* in the transmission of deviant patterns. Toby's theory of victim constituency (404) reflects an explicit interest in the identification process. Seeman's research on alienation (352) implies a concern for some type of negative reference other. Riesman's theory of character development considers the salience of the reference other within diverse industrial settings (321).

It is also possible to recast Lenski's statements on status crystallization (233) within a reference other perspective. One sociologist has already made this observation (123:59): "With the finding that both social class and crystallization provide a sharp delineation of attitudes one is led to compare this result to other research. Reference group theory seems to be the most useful research for comparative purposes. These data suggest that highly crystallized status in Lenski's terms refers to a status in which—for a given set of values—reference groups and membership groups coincide, while low status crystallization indicates lack of such coincidence. *In this regard* then crystallization is a measure of the coincidence of membership and reference group." It is not our task to explore specifically the ramifications of a more complete consideration of each of these works within the framework of the reference other orientation, but it is our judgment that such a strategy would result in substantial improvements in at least some of these instances. It should also be added that the well-known works of Erving Goffman have shown a concern for what we have referred to as salient reference others. It would certainly be beneficial to reconsider Goffman's symbolic others from the perspective of the reference other orientation.

The relationship of the work of early sociologists to the reference other orientation has not been emphasized in this book. The essential reasons for this were that, with the exception of the school of symbolic interactionism, a direct historical connection did not generally exist between the contributions of these sociologists and the emergence of the reference group concept, and that the theoretical contributions of their writings for the reference group perspective have not been considered in any exhaustive fashion. It was necessary for our purposes to specify some tentative parameters of the reference other orientation in terms of the more recent and explicit reference group literature.

It might now, however, be very beneficial to relate earlier sociological works to the reference other orientation. As the reference group concept has been more fully elaborated, there is an increased likelihood that significant implications could be obtained. More specifically, although the development and nurturance of reference relationships presupposes a sociological framework, studies explicitly based on this assumption have been at a premium. An approach of the type being suggested here might provide some new insights into the sociological aspects of reference relationships. For instance, Tarde's writings on the society-forming process have implications for the future development of the reference other orientation. This aspect of Tarde's work is discussed in (152).

One might be tempted to view earlier sociological writings as antiquated given modern advances, and, although this attitude could be justifiable, it is more scientific to let it remain an empirical question. Only recently, a sociologist suggested on the basis of his empirical findings that the rejection of certain of Simmel's ideas may have been premature (117:510 n): "The translator's comment that 'a literal translation of this phrase, "the intersection of social circles," is almost meaningless' is perhaps hasty, in the light of the development of set theory in modern algebra. It seems to this writer that Simmel was groping for (and just about making contact with) a conception of the individual representing an intersection of traits derived from association with a unique union of social sets (groups). This article follows this imagery in that it pictures the combined information resources of individuals in interaction as the union of information potential of all the groups with which they are associated."

Our final remarks will describe two valuable and contrasting approaches to the study of the reference other phenomenon. The first of these focuses upon the potential extension of the reference other orientation to "unique" areas in which it had not previously been extensively used. Various dimensions of the reference other orientation have been employed in the study of several aspects of songwriting (119; 120), LSD users (77), the prediction of delinquency (248), election jokes (308), national stereotypes (104), the Eskimo culture (179), the maintenance of the American patrician class (341), life in contemporary Appalachia (425), and the pool hustler (305). The Polsky study contains a good illustration of several reference others that in our terminology have a high or low salience in the "role-taking" or "taking into account" categories of the awareness dimension of the individual (305:52–71). Another interesting study that exemplifies this dimension of the individual is (135). The illustrations cited in this paragraph are important because they document the fact that the reference other orientation may be employed in the study of diverse areas.

At the same time, the reference other theorist should not ignore more common behaviors. Although the ethnomethodologist (96) is giving considerable attention to the routine activities of individuals, the reference group theorist has been wanting in this respect. This is unfortunate since, once one becomes aware of the ingredients of the reference other orientation, he begins to observe them rather frequently in everyday activities. The patterns exhibited by the American child are an example of this. (Young children and the aged in our society represent ideal populations for study. In fact, Romeis, Albert, and Acuff have just recently emphasized the importance of reference group theory for the disengagement theorist as well as for the interactionist theorist. See volume 1 of the *International Review of Sociology*, 1971, pp. 66–70.) A first-grade boy may hesitate to wear his raincoat to school because of a fear that his friends are not dressed in the same manner or argue that he should be permitted to stay up later because his friends are allowed this privilege. In later years, this same boy may fall far short of his academic potential due to the jibes of his classmates. The middle-class parents of an aging adolescent may ponder why their son is beginning to prefer the companionship of his friends on Sunday afternoons in preference to their traditional weekend drives, and if their son should turn to hard drugs they will immediately derogate themselves for *their* failure rather than recognize the possible influence of their son's adolescent friends. This is an important point. Deviant behavior among young populations is often attributed to problematic relationships between the child and his parents. One of the few studies employing a control group, however, found this not to be the case. See Vincent's study of unwed mothers (417). Hopefully these few thoughts will illustrate the fertile ground that everyday activities offer for the reference other theorist.

Bibliography
Index

Bibliography

1 Adams, Bert, "Occupational Position, Mobility, and the Kin of Orientation," *American Sociological Review*, 32 (1967), pp. 364–77.

2 Akers, Ronald L., "Problems in the Sociology of Deviance: Social Definitions and Behavior," *Social Forces*, 46 (1968), pp. 455–65.

3 Aldous, Joan and Leone Kell, "A Partial Test of Some Theories of Identification," *Marriage and Family Living*, 23 (1961), pp. 15–19.

4 Allport, Floyd H., "A Structuronomic Conception of Behavior: Individual and Collective: I. Structural Theory and the Master Problem of Social Psychology," *Journal of Abnormal and Social Psychology*, 64 (1962), pp. 3–30.

5 Allport, Gordon W., "The Psychologist's Frame of Reference," *Psychological Bulletin*, 37 (1940), pp. 1–28.

6 ———. "The Historical Background of Modern Social Psychology," in Gardner Lindzey (ed.), *Handbook of Social Psychology: 1. Theory and Method*, Reading, Mass.: Addison-Wesley, 1954, pp. 3–56.

7 ———. *Becoming: Basic Considerations for a Psychology of Personality*, New Haven: Yale Univ. Press, 1955.

8 Ames, Louise and Janet Learned, "Imaginary Companions and Related Phenomena," *Journal of Genetic Psychology*, 69 (1946), pp. 147–67.

9 Anderson, Charles H., *Toward a New Sociology: A Critical View*, Homewood, Ill.: Dorsey Press, 1971.

10 Aronfreed, Justin, *Conduct and Conscience: The Socialization of Internalized Control Over Behavior*, New York: Academic Press, 1968.

11 Arrowood, A. John and Ronald Friend, "Other Factors Determining the Choice of a Comparison Other," *Journal of Experimental Social Psychology*, 5 (1969), pp. 233–39.

12 Asch, Solomon E., Helen Block, and Max Hertzman, "Studies in the Principles of Judgments and Attitudes: I. Two Basic Principles of Judgment," *Journal of Psychology*, 5 (1938), pp. 219–51.

13 Asher, Steven R. and Vernon L. Allen, "Racial Preference and Social Comparison Processes," *Journal of Social Issues*, 25 (1969), pp. 157–66.

14 Babchuk, Nicholas and John Ballweg, "Primary Extended Kin Relations of Negro Couples," *Sociological Quarterly*, 12 (1971), pp. 69–77.

15 Backman, Carl W., Paul F. Secord, and Jerry R. Peirce, "Resistance to Change in the Self-Concept as a Function of Consensus Among Significant Others," *Sociometry*, 26 (1963), pp. 102–11.

16 Bagby, Philip H., "Culture and the Causes of Culture," *American Anthropologist*, 55 (1953), pp. 535–54.

17 Baker, Paul James, "A Critical Analysis of Selected Theoretical Problems in the Works of Howard P. Becker," Ph.D. dissertation, Duke Univ., 1967.

18 Baldwin, James M., "The Self-Conscious Person," in Chad Gordon and Kenneth J. Gergen (eds.), *The Self in Social Interaction*, New York: Wiley, 1968, pp. 161–69.

19 Ball, Donald W., "Toward a Sociology of Toys: Inanimate Objects, Socialization, and the Demography of the Doll World," *Sociological Quarterly*, 8 (1967), pp. 447–58.

20 Bandura, Albert, "The Role of Modeling Processes in Personality Development," in John M. Foley, Russell A. Lockhart, and David M. Messick (eds.), *Contemporary Readings in Psychology*, New York: Harper and Row, 1970, pp. 328–38.

21 Bandura, Albert and R. H. Walters, *Social Learning and Personality Development*, New York: Holt, Rinehart and Winston, 1963.

22 Barton, Allen H., "The Idea of Property-Space in Social Research," in Paul F. Lazarsfeld and Morris Rosenberg (eds.), *The Language of Social Research*, Glencoe, Ill.: Free Press, 1955, pp. 40–54.

23 Beattie, John, *Other Cultures: Aims, Methods, and Achievements in Social Anthropology*, New York: Free Press, 1964.

24 Becker, Howard P., *Through Values to Social Interpretation*, Durham: Duke Univ. Press, 1950.

25 Becker, Howard S., "Becoming a Marihuana User," *American Journal of Sociology*, 59 (1953), pp. 235–42.

26 Beezer, Robert H. and Howard F. Hjelm, *Factors Related to College Attendance*, Cooperative Research Monograph No. 8, U. S. Department of Health, Education, and Welfare, Office of Education, U. S. Government Printing Office, 1961.

27 Bender, Lauretta and B. Frank Vogel, "Imaginary Companions of Children," *American Journal of Orthopsychiatry*, 11 (1941), pp. 56–65.

28 Benson, Lee, *The Concept of Jacksonian Democracy: New York As a Test Case*, Princeton, N. J.: Princeton Univ. Press, 1961.

29 Berelson, Bernard and Gary A. Steiner, *Human Behavior: An Inventory of Scientific Findings*, New York: Harcourt, Brace and World, 1964.

30 Berger, Peter L., *Invitation to Sociology: A Humanistic Perspective*, Garden City, N. Y.: Doubleday Anchor Book, 1963.

31 Berger, Peter L. and Thomas Luckmann, *The Social Construction of Reality: A Treatise in the Sociology of Knowledge*, Garden City, N. Y.: Doubleday Anchor Book, 1966.

32 Berkowitz, Leonard and Richard M. Lundy, "Personality Characteristics

Related to Susceptibility to Influence by Peers or Authority Figures," *Journal of Personality*, 25 (1956), pp. 306–16.

33 Berreman, Gerald D., "Aleut Reference Group Alienation, Mobility, and Acculturation," *American Anthropologist*, 66 (1964), pp. 231–50.

34 Bierstedt, Robert, *The Social Order: An Introduction to Sociology*, 2nd ed., New York: McGraw-Hill, 1963.

35 Blalock, Hubert M., Jr., *Theory Construction: From Verbal to Mathematical Formulations*, Englewood Cliffs, N. J.: Prentice-Hall, 1969.

36 Blau, Peter M., "Social Mobility and Interpersonal Relations," *American Sociological Review*, 21 (1956), pp. 290–95.

37 Blau, Zena Smith, "Structural Constraints on Friendships in Old Age," *American Sociological Review*, 26 (1961), pp. 429–39.

38 Blum, Richard H. and Associates, *Students and Drugs—Drugs 2: College and High School Observations*, San Francisco: Jossey-Bass, 1969.

39 Blumer, Herbert, "What Is Wrong with Social Theory?" *American Sociological Review*, 19 (1954), pp. 3–10.

40 ———. "Sociological Analysis and the 'Variable,'" *American Sociological Review*, 21 (1956), pp. 683–90.

41 ———. "Society as Symbolic Interaction," in Arnold M. Rose (ed.), *Human Behavior and Social Processes*, Boston: Houghton Mifflin, 1962, pp. 179–92.

42 ———. *Symbolic Interactionism: Perspective and Method*, Englewood Cliffs, N. J.: Prentice-Hall, 1969.

43 Blumer, Herbert, with assistance from Alan Sutter, Samir Ahmed, and Roger Smith, *The World of Youthful Drug Use* (ADD Center Project Final Report), Berkeley: Univ. of California, School of Criminology, 1967.

44 Bolton, Charles D. and Kenneth C. W. Kammeyer, *The University Student: A Study of Student Behavior and Values*, New Haven, Conn.: College and Univ. Press, 1967.

45 Borgatta, Edgar F., "Role and Reference Group Theory," in Edgar F. Borgatta (ed.), *Social Psychology: Readings & Perspective*, Chicago: Rand McNally, 1969, pp. 286–96.

46 Bott, Elizabeth, "The Concept of Class as a Reference Group," *Human Relations*, 7 (1954), pp. 259–85.

47 Bowerman, Charles E. and John W. Kinch, "Changes in Family and Peer Orientation of Children Between the Fourth and Tenth Grades," *Social Forces*, 37 (1959), pp. 206–11.

48 Bredemeier, Harry C. and Richard M. Stephenson, *The Analysis of Social Systems*, New York: Holt, Rinehart and Winston, 1962.

49 Brim, Orville G., Jr., "Adult Socialization," in John A. Clausen (ed.), *Socialization and Society*, Boston: Little, Brown, 1968, pp. 182–226.

50 Brittain, Clay V., "Adolescent Choices and Parent-Peer Cross-Pressures," *American Sociological Review*, 28 (1963), pp. 385–91.

51 Bronfenbrenner, Urie, "Freudian Theories of Identification and Their Derivatives," *Child Development*, 31 (1960), pp. 15–40.

52 ———. "Parsons' Theory of Identification," in Max Black (ed.), *The Social Theories of Talcott Parsons*, Englewood Cliffs, N. J.: Prentice-Hall, 1961, pp. 191–213.

53 ———. *Two Worlds of Childhood: U. S. and U. S. S. R.*, New York: Russell Sage Foundation, 1970.

54 Brookover, Wilbur B. and Edsel L. Erickson, *Society, Schools and Learning*, Boston: Allyn and Bacon, 1969.

55 Brown, Judson S., "Principles of Intrapersonal Conflict," *Journal of Conflict Resolution*, 1 (1957), pp. 135–54.

56 Brown, Robert, *Explanation in Social Science*, Chicago: Aldine, 1963.

57 Brown, Roger, *Social Psychology*, New York: Free Press, 1965.

58 Bruner, Edward M., "Primary Group Experience and the Processes of Acculturation," *American Anthropologist*, 58 (1956), pp. 605–23.

59 Burchard, Waldo W., "Role Conflicts of Military Chaplains," *American Sociological Review*, 19 (1954), pp. 528–35.

60 Burchinal, Lee G., "Membership Groups and Attitudes Toward Cross-Religious Dating and Marriage," *Marriage and Family Living*, 22 (1960), pp. 248–53.

61 Buss, Arnold H. and Norman W. Portnoy, "Pain Tolerance and Group Identification," *Journal of Personality and Social Psychology*, 6 (1967), pp. 106–8.

62 Cain, Maureen E., "Some Suggested Developments for Role and Reference Group Analysis," *British Journal of Sociology*, 19 (1968), pp. 191–205.

63 Campbell, Donald T. and Julian C. Stanley, *Experimental and Quasi-Experimental Designs for Research*, Chicago: Rand McNally, 1963.

64 Campbell, Ernest Q., "The Internalization of Moral Norms," *Sociometry*, 27 (1964), pp. 391–412.

65 Campbell, Ernest Q. and C. Norman Alexander, "Structural Effects and Interpersonal Relationships," *American Journal of Sociology*, 71 (1965), pp. 284–89.

66 Campbell, Ernest Q. and Thomas F. Pettigrew, "Racial and Moral Crisis: The Role of Little Rock Ministers," *American Journal of Sociology*, 64 (1959), pp. 509–16.

67 Caplow, Theodore, *Principles of Organization*, New York: Harcourt, Brace and World, 1964.

68 ———. *Two Against One: Coalitions in Triads*, Englewood Cliffs, N. J.: Prentice-Hall, 1968.

69 Centers, Richard, *The Psychology of Social Classes: A Study of Class Consciousness*, Princeton: Princeton Univ. Press, 1949.

70 Chapman, Dwight W. and John Volkmann, "A Social Determinant of the Level of Aspiration," in Theodore M. Newcomb and Eugene L.

Hartley (eds)., *Readings in Social Psychology*, New York: Holt, 1947, pp. 90–99.

71 Charters, W. W., Jr., and Theodore M. Newcomb, "Some Attitudinal Effects of Experimentally Increased Salience of a Membership Group," in Eleanor E. Maccoby, Theodore M. Newcomb, and Eugene L. Hartley (eds.), *Readings in Social Psychology*, 3rd ed., New York: Holt, Rinehart and Winston, 1958, pp. 276–81.

72 Clark, Robert E., "Reference Group Theory and Delinquency," Unpublished manuscript, Pennsylvania State Univ., 1970

73 Clausen, John A. (ed.), *Socialization and Society*, Boston: Little, Brown, 1968.

74 Cohen, Albert K., "The Study of Social Disorganization and Deviant Behavior," in Robert K. Merton, Leonard Broom, and Leonard S. Cottrell, Jr. (eds.), *Sociology Today: Problems and Prospects*, New York: Basic Books, 1959, pp. 461–84.

75 ———. "The Sociology of the Deviant Act: Anomie Theory and Beyond," *American Sociological Review*, 30 (1965), pp. 5–14.

76 Cohen, Albert K. and James F. Short, Jr., "Juvenile Delinquency," in Robert Merton and Robert A. Nisbet (eds.), *Contemporary Social Problems*, New York: Harcourt, Brace and World, 1961, pp. 77–126.

77 Cohen, Allan Y., "Who Takes LSD and Why?", *New Society*, 8 (1966), pp. 226–28.

78 Cohen, Bernard P., "The Process of Choosing a Reference Group," in Joan H. Criswell, Herbert Solomon, and Patrick Suppes (eds.), *Mathematical Methods in Small Group Processes*, Stanford, Calif.: Stanford Univ. Press, 1962, pp. 101–18.

79 Coleman, James S., *The Adolescent Society: The Social Life of the Teenager and Its Impact on Education*, New York: Free Press of Glencoe, 1961.

80 ———. "The Methods of Sociology," in Robert Bierstedt (ed.), *A Design for Sociology: Scope, Objectives, and Methods*, Monograph 9, Philadelphia: The American Academy of Political and Social Science, 1969, pp. 86–114.

81 Cooley, Charles Horton, *Human Nature and the Social Order*, New York: Charles Scribner's Sons, 1902.

82 Coser, Rose Laub, "Insulation from Observability and Types of Social Conformity," *American Sociological Review*, 26 (1961), pp. 28–39.

83 Couch, Carl J. and John S. Murray, "Significant Others and Evaluation," *Sociometry*, 27 (1964), pp. 502–9.

84 Dai, Bingham, "A Socio-Psychiatric Approach to Personality Organization," *American Sociological Review*, 17 (1952), pp. 44–49.

85 Dashiell, J. F., "Experimental Studies of the Influence of Social Situations on the Behavior of Individual Human Adults," in C. A. Murchison (ed.), *Handbook of Social Psychology*, Worcester, Mass.: Clark Univ. Press, 1935, pp. 1097–1158.

86 Davis, Fred and Virginia L. Olesen, "Initiation into a Women's Profession: Identity Problems in the Status Transition of Coed to Student Nurse," *Sociometry*, 26 (1963), pp. 89–101.

87 Davis, James A., "A Formal Interpretation of the Theory of Relative Deprivation," *Sociometry*, 22 (1959), pp. 280–96.

88 ———. "Reference Groups and Relative Deprivation Among American Graduate Students," *Public Opinion Quarterly*, 25 (1961), pp. 455–56.

89 ———. "Structural Balance, Mechanical Solidarity, and Interpersonal Relations," *American Journal of Sociology*, 68 (1963), pp. 444–62.

90 ———. "The Campus as a Frog Pond: An Application of the Theory of Relative Deprivation to Career Decisions of College Men," *American Journal of Sociology*, 72 (1966), pp. 17–31.

91 Dawson, Richard E. and Kenneth Prewitt, *Political Socialization*, Boston: Little, Brown, 1969.

92 De Fleur, Melvin L., *Theories of Mass Communication*, 2nd ed., New York: David McKay, 1970.

93 De Fleur, Melvin L. and Frank R. Westie, "Attitude as a Scientific Concept," *Social Forces*, 42 (1963), pp. 17–31.

94 DeJong, Gordon F. and Coughenour C. Milton, "Reliability and Comparability of Two Instruments for Determining Reference Groups in Farm Practice Decisions," *Rural Sociology*, 25 (1960), pp. 298–307.

95 Denzin, Norman K., "The Significant Others of a College Population," *Sociological Quarterly*, 7 (1966), pp. 298–310.

96 ———. "Symbolic Interactionism and Ethnomethodology: A Proposed Synthesis," *American Sociological Review*, 34 (1969), pp. 922–34.

97 ———. *The Research Act: A Theoretical Introduction to Sociological Methods*, Chicago: Aldine, 1970.

98 ———. "The Methodologies of Symbolic Interaction: A Critical Review of Research Techniques," in Gregory P. Stone and Harvey A. Farberman (eds.), *Social Psychology Through Symbolic Interaction*, Waltham, Mass.: Ginn-Blaisdell, 1970, pp. 447–65.

99 ———. (ed.), *Sociological Methods: A Sourcebook*, Chicago: Aldine, 1970.

100 Deutsch, Morton and Robert M. Krauss, *Theories in Social Psychology*, New York: Basic Books, 1965.

101 Deutscher, Irwin, "Socialization for Postparental Life," in Jerold Heiss (ed.), *Family Roles and Interaction: An Anthology*, Chicago: Rand McNally, 1968, pp. 427–43.

102 ———. "Words and Deeds: Social Science and Social Policy," in William J. Filstead (ed.), *Qualitative Methodology: Firsthand Involvement with the Social World*, Chicago: Markham, 1970, pp. 27–51.

103 Dewey, John, *The Public and Its Problems*, New York: Holt, 1927.

104 Diab, Lutfy N., "National Stereotypes and the 'Reference Group' Concept," *Journal of Social Psychology*, 57 (1962), pp. 339–51.

105 Dickie-Clark, H. F., "The Marginal Situation: A Contribution to Marginality Theory," *Social Forces,* 44 (1966), pp. 363–70.

106 DiRenzo, Gordon J., "Toward Explanation in the Behavioral Sciences," in Gordon J. DiRenzo (ed.), *Concepts, Theory, and Explanation in the Behavioral Sciences,* New York: Random House, 1966, pp. 231–91.

107 Dorn, Dean S., "A Partial Test of the Delinquency Continuum Typology: Contracultures and Subcultures," *Social Forces,* 47 (1969), pp. 305–14.

108 Dornbusch, Sanford M. and Lauren C. Hickman, "Other-Directedness in Consumer-Goods Advertising: A Test of Riesman's Historical Theory," *Social Forces,* 38 (1959), pp. 99–102.

109 Drabek, Thomas E. and J. Eugene Haas, "Realism in Laboratory Simulation: Myth or Method?" *Social Forces,* 45 (1967), pp. 337–46.

110 Dubin, Robert, *Theory Building,* New York: Free Press, 1969.

111 Durkheim, Emile, *Socialism and Saint-Simon,* Yellow Springs, Ohio: Antioch Press, 1958.

112 Eberts, Paul and Kent P. Schwirian, "Metropolitan Crime Rates and Relative Deprivation," *Criminologica,* 5 (1968), pp. 43–52.

113 Ehrlich, Howard J., James W. Rinehart, and John C. Howell, "The Study of Role-Conflict: Explorations in Methodology," *Sociometry,* 25 (1962), pp. 85–97.

114 Eisenstadt, S. N., "Studies in Reference Group Behavior: I. Reference Norms and the Social Structure," *Human Relations,* 7 (1954), pp. 191–216.

115 ———. "Reference Group Behavior and Social Integration: An Explorative Study," *American Sociological Review,* 19 (1954), pp. 175–85.

116 England, George W. and Carroll I. Stein, "The Occupational Reference Group—A Neglected Concept in Employee Attitude Studies," *Personnel Psychology,* 14 (1961), pp. 299–304.

117 Erbe, William, "Gregariousness, Group Membership, and the Flow of Information," *American Journal of Sociology,* 67 (1962), pp. 502–16.

118 ———. "Social Involvement and Political Activity: A Replication and Elaboration," *American Sociological Review,* 29 (1964), pp. 198–215.

119 Etzkorn, K. Peter, "On Esthetic Standards and Reference Groups of Popular Songwriters," *Sociological Inquiry,* 36 (1966), pp. 39–47.

120 ———. "Social Context of Songwriting," *Ethnomusicology,* 7 (1963), pp. 96–106.

121 Ewens, William L., "Reference Other Support, Ethnic Attitudes, and Perceived Influence of Others in the Performance of Overt Acts," Ph.D. dissertation, Univ. of Iowa, 1969.

122 Faris, Robert E. L., *Chicago Sociology—1920–1932,* San Francisco: Chandler, 1967.

123 Fauman, S. Joseph, "Status Crystallization and Interracial Attitudes," *Social Forces*, 47 (1968), pp. 53–60.

124 Fendrich, James M., "Perceived Reference Group Support: Racial Attitudes and Overt Behavior," *American Sociological Review*, 32 (1967), pp. 960–70.

125 Festinger, Leon, "A Theory of Social Comparison Processes," *Human Relations*, 7 (1954), pp. 117–40.

126 Festinger, Leon, Henry W. Riecken, Jr., and Stanley Schachter, *When Prophecy Fails*, Minneapolis: Univ. of Minnesota Press, 1956.

127 Festinger, Leon, Stanley S. Schachter, and Kurt Back, "The Spatial Ecology of Group Formation," in Herbert H. Hyman and Eleanor Singer (eds.), *Readings in Reference Group Theory and Research*, New York: Free Press, 1968, pp. 268–77.

128 Festinger, Leon, Jane Torrey, and Ben Willerman, "Self-Evaluation as a Function of Attraction to the Group," *Human Relations*, 7 (1954), pp. 161–74.

129 Filstead, William J. (ed.), *Qualitative Methodology: Firsthand Involvement with the Social World*, Chicago: Markham, 1970.

130 Fishbein, Martin, "The Perception of Non-members—A Test of Merton's Reference Group Theory," *Sociometry*, 26 (1963), pp. 271–86.

131 Form, William H. and James A. Geschwender, "Social Reference Basis of Job Satisfaction: The Case of Manual Workers," *American Sociological Review*, 27 (1962), pp. 228–37.

132 Frankl, Viktor E., *Man's Search for Meaning: An Introduction to Logotherapy*, New York: Washington Square Press, 1963.

133 French, John R. P., Jr. and Bertram Raven, "The Bases of Social Power," in Dorwin Cartwright and Alvin Zander (eds.), *Group Dynamics: Research and Theory*, 2nd ed., New York: Harper and Row, 1953, pp. 607–23.

134 Friedham, Stanley, "Dialogue with James F. Short," *Issues in Criminology*, 5 (1970), pp. 25–41.

135 Gans, Herbert J., "The Creator-Audience Relationship in the Mass Media: An Analysis of Movie Making," in Bernard Rosenberg and David Manning White (eds.), *Mass Culture: The Popular Arts in America*, Glencoe, Ill.: Free Press, 1957, pp. 315–24.

136 Garabedian, Peter G., "Social Roles and Processes of Socialization in the Prison Community," *Social Problems*, 11 (1963), pp. 139–52.

137 Gerard, Harold B., "The Anchorage of Opinions in Face-to-Face Groups," *Human Relations*, 7 (1954), pp. 313–25.

138 Gerth, Hans and C. Wright Mills, *Character and Social Structure: The Psychology of Social Institutions*, New York: Harcourt, Brace, 1953.

139 Geschwender, James A. and Benjamin D. Singer, "Deprivation and the Detroit Riot," *Social Problems*, 17 (1970), pp. 457–63.

140 Getzels, J. W. and E. G. Guba, "Role, Role Conflict, and Effectiveness:

An Empirical Study," *American Sociological Review*, 19 (1954), pp. 164–75.

141 Glaser, Barney G. and Anselm L. Strauss, *The Discovery of Grounded Theory*, Chicago: Aldine, 1967.

142 ———. *Status Passage*, Chicago: Aldine-Atherton, 1971.

143 Glaser, Daniel, "Criminality Theories and Behavioral Images," *American Journal of Sociology*, 61 (1956), pp. 433–44.

144 Glass, Gene V., "How May Salience of a Membership Group Be Increased?" *Journal of Educational Measurement*, 1 (1964), pp. 125–29.

145 Glazer, Nathan, "'The American Soldier' as Science," *Commentary*, 8 (1949), pp. 487–96.

146 Golovensky, David I., "The Marginal Man Concept: An Analysis and Critique," *Social Forces*, 30 (1952), pp. 333–38.

147 Goode, William J., "A Theory of Role Strain," *American Sociological Review*, 25 (1960), pp. 483–96.

148 Gouldner, Alvin W., "Cosmopolitans and Locals: Toward an Analysis of Latent Social Roles," *Administrative Science Quarterly*, 2 (1957), pp. 281–306.

149 Greer, Scott A., *Social Organization*, New York: Random House, 1955.

150 Grindstaff, Carl F., "The Negro, Urbanization, and Relative Deprivation in the Deep South," *Social Problems*, 15 (1968), pp. 342–52.

151 Gross, Neal, Ward S. Mason, and Alexander W. McEachern, *Explorations in Role Analysis: Studies of the School Superintendency Role*, New York: Wiley, 1958.

152 Grupp, Stanley E., "The Sociology of Gabriel Tarde," *Sociology and Social Research*, 52 (1968), pp. 333–47.

153 Gullahorn, John T., "Measuring Role Conflict," *American Journal of Sociology*, 61 (1956), pp. 299–303.

154 Hadden, Jeffrey K. and Raymond C. Rymph, "Social Structure and Civil Rights Involvement: A Case Study of Protestant Ministers," *Social Forces*, 45 (1967), pp. 51–61.

155 Hadley, Robert G. and William V. Levy, "Vocational Development and Reference Groups," *Journal of Counseling Psychology*, 9 (1962), pp. 110–14.

156 Hamilton, Richard F., "Income, Class, and Reference Groups," *American Sociological Review*, 29 (1964), pp. 576–79.

157 Harris, Edward E., *Self-Attitude Critiques and Proposals*, New York: American Press, 1969.

158 Hartley, Eugene, "Psychological Problems of Multiple Group Membership," in John H. Rohrer and Muzafer Sherif (eds.), *Social Psychology at the Crossroads*, New York: Harper and Brothers, 1951, pp. 371–87.

159 Hartley, Eugene L. and Ruth E. Hartley, *Fundamentals of Social Psychology*, New York: Alfred A. Knopf, 1952.

160 Hartley, Ruth E., "Personal Characteristics and Acceptance of Secondary Groups as Reference Groups," *Journal of Individual Psychology,* 13 (1957), pp. 45–55.

161 ———. "Sex-Role Pressures and the Socialization of the Male Child," *Psychological Reports,* 5 (1959), pp. 457–68.

162 ———. "Norm Compatibility, Norm Preference, and the Acceptance of New Reference Groups," *Journal of Social Psychology,* 52 (1960), pp. 87–95.

163 ———. "Personal Needs and the Acceptance of a New Group as a Reference Group," *Journal of Social Psychology,* 51 (1960), pp. 349–58.

164 ———. "Relationships Between Perceived Values and Acceptance of a New Reference Group," *Journal of Social Psychology,* 51 (1960), pp. 181–90.

165 Haskell, Martin R., "Toward A Reference Group Theory of Juvenile Delinquency," *Social Problems,* 8 (1960–61), pp. 220–30.

166 Hauser, Philip M., "Comment on Coleman's Paper," in Robert Bierstedt (ed.), *A Design for Sociology: Scope, Objectives, and Methods,* Monograph 9, Philadelphia: The American Academy of Political and Social Science, 1969, pp. 122–28.

167 Heiss, Jerold (ed.), *Family Roles and Interaction: An Anthology,* Chicago: Rand McNally, 1968.

168 Henry, Andrew F. and James F. Short, Jr., *Suicide and Homicide,* Glencoe, Ill.: Free Press, 1954.

169 Hermann, Margaret G. and Nathan Kogan, "Negotiation in Leader and Delegate Groups," *Journal of Conflict Resolution,* 12 (1968), pp. 332–34.

170 Herriott, Robert E., "Some Social Determinants of Educational Aspiration," *Harvard Educational Review,* 33 (1963), pp. 157–77.

171 Hickman, C. Addison and Manford H. Kuhn, *Individuals, Groups, and Economic Behavior,* New York: Dryden Press, 1956.

172 Hinkle, Roscoe C., Jr., and Gisela J. Hinkle, *The Development of Modern Sociology: Its Nature and Growth in the United States,* New York: Random House, 1954.

173 Hochbaum, Godfrey M., "The Relation Between Group Members' Self-Confidence and Their Reactions to Group Pressures to Uniformity," *American Sociological Review,* 19 (1954), pp. 678–87.

174 Holden, David E. W., "Associations as Reference Groups: An Approach to the Problem," *Rural Sociology,* 30 (1965), pp. 63–74.

175 Holsti, Ole R., *Content Analysis for the Social Sciences and Humanities,* Reading, Mass.: Addison-Wesley, 1969.

176 Homans, George C., *The Human Group,* New York: Harcourt, Brace, 1950.

177 ———. "Contemporary Theory in Sociology," in Robert E. L. Faris

(ed.), *Handbook of Modern Sociology*, Chicago: Rand McNally, 1964, pp. 951–77.

178 Hsu, Francis L. K., "Kinship and Ways of Life: An Exploration," in Francis L. K. Hsu (ed.), *Psychological Anthropology: Approaches to Culture and Personality*, Homewood, Ill.: Dorsey Press, 1961, pp. 400–456.

179 Hughes, Charles Campbell, *An Eskimo Village in the Modern World*, Ithaca, N. Y.: Cornell Univ. Press, 1960.

180 Hughes, Everett C., "What Other?" in Arnold M. Rose (ed.), *Human Behavior and Social Processes*, Boston: Houghton Mifflin, 1962, pp. 119–27.

181 Humke, Ronald Gene, "Political Advertisements and Voting: An Empirical Analysis," Master's thesis, Illinois State Univ., 1970.

182 Hyman, Herbert Hiram, "*The Psychology of Status*," Archives of Psychology, no. 269 (1942).

183 ———. *Political Socialization: A Study in the Psychology of Political Behavior*, Glencoe, Ill.: Free Press, 1959.

184 ———. "Reflections on Reference Groups," *Public Opinion Quarterly*, 24 (1960), pp. 383–96.

185 ———. "Reference Groups," in David L. Sills (ed.), *International Encyclopedia of the Social Sciences*, Vol. 13, United States: Macmillan and Free Press, 1968, pp. 353–61.

186 Hyman, Herbert H. and Eleanor Singer (eds.), *Readings in Reference Group Theory and Research*, New York: Free Press, 1968.

187 Hyman, Herbert H. and Charles R. Wright, "Voluntary Association Memberships of American Adults: Evidence from National Sample Surveys," *American Sociological Review*, 23 (1958), pp. 284–94.

188 Inkeles, Alex, "Personality and Social Structure," in Robert K. Merton, Leonard Broom, and Leonard S. Cottrell, Jr. (eds.), *Sociology Today: Problems and Prospects*, New York: Basic Books, 1959, pp. 249–76.

189 ———. "Sociology and Psychology," in Sigmund Koch (ed.), *Psychology: A Study of a Science*, Vol. 6, New York: McGraw-Hill, 1963, pp. 317–87.

190 ———. "Social Structure and the Socialization of Competence," *Harvard Educational Review*, 36 (1966), pp. 265–83.

191 ———. "Society, Social Structure, and Child Socialization," in John A. Clausen (ed.), *Socialization and Society*, Boston: Little, Brown, 1968, pp. 73–129.

192 Irwin, John, "Notes on the Present Status of the Concept Subculture," in David O. Arnold (ed.), *The Sociology of Subcultures*, Berkeley: Glendessary Press, 1970, pp. 164–70.

193 Israel, Joachim, *Self-Evaluation and Rejection in Groups*, Stockholm: Almqvist and Wiksell, 1956.

194 Jackman, Norman R., "Survival in the Concentration Camp," *Human Organization*, 17 (1958), pp. 23–26.

195 Jackson, Jay M., "A Space for Conceptualizing Person-Group Relationships," *Human Relations,* 12 (1959), pp. 3–15.

196 ———. "Reference Group Processes in a Formal Organization," *Sociometry,* 22 (1959), pp. 307–27.

197 Jahoda, Marie, "Conformity and Independence: A Psychological Analysis," *Human Relations,* 12 (1959), pp. 99–120.

198 Jahoda, Marie, Morton Deutsch, and Stuart W. Cook, *Research Methods in Social Relations: 1. Basic Processes,* New York: Dryden Press, 1951.

199 James, William, "The Self," in Chad Gordon and Kenneth J. Gergen (eds.), *The Self in Social Interaction,* New York: Wiley, 1968, pp. 41–49.

200 Janis, Irving L., "Personality Correlates of Susceptibility to Persuasion," *Journal of Personality,* 22 (1954), pp. 504–18.

201 Jennings, Helen Hall, "Sociometric Structure in Personality and Group Formation," in Muzafer Sherif and M. O. Wilson (eds.), *Group Relations at the Crossroads,* New York: Harper and Brothers, 1953, pp. 332–65.

202 Jones, Edward E. and Harold B. Gerard, *Foundations of Social Psychology,* New York: Wiley, 1967.

203 Jones, W. T., *The Romantic Syndrome: Toward a New Method in Cultural Anthropology and History of Ideas,* The Hague, Netherlands: Martinus Nijhoff, 1961.

204 Jourard, Sidney M., *The Transparent Self: Self-Disclosure and Well-Being,* Princeton, N. J.: D. Van Nostrand, 1964.

205 Kagan, Jerome, and William Phillips, "Measurement of Identification: A Methodological Note," *Journal of Abnormal and Social Psychology,* 69 (1964), pp. 442–44.

206 Kahn, Robert L., Donald M. Wolfe, Robert P. Quinn, J. Diedrick Snoek, and Robert A. Rosenthal, "Adjustment to Role Conflict and Ambiguity in Organizations," in Bruce J. Biddle and Edwin J. Thomas (eds.), *Role Theory: Concepts and Research,* New York: Wiley, 1966, pp. 277–82.

207 Kandel, Denise B. and Gerald S. Lesser, "Parental and Peer Influences on Educational Plans of Adolescents," *American Sociological Review,* 34 (1969), pp. 213–23.

208 Kanin, Eugene J., "Reference Groups and Sex Conduct Norm Violations," *Sociological Quarterly,* 8 (1967), pp. 495–504.

209 Kaplan, Abraham, *The Conduct of Inquiry: Methodology for Behavioral Science,* Scranton, Pa.: Chandler, 1964.

210 Kaplan, Norman, "Reference Group Theory and Voting Behavior," Ph.D. dissertation, Columbia Univ., 1955.

211 Katz, Elihu, and Paul F. Lazarsfeld, *Personal Influence: The Part Played by People in the Flow of Mass Communications,* Glencoe, Ill.: Free Press, 1955.

212 Kelley, Harold H., "Salience of Membership and Resistance to Change of Group-Anchored Attitudes," *Human Relations*, 8 (1955), pp. 275–89.

213 ———. "Two Functions of Reference Groups," in Herbert H. Hyman and Eleanor Singer (eds.), *Readings in Reference Group Theory and Research*, New York: Free Press, 1968, pp. 77–83.

214 Kelman, Herbert C., "Compliance, Identification and Internalization: Three Processes of Attitude Change," *Journal of Conflict Resolution*, 2 (1958), pp. 51–60.

215 ———. "Processes of Opinion Change," *Public Opinion Quarterly*, 25 (1961), pp. 57–78.

216 Kemper, Theodore D., "Self-Conceptions and the Expectations of Significant Others," *Sociological Quarterly*, 7 (1966), pp. 323–43.

217 ———. "Reference Groups, Socialization and Achievement," *American Sociological Review*, 33 (1968), pp. 31–45.

218 Kephart, William M., "A Quantitative Analysis of Intragroup Relationships," *American Journal of Sociology*, 55 (1950), pp. 544–49.

219 Killian, Lewis M., "The Significance of Multiple-Group Membership in Disaster," *American Journal of Sociology*, 57 (1952), pp. 309–14.

220 Klapp, Orrin E., *Symbolic Leaders: Public Dramas and Public Men*, Chicago: Aldine, 1964.

221 ———. *Collective Search for Identity*, New York: Holt, Rinehart and Winston, 1969.

222 Klein, Alan F., "Role and Reference Group Theory: Implications for Social Group Work Research," in L. Kegan (ed.), *Social Science Theory and Social Work Research*, New York: National Association of Social Workers, 1960, pp. 32–45.

223 Koch, Sigmund (ed.), *Psychology: A Study of a Science*, Vol. 5, New York: McGraw-Hill, 1963.

224 Komarovsky, Mirra, *Blue-Collar Marriage*, New York: Random House, 1962.

225 Krieger, Alex D., "The Typological Concept," *American Antiquity*, 3 (1944), pp. 271–88.

226 Kuhn, Manford, "Reference Group," in Julius Gould and William L. Kolb (eds.), *A Dictionary of the Social Sciences*, New York: Free Press of Glencoe, 1964, pp. 580–81.

227 ———. "Social Object," in Julius Gould and William L. Kolb (eds.), *A Dictionary of the Social Sciences*, Glencoe, Ill.: Free Press, 1964, pp. 659–60.

228 ———. "Major Trends in Symbolic Interaction Theory in the Past Twenty-Five Years," *Sociological Quarterly*, 5 (1964), pp. 61–84.

229 ———. "The Reference Group Reconsidered," *Sociological Quarterly*, 5 (1964), pp. 5–21.

230 Lazarsfeld, Paul F., Bernard Berelson and Hazel Gaudet, *The People's Choice*, New York: Columbia Univ. Press, 1944.

231 Lefcourt, Herbert M. and Gordon W. Ladwig, "The Effect of Reference

Group Upon Negroes' Task Persistence in a Biracial Competitive Game," *Journal of Personality and Social Psychology*, 1 (1965), pp. 668–71.

232 Lemert, Edwin M., "Social Structure, Social Control, and Deviation," in Marshall B. Clinard (ed.), *Anomie and Deviant Behavior*, New York: Free Press, 1964, pp. 57–97.

233 Lenski, Gerhard E., "Status Crystallization: A Non-Vertical Dimension of Social Status," *American Sociological Review*, 19 (1954), pp. 405–13.

234 Leontief, Wassily, "Note on the Pluralistic Interpretation of History and the Problem of Interdisciplinary Cooperation," *Journal of Philosophy*, 45 (1948), pp. 617–24.

235 Levinson, Daniel J., "Role, Personality, and Social Structure in the Organizational Setting," *Journal of Abnormal and Social Psychology*, 58 (1959), pp. 170–80.

236 Levy, Marion J., *The Structure of Society*, Princeton, N. J.: Princeton Univ. Press, 1952.

237 Lewin, Kurt, "Psycho-Sociological Problems of a Minority Group," *Character and Personality*, 3 (1935), pp. 175–87.

238 ———. *Resolving Social Conflicts: Selected Papers on Group Dynamics*, New York: Harper and Brothers, 1948.

239 Lindesmith, Alfred R. and Anselm L. Strauss, *Social Psychology*, 3rd ed., New York: Holt, Rinehart and Winston, 1968.

240 Linn, Erwin L., "Reference Group: A Case Study in Conceptual Diffusion," *Sociological Quarterly*, 7 (1966), pp. 489–99.

241 Linn, Lawrence S., "Social Identification and the Use of Marijuana," *International Journal of the Addictions*, 6 (1971), pp. 79–107.

242 Linton, Ralph, *The Study of Man*, New York: Appleton-Century-Crofts, 1936.

243 Lipset, Seymour Martin and Martin Trow, "Reference Group Theory and Trade Union Wage Policy," in Mirra Komarovsky (ed.), *Common Frontiers of the Social Sciences*, Glencoe, Ill.: Free Press, 1957, pp. 391–411.

244 Litwak, Eugene, "Group Pressure and Family Breakup: A Study of German Communities," *American Journal of Sociology*, 61 (1956), pp. 345–54.

245 ———. "Reference Group Theory, Bureaucratic Career, and Neighborhood Primary Group Cohesion," *Sociometry*, 23 (1960), pp. 72–83.

246 Liu, William T., "The Community Reference System, Religiosity and Race Attitudes," *Social Forces*, 39 (1961), pp. 324–28.

247 Louch, A. R., *Explanation and Human Action*, Berkeley: Univ. of California Press, 1966.

248 Lowe, Jay, "Prediction of Delinquency With an Attitudinal Configuration Model," *Social Forces*, 45 (1966), pp. 106–13.

249 McCall, George J., Michal M. McCall, Norman K. Denzin, Gerald D.

Suttles, and Suzanne B. Kurth (eds.), *Social Relationships*, Chicago: Aldine, 1970.

250 McCall, George J. and J. L. Simmons, *Identities and Interactions: An Examination of Human Associations in Everyday Life*, New York: Free Press, 1966.

251 McCall, George J. and J. L. Simmons (eds.), *Issues in Participant Observation: A Text and Reader*, Reading, Mass.: Addison-Wesley, 1969.

252 McDill, Edward L. and James Coleman, "Family and Peer Influences in College Plans of High Schools Students," *Sociology of Education*, 38 (1965), pp. 112–26.

253 Mack, Raymond W., "Riot, Revolt, or Responsible Revolution: Of Reference Groups and Racism," *Sociological Quarterly*, 10 (1969), pp. 147–56.

254 McKinney, John C., *Constructive Typology and Social Theory*, New York: Meredith, 1966.

255 ———. "Typification, Typologies, and Sociological Theory," *Social Forces*, 48 (1969), pp. 1–12.

256 Madge, John, *The Origins of Scientific Sociology*, New York: Free Press of Glencoe, 1962.

257 Manis, Jerome G. and Bernard N. Meltzer (eds.), *Symbolic Interaction: A Reader in Social Psychology*, Boston: Allyn and Bacon, 1967.

258 Mannheim, Bilha F., "Reference Groups, Membership Groups and the Self Image," *Sociometry*, 29 (1966), pp. 265–79.

259 Martindale, Don, *The Nature and Types of Sociological Theory*, Boston: Houghton Mifflin, 1960.

260 Matthews, Victor, "Differential Identification: An Empirical Note," *Social Problems*, 15 (1968), pp. 376–83.

261 Matza, David, *Delinquency and Drift*, New York: Wiley, 1964.

262 ———. "Poverty and Disrepute," in Robert K. Merton and Robert A. Nisbet (eds.), *Contemporary Social Problems*, 2nd ed., New York: Harcourt, Brace and World, 1966, pp. 619–69.

263 ———. *Becoming Deviant*, Englewood Cliffs, N. J.: Prentice-Hall, 1969.

264 Mauss, Armand L., "Anticipatory Socialization Toward College as a Factor in Adolescent Marijuana Use," *Social Problems*, 16 (1969), pp. 357–64.

265 May, Francis C., Jr., "Book Review of *Readings in Reference Group Theory and Research* edited by Herbert H. Hyman and Eleanor Singer," *Social Forces*, 47 (1969), p. 373.

266 Meltzer, Bernard N., "Mead's Social Psychology," in Jerome G. Manis and Bernard N. Meltzer (eds.), *Symbolic Interaction: A Reader in Social Psychology*, Boston: Allyn and Bacon, 1967, pp. 5–24.

267 Meltzer, Bernard N. and John W. Petras, "The Chicago and Iowa Schools of Symbolic Interactionism," in Tamotsu Shibutani (ed.),

Human Nature and Collective Behavior: Papers in Honor of Herbert Blumer, Englewood Cliffs, N. J.: Prentice-Hall, 1970, pp. 3–17.

268 Merrill, Francis E., "The Self and the Other: An Emerging Field of Social Problems," *Social Problems,* 4 (1957), pp. 200–207.

269 ———. "Stendhal and the Self: A Study in the Sociology of Literature," *American Journal of Sociology,* 66 (1961), pp. 446–53.

270 Merton, Robert K., "The Role-Set: Problems in Sociological Theory," *British Journal of Sociology,* 8 (1957), pp. 106–20.

271 ———. *Social Theory and Social Structure,* 2nd ed., Glencoe, Ill.: Free Press, 1957.

272 Merton, Robert K. and Alice S. Kitt, "Contributions to the Theory of Reference Group Behavior," in Robert K. Merton and Paul F. Lazarsfeld (eds.), *Continuities in Social Research: Studies in the Scope and Method of "The American Soldier,"* Glencoe, Ill.: Free Press, 1950, pp. 40–105.

273 Miller, Delbert C. and Fremont A. Shull, Jr., "The Prediction of Administrative Role Conflict Resolutions," *Administrative Science Quarterly,* 7 (1962), pp. 143–60.

274 Mirande, Alfred M., "Reference Group Theory and Adolescent Sexual Behavior," *Journal of Marriage and the Family,* 30 (1968), pp. 572–77.

275 Mishler, Elliot G., "Personality Characteristics and the Resolution of Role Conflicts," *Public Opinion Quarterly,* 17 (1953), pp. 115–35.

276 Miyamoto, S. Frank, "Self, Motivation, and Symbolic Interactionist Theory," in Tamotsu Shibutani (ed.), *Human Nature and Collective Behavior: Papers in Honor of Herbert Blumer,* Englewood Cliffs, N. J.: Prentice-Hall, 1970, pp. 271–85.

277 Miyamoto, S. Frank and Sanford M. Dornbusch, "A Test of Interactionist Hypotheses of Self-Conception," *American Journal of Sociology,* 61 (1956), pp. 399–403.

278 Moore, Harvey Allan, "The Significant Others of a College Population: A Replication and Extension of Research," Master's thesis, Illinois State Univ., 1969.

279 Murdock, George Peter, *Social Structure,* New York: Macmillan, 1949.

280 Mussen, Paul and Luther Distler, "Masculinity, Identification, and Father-Son Relationship," *Journal of Abnormal and Social Psychology,* 59 (1959), pp. 350–56.

281 Nadel, S. F., *The Theory of Social Structure,* Glencoe, Ill.: Free Press, 1957.

282 Nahemow, Lucille and Ruth Bennett, "Conformity, Persuasibility and Counternormative Persuasion," *Sociometry,* 30 (1967), pp. 14–25.

283 Nelson, Harold A., "A Tentative Foundation for Reference Group Theory," *Sociology and Social Research,* 45 (1961), pp. 274–80.

284 Newcomb, Theodore M., *Personality and Social Change: Attitude Formation in a Study Community,* New York: Dryden Press, 1943.

285 ———. *Social Psychology*, New York: Holt, 1950.

286 ———. "Book Review of *Continuities in Social Research: Studies in the Scope and Method of 'The American Soldier'* edited by Robert K. Merton and Paul F. Lazarsfeld," *American Journal of Sociology*, 57 (1951), pp. 90–92.

287 ———. "Attitude Development as a Function of Reference Groups: The Bennington Study," in Herbert H. Hyman and Eleanor Singer (eds.), *Readings in Reference Group Theory and Research*, New York: Free Press, 1968, pp. 374–86.

288 Newcomb, Theodore M., Kathryn E. Koenig, Richard Flacks, and Donald P. Warwick, *Persistence and Change: Bennington College and Its Students After Twenty-five Years*, New York: Wiley, 1967.

289 Olmsted, Michael S., *The Small Group*, New York: Random House, 1959.

290 Olsen, Marvin E., *The Process of Social Organization*, New York: Holt, Rinehart and Winston, 1968.

291 Parker, Seymour and Robert Kleiner, "Status Position, Mobility, and Ethnic Identification of the Negro," *Journal of Social Issues*, 20 (1964), pp. 85–102.

292 ———. *Mental Illness in the Urban Negro Community*, New York: Free Press, 1966.

293 Parsons, Talcott, *The Social System*, Glencoe, Ill.: Free Press, 1951.

294 ———. "Cooley and the Problem of Internalization," in Albert J. Reiss, Jr. (ed.), *Cooley and Sociological Analysis*, Ann Arbor: Univ. of Michigan Press, 1968, pp. 48–67.

295 Patchen, Martin, "The Effect of Reference Group Standards on Job Satisfactions," *Human Relations*, 11 (1958), pp. 303–14.

296 ———. "A Conceptual Framework and Some Empirical Data Regarding Comparisons of Social Rewards," *Sociometry*, 24 (1961), pp. 136–56.

297 Paynton, Clifford T., "A Suggestion for Reference Group Theory: Ideational Referents and Group Referents," *Canadian Review of Social Anthropology*, 3 (1966), pp. 214–23.

298 Perry, Helen Swick, Introduction to "Schizophrenia as a Human Process," in Helen Swick Perry (ed.), *The Collected Works of Harry Stack Sullivan, M.D.*, Vol. 2, New York: W. W. Norton, 1964, pp. xi–xxxi.

299 Petroni, Frank A., "Significant Others and Illness Behavior: A Much Neglected Sick Role Contingency," *Sociological Quarterly*, 10 (1969), pp. 32–41.

300 Pettigrew, Thomas F., "Social Evaluation Theory: Convergences and Applications," in *Nebraska Symposium on Motivation*, Lincoln: Univ. of Nebraska Press, 1967, pp. 241–311.

301 Pilisuk, Marc, "Book Review of *Readings in Reference Group Theory*

and Research edited by Herbert H. Hyman and Eleanor Singer," *American Sociological Review,* 34 (1969), pp. 118–19.

302 Plotnicov, Leonard, "Fixed Membership Groups: The Locus of Culture Processes," *American Anthropologist,* 64 (1962), pp. 97–103.

303 Pollis, Nicholas P., "Reference Group Re-Examined," *British Journal of Sociology,* 19 (1968), pp. 300–307.

304 Pollis, Nicholas P. and Carol A. Pollis, "Sociological Referents of Social Norms," *Sociological Quarterly,* 11 (1970), pp. 230–42.

305 Polsky, Ned, *Hustlers, Beats, and Others,* Garden City, N. Y.: Double-day Anchor Book, 1967.

306 Pool, Ithiel de Sola and Irwin Shulman, "Newsmen's Fantasies, Audiences, and Newswriting," *Public Opinion Quarterly,* 23 (1959), pp. 145–58.

307 Preiss, Jack J. and Howard J. Ehrlich, *An Examination of Role Theory: The Case of the State Police,* Lincoln: Univ. of Nebraska Press, 1966.

308 Priest, Robert F., "Election Jokes: The Effects of Reference Group Membership," *Psychological Reports,* 18 (1966), pp. 600–602.

309 ———. "Book Review of *Readings in Reference Group Theory and Research* edited by Herbert H. Hyman and Eleanor Singer," *Sociology and Social Research,* 53 (1969), pp. 555–57.

310 Quarantelli, E. L. and Joseph Cooper, "Self-Conceptions and Others: A Further Test of Meadian Hypotheses," *Sociological Quarterly,* 7 (1966), pp. 281–97.

311 Quinney, Richard, *The Problem of Crime,* New York: Dodd, Mead, 1970.

312 Raven, Bertram H. and Philip S. Gallo, "The Effects of Nominating Conventions, Elections, and Reference Group Identification upon the Perception of Political Figures," *Human Relations,* 18 (1965), pp. 217–29.

313 Redfield, Robert, "The Folk Society," *American Journal of Sociology,* 52 (1947), pp. 293–308.

314 ———. "The Natural History of the Folk Society," *Social Forces,* 31 (1953), pp. 224–28.

315 Reeder, Leo G., George A. Donohue and Arturo Biblarz, "Conceptions of Self and Others," *American Journal of Sociology,* 66 (1960), pp. 153–59.

316 Reiss, Albert J., Jr. and A. Lewis Rhodes, "An Empirical Test of Differential Association Theory," *Journal of Research in Crime and Delinquency,* 1 (1964), pp. 5–18.

317 Reiss, Ira L., *The Social Context of Premarital Sexual Permissiveness,* New York: Holt, Rinehart and Winston, 1967.

318 Rescher, Nicholas, "Fundamental Problems in the Theory of Scientific Explanation," in Bernard Baumrin (ed.), *Philosophy of Science: The Delaware Seminar,* Vol. 2, New York: Interscience Publishers, 1963, pp. 41–60.

319 Rhodes, Lewis, "Anomia, Aspiration, and Status," *Social Forces*, 42 (1964), pp. 434–40.

320 Rice, Stuart A., *Quantitative Methods in Politics*, New York: Knopf, 1928.

321 Riesman, David, Nathan Glazer, and Reuel Denney, *The Lonely Crowd: A Study of the Changing American Character*, Garden City, N. Y.: Doubleday Anchor Book, 1950.

322 Riley, Matilda White, *Sociological Research*: 1. *A Case Approach*, New York: Harcourt, Brace and World, 1963.

323 Robinson, W. S., "The Logical Structure of Analytic Induction," *American Sociological Review*, 16 (1951), pp. 812–18.

324 Rogers, Everett M., "Reference Group Influences on Student Drinking Behavior," *Quarterly Journal of Studies on Alcohol*, 19 (1958), pp. 244–54.

325 Rokeach, Milton, *The Three Christs of Ypsilanti: A Psychological Study*, New York: Knopf, 1964.

326 Rommetveit, Ragnar, *Social Norms and Roles: Explorations in the Psychology of Enduring Social Pressures*, Minneapolis: Univ. of Minnesota Press, 1955.

327 Roper, Elmo, "Classifying Respondents by Economic Status," *Public Opinion Quarterly*, 4 (1940), pp. 270–72.

328 Rose, Arnold M., "Reference Groups of Rural High School Youth," *Child Development*, 27 (1956), pp. 351–63.

329 ———. "A Systematic Summary of Symbolic Interaction Theory," in Arnold M. Rose (ed.), *Human Behavior and Social Processes: An Interactionist Approach*, Boston: Houghton Mifflin, 1962, pp. 3–19.

330 ——— (ed.). *Human Behavior and Social Processes: An Interactionist Approach*, Boston: Houghton Mifflin, 1962.

331 Rose, Jerry D., "The Role of the Other in Self-Evaluation," *Sociological Quarterly*, 10 (1969), pp. 470–79.

332 Rosen, Bernard C., "Conflicting Group Membership: A Study of Parent-Peer Group Cross-Pressures," *American Sociological Review*, 20 (1955), pp. 155–61.

333 ———. "The Reference Group Approach to the Parental Factor in Attitude and Behavior Formation," *Social Forces*, 34 (1955), pp. 137–44.

334 Rosenberg, George S., *The Worker Grows Old*, San Francisco: Jossey-Bass, 1970.

335 Rosenman, Stanley, "The Similarity and the Coding of the Self-Concept and the Other-Concept," *Journal of General Psychology*, 56 (1957), pp. 243–50.

336 Rouse, Irving, "The Classification of Artifacts in Archaeology," *American Antiquity*, 25 (1960), pp. 313–23.

337 Runciman, Walter Garrison, *Relative Deprivation and Social Justice: A*

Study of Attitudes to Social Inequality in Twentieth-Century England, Berkeley: Univ. of California Press, 1966.

338 ⸺. "Problems of Research on Relative Deprivation," in Herbert H. Hyman and Eleanor Singer (eds.), *Readings in Reference Group Theory and Research*, New York: Free Press, 1968, pp. 69–76.

339 Sampson, Samuel Franklin, "A Historical Review and Critical Appraisal of the Reference Group Concept in Psychology and Sociology," Master's thesis, Univ. of Oklahoma, 1961.

340 Sanford, Nevitt, "The Dynamics of Identification," *Psychological Review*, 62 (1955), pp. 106–18.

341 Saveth, Edward N., "The American Patrician Class: A Field of Research," *American Quarterly*, 15 (1963), pp. 235–52.

342 Schachter, Stanley, *The Psychology of Affiliation: Experimental Studies of the Sources of Gregariousness*, Stanford, Calif.: Stanford Univ. Press, 1959.

343 Schachter, S. and J. E. Singer, "Cognitive, Social and Physiological Determinants of Emotional State," *Psychological Review*, 69 (1962), pp. 379–99.

344 Schmitt, Raymond L., "Major Role Change and Self Change," *Sociological Quarterly*, 7 (1966), pp. 311–22.

345 ⸺. "A Note on the Value of the Stimulus in Experimental Situations," *Sociological Quarterly*, 8 (1967), pp. 407–10.

346 Schmitt, Raymond L. and B. R. Audas, "A Descriptive Study of Internalized Audiences," *Sociological Focus*, 1 (1968), pp. 1–21.

347 Scriven, Michael, "Explanation and Prediction in Evolutionary Theory," *Science*, 130 (1959), pp. 477–82.

348 ⸺. "The Limits of Physical Explanation," in Bernard Baumrin (ed.), *Philosophy of Science: The Delaware Seminar*, Vol. 2, New York: Interscience Publishers, 1963, pp. 107–35.

349 Sears, Robert R., Eleanor E. Maccoby, and Harry Levin, *Patterns of Child Rearing*, Evanston, Ill.: Row, Peterson, 1957.

350 Secord, Paul F. and Carl W. Backman, *Social Psychology*, New York: McGraw-Hill, 1964.

351 Seeman, Melvin, "Role Conflict and Ambivalence in Leadership," *American Sociological Review*, 18 (1953), pp. 373–80.

352 ⸺. "On the Meaning of Alienation," *American Sociological Review*, 24 (1959), pp. 783–91.

353 Seeman, Melvin and John W. Evans, "Apprenticeship and Attitude Change," *American Journal of Sociology*, 67 (1962), pp. 365–78.

354 Selltiz, Claire, Marie Jahoda, Morton Deutsch, and Stuart W. Cook, *Research Methods in Social Relations*, 2nd ed., New York: Holt, Rinehart and Winston, 1959.

355 Sewell, William H., "Community of Residence and College Plans," *American Sociological Review*, 29 (1964), pp. 24–38.

356 Sewell, William H. and Vimal P. Shah, "Social Class, Parental Encourage-

ment, and Educational Aspirations," *American Journal of Sociology*, 73 (1968), pp. 559–72.

357 Sharples, G. E. Ned, "Insignificant Others and the Social Role of the Disabled," Unpublished paper, Univ. of Michigan, 1970.

358 Shaw, Marvin E. and Philip R. Costanzo, *Theories of Social Psychology*, New York: McGraw-Hill, 1970.

359 Shaw, Marvin E. and Jack M. Wright, *Scales for the Measurement of Attitudes*, New York: McGraw-Hill, 1967.

360 Sherif, Muzafer, *The Psychology of Social Norms*, New York: Harper and Brothers, 1936.

361 ———. *An Outline of Social Psychology*, New York: Harper and Brothers, 1948.

362 ———. *Social Interaction: Process and Products*, Chicago: Aldine, 1967.

363 Sherif, Muzafer and Hadley Cantril, *The Psychology of Ego-Involvements: Social Attitudes and Identifications*, New York: Wiley, 1947.

364 Sherif, Muzafer and Carolyn W. Sherif, *Groups in Harmony and Tension: An Integration of Studies on Intergroup Relations*, New York: Harper and Brothers, 1953.

365 ———. *Reference Groups: Exploration into Conformity and Deviation of Adolescents*, New York: Harper and Row, 1964.

366 ———. *Social Psychology*, New York: Harper and Row, 1969.

367 Sherman, Richard B., "Status Revolution and Reference Group Theory," in Edward N. Saveth (ed.), *American History and the Social Sciences*, New York: Free Press of Glencoe, 1964, pp. 196–201.

368 Sherwood, John J., "Self Identity and Referent Others," *Sociometry*, 28 (1965), pp. 66–81.

369 Shibutani, Tamotsu, "Reference Groups as Perspectives," *American Journal of Sociology*, 60 (1955), pp. 562–69.

370 ———. *Society and Personality: An Interactionist Approach to Social Psychology*, Englewood Cliffs, N. J.: Prentice-Hall, 1961.

371 ———. "Reference Groups and Social Control," in Arnold M. Rose (ed.), *Human Behavior and Social Processes*, Boston: Houghton Mifflin, 1962, pp. 128–47.

372 Siegel, Alberta Engvall and Sidney Siegel, "Reference Groups, Membership Groups, and Attitude Change," *Journal of Abnormal and Social Psychology*, 55 (1957), pp. 360–64.

373 Simmel, Edward C., Ronald A. Hoppe and G. Alexander Milton, *Social Facilitation and Imitative Behavior*, Boston: Allyn and Bacon, 1968.

374 Simmel, Georg, "Sur quelques relations de la pensée théoriques avec les intérêts pratiques," *Revue de Métaphysique et de Morale*, 4, No. 2 (1896), pp. 160–78.

375 ———. *Conflict and The Web of Group-Affiliations*, Glencoe, Ill.: Free Press, 1955, pp. 125–95.

376 Simmons, Roberta G., "The Experimentally-Increased Salience of Ex-

treme Comparative Reference Groups," *Sociology and Social Research,* 53 (1969), pp. 490–99.

377 Simon, Julian L., "Doctors, Smoking, and Reference Groups," *Public Opinion Quarterly,* 31 (1967), pp. 646–47.

378 Simpson, Richard L., "Parental Influence, Anticipatory Socialization, and Social Mobility," *American Sociological Review,* 27 (1962), pp. 517–22.

379 Singer, Jerome E., "Social Comparison—Progress and Issues," *Journal of Experimental Social Psychology,* 2, Suppl. 1 (1966), pp. 103–10.

380 Slocum, W. L., "Some Sociological Aspects of Occupational Choice," *American Journal of Economics and Sociology,* 18 (1959), pp. 139–47.

381 Smelser, Neil J., "The Optimum Scope of Sociology," in Robert Bierstedt (ed.), *A Design for Sociology: Scope, Objectives, and Methods,* Philadelphia: The American Academy of Political and Social Science, 1969, pp. 1–21.

382 Smith, David Horton, "A Parsimonious Definition of 'Group': Toward Conceptual Clarity and Scientific Utility," *Sociological Inquiry,* 37 (1967), pp. 141–67.

383 Spitzer, Stephan, Carl Couch, and John Stratton, *The Assessment of the Self,* Iowa City, Iowa: Sernoll, 1971.

384 Spitzer, Stephan P. and Robert M. Swanson, "Sociological Perspectives on the Person," in Stephan P. Spitzer (ed.), *The Sociology of Personality,* New York: Van Nostrand Reinhold, 1969, pp. 189–207.

385 Stern, Eric and Suzanne Keller, "Spontaneous Group Reference in France," *Public Opinion Quarterly,* 17 (1963), pp. 208–17.

386 Stinchcombe, Arthur L., *Constructing Social Theories,* New York: Harcourt, Brace and World, 1968.

387 Stone, Gregory P., "Book Review of *Social Theory and Social Structure* (2nd ed.) by Robert K. Merton," *Administrative Science Quarterly,* 2 (1958), pp. 556–62.

388 Stone, Gregory P. and Harvey A. Farberman, *Social Psychology Through Symbolic Interaction,* Waltham, Mass.: Ginn-Blaisdell, 1970.

389 Stouffer, Samuel A., "An Analysis of Conflicting Social Norms," *American Sociological Review,* 14 (1949), pp. 707–17.

390 ———. "Some Afterthoughts of a Contributor to 'The American Soldier,'" in Robert K. Merton and Paul F. Lazarsfeld (eds.), *Continuities in Social Research: Studies in the Scope and Method of "The American Soldier,"* Glencoe, Ill.: Free Press, 1950, pp. 197–211.

391 ———. *Social Research to Test Ideas,* New York: Free Press of Glencoe, 1962.

392 Stouffer, Samuel A., Edward A. Suchman, Leland C. DeVinney, Shirley A. Star, and Robin M. Williams, Jr., *The American Soldier: Adjustment During Army Life,* Vol. 1, Princeton, N. J.: Princeton Univ. Press, 1949.

393 Stouffer, Samuel A. and Jackson Toby, "Role Conflict and Personality," *American Journal of Sociology*, 56 (1951), pp. 395–406.

394 Stratton, John R., "Differential Identification and Attitudes Toward the Law," *Social Forces*, 46 (1968), pp. 256–62.

395 Strauss, Anselm L., *Mirrors and Masks: The Search for Identity*, Glencoe, Ill.: Free Press, 1959.

396 Strauss, Helen May, "Reference Group and Social Comparison Processes Among the Totally Blind," in Herbert H. Hyman and Eleanor Singer (eds.), *Readings in Reference Group Theory and Research*, New York: Free Press, 1968, pp. 222–37.

397 Stryker, Sheldon, "Identity Salience and Role Performance: The Relevance of Symbolic Interaction Theory for Family Research," *Journal of Marriage and the Family*, 30 (1968), pp. 558–64.

398 Sullivan, Harry Stack, *Conceptions of Modern Psychiatry*, New York: W. W. Norton, 1940.

399 Sumner, William Graham, *Folkways*, New York: Mentor, 1960.

400 Sutherland, Edwin H., *Principles of Criminology*, 3rd ed., Philadelphia: J. B. Lippincott, 1939.

401 Thomas, Edwin J. and Bruce J. Biddle, "The Conceptual Structure" (Chs. 2 and 3), in Bruce J. Biddle and Edwin J. Thomas (eds.), *Role Theory: Concepts and Research*, New York: Wiley, 1966, pp. 23–51.

402 Thoreau, Henry David, *Walden or Life in the Woods*, New York: New American Library, 1942.

403 Toby, Jackson, "Some Variables in Role Conflict Analysis," *Social Forces*, 30 (1951), pp. 323–27.

404 ———. "Is Punishment Necessary?", *Journal of Criminal Law, Criminology and Police Science*, 55 (1964), pp. 332–37.

405 Tomeh, Aida K., "The Impact of Reference Groups on the Educational and Occupational Aspirations of Women College Students," *Journal of Marriage and the Family*, 30 (1968), pp. 102–10.

406 ———. "Reference-Group Supports Among Middle Eastern College Students," *Journal of Marriage and the Family*, 32 (1970), pp. 156–66.

407 Triplett, N., "The Dynamogenic Factors in Pacemaking and Competition," *American Journal of Psychology*, 9 (1897), pp. 507–33.

408 Turner, Ralph H., "Self and Other in Moral Judgment," *American Sociological Review*, 19 (1954), pp. 249–59.

409 ———. "Reference Groups of Future-Oriented Men," *Social Forces*, 34 (1955), pp. 130–36.

410 ———. "Role-Taking, Role Standpoint, and Reference-Group Behavior," *American Journal of Sociology*, 61 (1956), pp. 316–28.

411 ———. "Role-Taking: Process Versus Conformity," in Arnold M. Rose (ed.), *Human Behavior and Social Processes*, Boston: Houghton Mifflin, 1962, pp. 20–40.

412 Turner, Ralph H., "Upward Mobility and Class Values," *Social Problems,*
11 (1964), pp. 359–71.

413 Vander Zanden, James W., *American Minority Relations: The Sociology
of Race and Ethnic Groups,* New York: Ronald Press, 1963.

414 ———. *Sociology: A Systematic Approach,* New York: Ronald Press,
1965.

415 Verba, Sidney, *Small Groups and Political Behavior: A Study of Leadership,* Princeton, N. J.: Princeton Univ. Press, 1961.

416 Videbeck, Richard, "Self-Conception and the Reactions of Others," *Sociometry,* 23 (1960), pp. 351–59.

417 Vincent, Clark, *Unmarried Mothers,* New York: Free Press of Glencoe,
1961.

418 Wallace, Samuel E., "Reference Group Behavior in Occupational Role
Socialization," *Sociological Quarterly,* 7 (1966), pp. 366–72.

419 Wallace, Walter L. (ed.), *Sociological Theory,* Chicago: Aldine, 1969.

420 Warnecke, Richard B. and Kurt W. Back, "Dropouts from a Collegiate
Nursing Program: An Attempt at Quantifying Typologies," Unpublished paper, Duke Univ., 1966.

421 Warriner, Charles K., "Groups Are Real: A Reaffirmation," *American
Sociological Review,* 21 (1956), pp. 549–54.

422 Warshay, Leon H., "The Current State of Sociological Theory: Diversity,
Polarity, Empiricism, and Small Theories," *Sociological Quarterly,*
12 (1971), pp. 23–45.

423 Watson, Goodwin, *Social Psychology: Issues and Insights,* Philadelphia
and New York: J. B. Lippincott, 1966.

424 Webb, Eugene J., Donald T. Campbell, Richard D. Schwartz, and Lee
Sechrest, *Unobtrusive Measures: Nonreactive Research in the Social
Sciences,* Chicago: Rand McNally, 1966.

425 Weller, Jack E., *Yesterday's People: Life in Contemporary Appalachia,*
Lexington, Ky.: Univ. of Kentucky Press, 1965.

426 Wheeler, Ladd, *Interpersonal Influence,* Boston: Allyn and Bacon, 1970.

427 Wheeler, Ladd, Kelly G. Shaver, Russell A. Jones, George R. Goethals,
Joel Cooper and James E. Robinson, Charles L. Gruder, and Kent W.
Butzine, "Factors Determining Choice of a Comparison Other," *Jour-
nal of Experimental Social Psychology,* 5 (1969), pp. 219–32.

428 Wheeler, Stanton, "Socialization in Correctional Communities, *American Sociological Review,* 26 (1961), pp. 697–712.

429 Whitehurst, Robert N., "Premarital Reference-Group Orientations and
Marriage Adjustment," *Journal of Marriage and the Family,* 30
(1968), pp. 397–401.

430 Wilensky, Harold L., "The Moonlighter: A Product of Relative Deprivation," *Industrial Relations,* 3 (1963), pp. 105–24.

431 Williams, Margaret Aasterud, "Reference Groups: A Review and Commentary," *Sociological Quarterly,* 11 (1970), pp. 545–54.

432 Wilson, Alan B., "Residential Segregation of Social Classes and Aspirations of High School Boys," *American Sociological Review*, 24 (1959), pp. 836–45.

433 Winch, Robert F., "Heuristic and Empirical Typologies: A Job for Factor Analysis," *American Sociological Review*, 12 (1947), pp. 68–75.

434 Woelfel, Joseph and Archibald O. Haller, "Significant Others, the Self-Reflexive Act and the Attitude Formation Process," *American Sociological Review*, 36 (1971), pp. 74–87.

435 Wolff, Kurt H., "The Sociology of Knowledge and Sociological Theory," in James E. Curtis and John W. Petras (eds.), *The Sociology of Knowledge*, New York: Praeger Publishers, 1970, pp. 545–56.

436 Wood, S. M., "Uniform—Its Significance as a Factor in Role-Relationships," *Sociological Review*, 14 (1966), pp. 139–51.

437 Wrong, Dennis H., "The Over-Socialized Conception of Man in Modern Sociology," *American Sociological Review*, 26 (1961), pp. 183–93.

438 Wylie, Ruth C., *The Self Concept: A Critical Survey of Pertinent Research Literature*, Lincoln: Univ. of Nebraska Press, 1961.

439 Yinger, J. Milton, "Contraculture and Subculture," *American Sociological Review*, 25 (1960), pp. 625–35.

440 Zetterberg, Hans, *On Theory and Verification in Sociology*, Totawa, N. J.: Bedminister Press, 1963.

441 Zimmerman, Claire and Raymond A. Bauer, "The Effect of an Audience Upon What Is Remembered," *Public Opinion Quarterly*, 20 (1956), pp. 238–48.

442 Zurcher, Louis A., Jr., David W. Sonenschein, and Eric L. Metzner, "The Hasher: A Study of Role Conflict," *Social Forces*, 44 (1966), pp. 505–14.

Index

in relationship to study of reference others, 182–83

Moore, Harvey Allan: studied orientational and role-specific reference others, 69, 86, 157

Motivation: and reference group studies of educational plans, 126–28; reference group socialization theory related to, 138; part of Kemper's achievement explanation, 152–53; related to reference group theory by Kuhn in one of few symbolic interactional efforts to emphasize structure, 186

Multiple reference groups: in Merton and Kitt effort, 34, 97. *See also* Multiple reference others

Multiple reference others: and expansion of reference set, 97; and reference relationship formation, 97–98; and differential influence of, 97–98; and identification-object reference relationship conflict, 98–99; and normative reference relationship conflict, 101–2; and consensus of reference others in conflict resolution, 111; and size of reference set in conflict resolution, 112–13; and significance of the future study of the relative importance of reference others in reference sets, 188

Multivariate statistical techniques: method of controlling extraneous variables, 167; and importance for reference other theorist, 169; limitations of, 169

Murdock, George Peter: work shows influence of social structure upon reference relationship formation process, 78–79

Murray, John S., 85, 115

Mussen, Paul, 93

Nadel, S. F., 76, 85

Nahemow, Lucille: source relating reference group theory to conformity, 10, 137

National stereotypes: reference group study of, 190

Negative identification-object reference relationship: defined, 60; discussed, 60–63; sociometric techniques used to measure, 170–71; suggested research, 187. *See also* Alienation; Negative reference group concept

Negative nonmembership reference group: in Sumner's work, 26

Negative reference group concept: in Bennington study, 31; clarified by Newcomb, 31; and voting behavior, 150, 151; authors urging more study, 187; discussed, 187. *See also* Alienation; Negative identification-object reference relationship

Negative reference power: reference on, 187

Negotiations: reference group study of, 10

Negro discontent: relative deprivation writings on, 128, 129–30

Nelson, Harold A.: and tentative foundation for reference group theory, 76

Newcomb, Theodore M.: and social psychological character of reference group concept, 8; and Bennington College study, 30–31, 120, 123; and work used by Kelley, 36; definitions of positive and negative reference group, 41; and laboratory study of salient reference groups, 43, 106–7, 163, 168; and Sherifs' reaction to negative reference group concept, 62; and negative reference other, 187

Non-awareness: in table four, 51; defined, 72; discussed, 72–73

Nonexperimental procedures: types noted, 167; and relevance for reference other theorist, 167

Nonmembership affiliation: definition, 58; discussed, 58–59. *See also* Nonmembership group; Nonmembership other

Nonmembership group: importance explicated by Merton, 19; importance anticipated by early symbolic interactionists, 21. *See also* Nonmembership affiliation; Nonmembership other

Nonmembership nonreference other: discussed, 5; example, 5

Nonmembership other: importance recognized, 15; in Mead's work, 19; in Fishbein's theory, 154–55; and need for additional study, 188. *See also* Nonmembership affiliation; Nonmembership group

Nonmembership reference other: distinguishing function, 4, 5; discussed, 4–5; example, 4–5; in mass societies,